The Transformation of Employment Relations in Europe

T0295830

Since the 1980s, the process of European economic integration, within a wider context of globalization, has accelerated employment change and placed a new premium on 'flexible' forms of work organization. The institutions of employment relations, specifically those concerning collective bargaining between employers and trade unions, have had to adapt accordingly. *The Transformation of Employment Relations* focuses not just on recent change, but also charts the strategic choices that have influenced employment relations and examines these key developments in a comparative perspective.

A historical and cross-national analysis of the most important and controversial 'issues' explores the motivation of the actors, the implementation of change, and its evolution in a diverse European context. The book highlights the policies and the roles played by different institutional and social actors (employers, management, trade unions, professional associations and governments) and assesses the extent to which these policies and roles have had significant effects on outcomes. This comparative analysis of the transformation of work and employment regulation, within the context of a quarter-century timeframe, has not been undertaken in any other book. But this is no comparative handbook in which changes are largely described on a country-by-country basis; instead, *The Transformation of Employment Relations* is focused thematically. As Europe copes with a serious economic crisis, understanding of the dynamics of work transformation has never been more important.

James Arrowsmith is Professor in the School of Management at Massey University, New Zealand.

Valeria Pulignano is Professor in Sociology of Labor and Industrial Relations at the Catholic University of Leuven, Belgium.

Routledge Research in Employment Relations

Series editors: Rick Delbridge and Edmund Heery *Cardiff Business School, UK*

Aspects of the employment relationship are central to numerous courses at both undergraduate and postgraduate level.

Drawing from insights from industrial relations, human resource management and industrial sociology, this series provides an alternative source of research-based materials and texts, reviewing key developments in employment research.

Books published in this series are works of high academic merit, drawn from a wide range of academic studies in the social sciences.

The Transformation of Employment Relations in Europe

Institutions and Outcomes in the Age of Globalization

Edited by James Arrowsmith and Valeria Pulignano

Routledge
Taylor & Francis Group

NEW YORK AND LONDON

First published 2013
by Routledge
711 Third Avenue, New York, NY 10017

Simultaneously published in the UK
by Routledge
2 Park Square, Milton Park, Abingdon, Oxon OX14 4RN

First issued in paperback 2018

*Routledge is an imprint of the Taylor & Francis Group,
an informa business*

Library of Congress Cataloging-in-Publication Data

The transformation of employment relations in Europe : institutions and
    outcomes in the age of globalisation / edited by James Arrowsmith and
    Valeria Pulignano.
        pages cm — (Routledge research in employment relations ; 31)
    Includes bibliographical references and index.
    1. Industrial relations—Europe.   I. Arrowsmith, James, 1968–
II. Pulignano, Valeria, 1968–
    HD8376.5.T72 2013
    331.094—dc23
    2013001764

ISBN 13: 978-1-138-34081-7 (pbk)
ISBN 13: 978-0-415-87593-6 (hbk)

Typeset in Sabon
by Apex CoVantage, LLC

Thanks to our families for their support in this project—
Jane, James, and Jessica and Luc and Luca. Thanks also
to Giuseppe Della Rocca for his guiding contribution to the
formative stages of this project.
Both Valeria and Jim would also like to acknowledge
the Warwick Industrial Relations Research Unit (IRRU) for
its unique contribution to Employment Relations scholarship
over the past 43 years. Without IRRU, this book—and so many
others—would not have been possible.

Contents

Figures

Tables

Foreword

This book was originally devised just before the onset of the global financial crisis (GFC) in 2007–2008. Its purpose of identifying and discussing the main trends and transformations in European employment relations, since the onset of the European Union project some twenty years before, was only made more pertinent by this cataclysmic event. The chapters in this volume serve to locate the recent tensions around austerity and the very future of the euro, and their implications for industrial relations, in a broader context of unfolding change.

The question of the future of industrial relations as a method of regulating employment and as a channel of citizenship in capitalist societies today is crucial. One view is that globalization reintroduces the '*open shop*' in labor relations on a huge scale, allowing the enterprise (especially multinationals) to utilize labor with fewer and fewer restrictions (Cella 2012). Globalization introduces instability in the form of wage competition, collective-bargaining decentralization and the deregulation of labor standards, undermining relationships between employers, trade unions and the state at sector and national levels. As also explained in this volume, this has proceeded along with structural changes between and within sectors, including tertiarization; the declining size of production units; the creation of national and international production and services networks; and changes in work organization, hierarchical structures, and personnel policies related to technological transformations and the weakening of the Fordist model. These are all phenomena that give rise to a greater fragmentation of work, and a greater diversity and dispersion of the workforce, which raises serious problems for traditional models of regulation.

Addressing these developments introduces the issue of variety and convergence among national industrial relations systems. The sociotechnical innovations referred to above are more or less generalized and have similar effects in many European countries. However, as several of our contributors show, institutional divergence remains. In particular, the strength and role of trade unions varies significantly (Crouch 2012), and public-sector industrial relations shows significant signs of path dependency and thus diversity (Bach and Bordogna 2011). At the same time, the processes and outcomes of industrial relations have been subject to significant change. This supports new versions of the theory of convergence, in which industrial relations institutions remain in place but change their meaning and functions in a logic of neoliberal adjustment (Baccaro and Howell 2010). The emphasis is increasingly and commonly (if not uniformly) on the flexibility of labor markets, wages and working hours with, in many cases, the reshaping of the structure of the national industrial relations system due to the decline of unions and employers' associations.

These questions concerning convergence or diversity, and indeed the very future of industrial relations, are well documented in this book. It also identifies a space for further research, especially to assess the importance of institutional differences between countries. These include addressing, at both the national and the European level, the role and effects of law and culture in, for example, the regulation of wages and in legitimizing the participation of employees' representatives. For instance, the *Betriebrate* in Germany often allowed, regardless of concession agreements, intelligent solutions to avoid heavy layoffs during the recent corporate crises. Hence, research also needs to take a closer examination of the content and procedures of local agreements to establish which outcomes amount to a mere defeat of contractual regulation, and which can be considered as a protection of labor in profoundly difficult times. This is a pressing issue for industrial relations practitioners as well as academics, not least because the balance of power is now so unfavorable to the trade union movement.

Giuseppe Della Rocca
September 2012

REFERENCES

Baccaro, L. and Howell, C. 2011. 'A common neoliberal trajectory: The transformation of industrial relations in advanced capitalism', *Politics and Society*, 39:4. 521–563.

Bach, S. and Bordogna, L. 2011. 'Varieties of new public management or alternative methods? The reform of public service employment relations in industrialized democracies', *The International Journal of Human Resource Management*, 22:11. 2281–2294.

Cella, G. P. 2012. 'Difficoltà crescenti per le relazioni industriali europee e italiane' (Growing difficulties in European and Italian industrial relations), *Stato e Mercato*, 1. 29–54.

Crouch, C. 2012. 'Il Declino delle relazioni industriali nell'odierno capitalismo' (The decline of industrial relations in contemporary capitalism), *Stato e Mercato*, 1. 55–76.

1   Introduction

James Arrowsmith and Valeria Pulignano

The European Union (EU) was born following the consummation of the Treaty on European Union at Maastricht in 1992. It was the culmination of a process initiated by the 1986 Single European Act. An important goal of the Treaty was to promote growth, employment and rising living standards, not only by the removal of barriers to the movement of capital, goods and labor across internal borders, but also ultimately through monetary union. The common currency, and a singular monetary policy, was introduced in 1999. This profound 'deepening' of the EU was also accompanied by a relatively swift 'widening'. The twelve Maastricht signatories were joined by Austria, Finland and Sweden in 1995 and by ten new member states (NMS) in 2004, mainly former communist countries in Central and Eastern Europe (CEE). By 2013 the EU had grown to twenty-eight member states, with most (seventeen) adopting the euro as their currency. In the course of a generation, therefore, the EU became a heterogeneous collection of states, diverse in terms of history and culture, economic development, fiscal regimes and welfare and employment institutions, yet economically bound to each other in ways never before seen on the continent outside of conquest.

The scale, pace and fundamental disconnections of this process had powerful implications for industrial relations (IR) in Europe. Most particularly, the bargaining power of organized labor became weakened by the combined effects of heightened competition (between firms in countries with very different labor cost and regulatory configurations) and increased capital concentration and mobility. The internationalization and intensification of competition unleashed intense pressures on nationally based IR systems, especially in manufacturing, which often set the pattern for negotiations in other sectors. Firms sought looser multiemployer arrangements to facilitate flexibility in determining employment conditions and restructuring. The governance capacity of national, usually sector-based, IR institutions was also diminished by the spectacular growth of multinational companies (MNCs), which followed the integration of EU product and capital markets; annual cross-border mergers and acquisitions soared from around 750 in 1992 to 3,000 at the turn of that decade (Garnier 2007). Collective bargaining agenda were thus increasingly informed by competitive benchmarking and more or less explicit threats to relocate production or investment abroad, which intensified in the run up to the 2004 enlargement (Arrowsmith and Marginson 2006).

Throughout this period there were other profound, and reinforcing, challenges for trade unions. First, the continued shift of employment from (labor-intensive) manufacturing to services meant that the workforce became increasingly diverse and dispersed. The gender and occupational recomposition of the labor force, as well as the accompanying fragmentation of employment across smaller workplaces and 'atypical' forms, caused profound problems for traditional modes of organization and contributed to declining membership density. Second, the information and communication technology (ICT) revolution increased the pace of change within organizations, encouraging new forms of flexible work organization that challenged established norms. Third, labor management was increasingly informed by the philosophies and practices of 'human resource management' (HRM), which emphasized employee flexibility and performance and showed less concern for traditional, collective forms of labor regulation. Fourth, in the political arena, a deregulation agenda, which was informed by neoliberal market ideologies, emerged (Baccaro and Howell 2011). This was manifest in the removal of restrictions (such as those concerning opening hours) on private sectors such as retail and banking, in labor market and welfare reform, and in the privatization and commercialization of public sector organizations. As discussed below, this process intensified with the austerity measures introduced to address the severe Eurozone sovereign debt problems in the years following the 2007–2008 global financial crisis (GFC).

The surface paradox is that the European project began with radical political intentions, and it remains stamped with progressive rhetoric (Anderson 2009). The founding principles of the postwar Community were peace and prosperity, to which might now be added the goals of inclusivity, social protection and quality of life. In particular, the Maastricht Treaty elaborated the concept of 'social Europe' in two main ways. First, it extended qualified majority voting to areas such as equal opportunities, the information and consultation of workers, and policies to help the unemployed. The 'social protocol' and acknowledgment in the Treaty of the 1989 declaration of the Community Charter of the Fundamental Social Rights of Workers led to directives concerning pregnancy and maternity rights (1992), working time (1993) and European works councils (1994). Maastricht also institutionalized mechanisms of 'social dialogue', allowing trade union and employer representatives to inform and implement relevant regulation. Framework agreements between the intersectoral social partners led to directives on parental leave (1996), part-time work (1997) and fixed-term work (1999). Social dialogue at the European sector level also intensified after the Commission's decision to support the establishment of sectoral social dialogue committees (SSDCs) in 1998.

However, the 'social dimension' has always been feeble compared to the economic imperative of European integration. It has withered further as the EU has grown. The increased diversity of the EU placed greater emphasis on 'subsidiarity' and looser forms of coordination. Hence, subsequent framework agreements tend to relate to less contentious areas of employment—telework (2002), work-related stress (2004), harassment and violence at work (2007) and inclusive labor markets (2010)—and were not transformed into directives. Much of the work of the SSDCs has a similar focus around joint concerns and exhortation, and the case of temporary agency work (which eventually led to a directive) illustrates how employers can frustrate progress toward agreement when there are 'harder' issues to negotiate. The European Trade Union Institute (ETUI) attributes much of these shortcomings 'to heavy (business) lobbying of the European institutions in the context of widespread determination to deregulate and flexibilise labour law' (Clauwaert et al. 2009, p.76).

The influence of organized labor has, therefore, diminished in the social (let alone the economic) policy sphere, as well as at the enterprise and workplace levels. Maastricht opened Pandora's box, giving free rein to capital and undermining the pillars of the European social model on which the loftier social and employment aspirations of the EU depend. Notwithstanding the political complexion of national governments, the existence of the internal market places pressure on member states to pursue ever more business-friendly social, fiscal and labor market policies, all within an EU policy framework that favors a conservative approach to macroeconomic and market governance.

OBJECTIVES OF THE BOOK

It is in this context that this book takes as its main themes not only the challenges that the above developments pose for labor markets and industrial and employment relations 'models' in Europe, but also the main strategies involved and the outcomes of change since the end of the 1980s. It is designed to be original in two ways. First, its focus is not only on recent changes, but it also concerns the transformation of work, employment relations and labor markets in the first two decades of the EU: by taking a recent historical perspective, the patterns of change across different sectoral and national-institutional contexts can better be understood. Second, it is organized thematically rather than compiled as a comparative handbook, in which changes are largely described on a country-by-country basis. Though this means that not all countries or important issues can be addressed (an impossible task in any case), it aims to provide analytical consistency in that the chapters collectively contribute to a deeper understanding of the bigger picture over time, while also addressing important topics in their own right.

Two objectives are central to this volume. First, we aim to identify the key trends and changes that have occurred in employment relationships, labor markets and industrial relations systems in Europe since the formation of the EU in the early 1990s. This is done by connecting (a) the nature of the processes through which these changes have materialized across different countries (such as the evolution of the structure of collective bargaining and systems of collective representation, the enlargement of the EU, the restructuring of employment relations in the public sector) with (b) the outcomes to which these processes have contributed, particularly in terms of working conditions (wages, working time and work organization), and finally, with (c) the social and employment policy discourses (such as flexicurity and employability), which have followed and reinforced these transformations at both European and national levels.

Second, we want to explain the nature of these transformations and explore the conditions underpinning them. Here the various chapter contributions reveal that similar trends can be observed across countries that reiterate a move toward market liberalization. Though manifested in various ways, the common process emerges of a dynamic promoting the flexibilization and deregulation of the employment relationship. As will be shown in the chapters that follow, this has developed progressively in Europe over the past twenty years but, in the context of the recent multidimensional (economic, financial, social and political) crisis, is now something more compelling and novel, to such a degree that relevant aspects of working conditions (in particular, wages) are explicitly seen as adjustment variables for redressing economic imbalances and national competitiveness in Europe. As recalled in chapter 9 by Pulignano in this book, the European Commission (2011, p.20) put it clearly in expressing its new European economic governance policy: 'reforms of labour markets and in particular in relation to wage-setting mechanisms need to ensure efficient adjustment of labour costs in order to facilitate absorption of macroeconomic imbalances and to reduce unemployment'. The liberalizing developments and trends identified in this book are thus anticipated, by policy makers at least, to continue apace in the near future and beyond.

The basis of our thematic approach is a recognition that focusing on national institutional settings, especially in comparative perspective, is a necessary but incomplete way to understand the multilayered nature of change in Europe, and in particular the changing roles and strategies of the key actors. In the past decade or so, a stream of literature associated with 'neo-institutionalist' perspectives has made significant contributions to our understanding of the nature of employment and industrial relations systems. The 'varieties of capitalism' approach, for example, analyses the broadly contrasting employment policies of firms in coordinated or liberal market economies (Soskice and Hall 2000). Another highly influential way of understanding different forms of labor market regulation has been the analysis of differences between social democratic and liberal welfare state systems (Esping-Andersen 1999). These models provide valuable insights into the institutional similarities and differences between countries but have been criticized for a functionalist emphasis on complementary and path dependency (Heyes et al. 2012).

Two further sets of contributions emphasize the need for a dynamic and actor-centered approach to the political economy of labor regulation. First, Marginson and Sisson (2004) highlight the complex and multilevel nature of the governance of European employment systems, which leads to varying (and variable) degrees of integration. They also emphasize the need to focus on intra- and intercountry dynamics through the lens of the sector, following the approach of Katz and Derbishire (2000). Their research identified a tendency toward 'converging divergences', whereby sector-level employment regulation and outcomes come to look increasingly similar across countries, which at the same time helps to promote increased differentiation between sectors within countries. An important element in shaping this process was collective-bargaining decentralization and, in particular, declining trade union power, even if many of the institutions formally regulating employment appeared to retain their chief distinguishing characteristics (Katz 1993; 2005). This leads to the second key contribution, which is the importance of a longitudinal perspective. A focus on evolving power relations shows how radical, and to some degree convergent, change can be wrought incrementally within national systems that appear more or less formally continuous and distinct (Crouch and Farrell 2004; Streeck and Thelen 2005; Thelen 2003; Pontusson 2005).

Hence, there is a need to simultaneously focus on the key drivers and outcomes within and between countries, especially the role of the actors, if we are to arrive at a more thorough understanding of the dynamics of change (Bosch et al. 2009). This is why we have invited our contributors to provide an integrated analysis of some of the main transformations that have occurred in the European employment space, rather than produce a series of discrete country cases. Our focus is threefold: the primary *processes* driving change within and across countries; the main *outcomes* that they have produced in terms of IR arrangements, working conditions and labor standards for employees; and the *policy* discourses which have both sustained and followed these developments.

PLAN OF THE BOOK

The contributions in part 1 analyze institutional developments in the private sector at national and at firm levels, in the public sector and in the NMS. They demonstrate that the formal institutional continuity that largely characterizes industrial relations in the EU masks fundamental changes that disadvantage organized labor. Part 2 explores outcomes in terms of the triple nexus of the 'wage-effort bargain', namely, pay, working time and the organization of work. The common theme is one of heightened employer control under the banner of flexibility. Competition and decentralization have been the principal drivers of an increased moderation and differentiation of wages, more irregular working patterns and work intensification throughout much of Europe. Part 3 looks at the EU-level policy dimension. On the face of it, the social dimension has been articulated through the social dialogue process and by the emergence of a portfolio of regulations around areas such as antidiscrimination and collective representation. But there has also been a shift to increasingly 'soft' forms of coordination centered on an ambiguous but implicitly deregulatory agenda of 'employability' and 'flexicurity'. The overall verdict of part 3—indeed, of the book overall—is one of unfulfilled promise, of social Europe *manqué*.

Part 1—Processes

In chapter 2, Keith Sisson analyses institutional developments in collective bargaining in the private sectors of the major Western European economies. He argues that the common and defining feature of IR in these countries—multiemployer bargaining (MEB)—is now seriously under threat. This is largely because the internationalization of markets and competition from the early 1990s, along with changes in the scale and structure of business, undermined the institutional compromise that MEB represented. Sisson identifies a process whereby sector-based MEB became increasingly narrower in scope and weaker in substance, concerned with a competitiveness agenda also served by national-level 'social pacts'. He concludes that the institutional structures of MEB are likely to endure, not least as they remain embedded within wider social contracts that often include statutory entitlements for trade unions, but that they are also likely to become increasingly hollow without a renewal of the political will on which they have come to depend.

This theme is further explored by Miguel Martínez Lucio and Maria González Menéndez in their examination of developments at workplace level. Works Councils continue to play an important role in the IR systems of the EU (the NMS and Anglophone countries apart), but this apparent continuity is deceptive. Overall, the original logic of class compromise that institutionalized collective representation in the workplace has been undermined by employers' heightened competitiveness concerns and trade union membership decline. Perhaps even more fundamentally, the authors also explain how a series of 'fracturing processes' have introduced new fissures within collective representation. This is linked to changing relations between the sector and firm levels of collective bargaining, between works councils and trade unions, between collective and direct forms of representation, and between different constituent units of the firm. Though there are different trajectories between national systems, there is a common tendency to fragmentation that, the authors suggest, might ultimately and perversely pose challenges for management, as well as for unions at local levels, in dealing with workplace labor issues.

Attention shifts to the public sector in chapter 4. Here, trade union growth was historically linked to the expansion of the welfare state and a benign support for social corporatism in many European countries. However in recent decades trade unions and collective bargaining have been threatened by the market-oriented tenets of 'New Public Management' (NPM). Giuseppe Della Rocca charts how varieties of NPM emerged across Europe, fueled by concerns with the cost and quality of public service and implemented by means of decentralization and employment practices such as performance management and variable pay. The overall picture is one of a hybridization of employment regulation between market and administrative forms and involving a mix of collective bargaining and unilateral practice—with the latter most obvious in the wave of austerity responses to the post–GFC crisis. A common theme is the undermining of the status and employment terms and conditions of public servants. Della Rocca argues that this represents a fragmented and fluctuating process of partial convergence between sectors and countries.

In chapter 5, Guglielmo Meardi examines the emerging systems of IR in the NMS. These remain largely disorganized and market-oriented; though there are differences between these countries, they each maintain weak collective bargaining institutions at all levels, especially in the private sector, and offer much lower standards of labor protection and welfare than in Western Europe. For this reason, developments in the CEE countries are not only of regional interest—their labor market and employment systems also fundamentally challenge the core assumptions of the 'European Social Model'. The argument of this chapter is that accession to the EU has not prompted convergence toward Western European patterns, and efforts to graft on social dialogue, such as in the form of national social pacts, have largely served to incorporate trade unions and undermine their mobilization capacity. Furthermore, Meardi demonstrates that EU accession was deleterious for workers even before the GFC, contributing to large-scale emigration and a level of social disenfranchisement that questions the social sustainability of what he describes as an extreme neoliberal experiment in these countries.

Part 2—Outcomes

In chapter 6 Maarten Keune and Kurt Vandaele show how 'solidaristic wage policies', premised on a degree of horizontal and vertical wage standardization within countries, have given way to competition-oriented arrangements geared to wage moderation and flexibility. Pay inequality and variability tends to be greatest in countries with single-employer bargaining arrangements, but even with MEB arrangements there is greater use of performance-related pay schemes and a declining wage share. This is explained by the pressures introduced by economic integration both at national and firm levels. Essentially, pay restraint and variability were the product of tripartite 'social pacts' and collective-bargaining decentralization in a context of increased competition and declining trade unions. In this context, schemes such as minimum wages have had little purchase on maintaining solidarity in national wage systems.

Developments in working time patterns and regulation are reviewed in chapter 7. The duration of working time, especially long hours and part-time hours, is heavily gendered. It is also fragmented by sector- and country-level factors such as the level of economic development and productivity, tax and benefits systems, social norms and regulation by law and collective bargaining. Amidst this diversity, Arrowsmith highlights a widespread growth in flexible working time arrangements, which has helped normalize 'atypical' and irregular work. Reduced hours has been a historic goal of trade unions, and greater control over scheduling has become increasingly important to improve quality of working life. However, in recent decades increased competition, the growth of MNCs, persistent unemployment and IR decentralization have conspired to shift the working-time agenda away from union interests to serving employers' flexibility needs, and the GFC also furthered concession bargaining over working time in the cause of saving jobs. Arrowsmith also argues that the history of the Working Time Directive (and regulatory developments in countries such as France) demonstrates the political hegemony of employers' interests in this vital area.

The transformation of work organization over the past two decades, and its relationship to labor regulation, is analyzed by Ludger Pries in chapter 8. The shift from manual to white-collar and professional work, the introduction of new forms of ICT and the internationalization of markets and organizations have helped drive new forms of work organization espousing employee participation and collaboration in the pursuit of innovation and change. However, Pries argues that rather than humanizing work, the reality is more often one of an intensification masked by superficial de-Taylorization. Interfirm competition, and the decentralization and marketization of intrafirm relations, have increased work demands—including at the normative level—while new forms of working such as teamwork are concerned to enhance managerial control. Given that the organization of work is not an objectively neutral activity but is shaped by power relations, these changes in work organization are facilitated by, and contribute to, changes in modes of labor regulation. Pries concludes that, while there is much potential for a cooperative mode of work organization based on innovation, employee participation and high labor standards, much will depend on developments in the politics of labor regulation, and these do not appear favorable at the present time.

Part 3—Policy

The changing nature of European social and employment policy is the focus of chapter 9. Valeria Pulignano charts a growing disconnection between market and social integration as the former introduces greater complexity, diversity and uncertainty into the European employment space. The policy response was to move from the legislative approach, originally associated with 'harmonization', to 'soft' forms of employment and labor market coordination such as social dialogue and the 'open method of coordination'. European regulation thus appears increasingly limited and tentative at a time when fears of 'social dumping' and 'regime competition' have become more acute. Nevertheless, Pulignano argues that the emergence of these new mechanisms, positioned as they are to involve and influence the social actors, has at least the potential to improve governance capacity. The key is to develop integrated and complementary approaches that deliver the authority of traditional instruments with the flexibility and stakeholder engagement associated with looser forms of regulation. Again, however, recent developments suggest this is unlikely at the current time.

The next chapters focus on two important policy goals that arguably define the current EU employment policy agenda. The concept and practicalities of 'employability' are analyzed by Jonathan Winterton and Nigel Haworth in chapter 10. The term emerged in the 1980s and reflects the concern of supply-side economics with labor market reform. The authors chart how, and with what implications, it became an increasingly important focus of the European Employment Strategy as it emerged in the early 1990s. Its attractiveness to policy makers is twofold. First, it serves an ideological function in reproblematizing unemployment in terms of the performance of individuals and markets. Second, it permits looser economic coordination in the form of guidelines and reporting linked to employment (not unemployment) targets. In terms of effects, Winterton and Haworth analyze national reports to demonstrate a diversity of practice at member-state level (whilst acknowledging the subsidiarity principle built in to the framework) in addition to a generic concern to 'modernize' labor market institutions in pursuit of greater flexibility. The authors argue that this focus fails to tackle the fundamental problems associated with deficiencies in the demand side of the European economy.

We close with an equally innovative analysis of another concept that has dominated the European employment discourse since the early 1990s—flexicurity. This term is related to employability but has a more explicit focus on the role of the social partners at firm and sector levels. The authors, Ton Wilthagen, Ruud Muffels and Heejung Chung, introduce a conceptual model of national labor market performance, which they then test using empirical data. They observe a number of familiar country clusters along a range of different dimensions, with no strong evidence of convergence. They conclude that it is countries with the most robust and articulated industrial relations systems, such as the 'Continental' and 'Nordic' blocs, that are better able to balance flexibility and security; elsewhere, it is flexibility that tends to hold sway.

CONCLUSIONS

The overall theme to emerge from these contributions is that the IR dimension of the EU project involves a combination of undoing and reconstruction that leaves organized labor increasingly vulnerable. This is less a matter of institutional deconfiguration, or convergence, than the product of processes that have fundamentally transformed the power resources of capital and labor. Though employment deregulation, albeit within existing institutional boundaries, is a common theme, the overarching narrative is of an ever more aggressive pursuit of 'flexibility' by employers and the state in the context of trade union retreat. This process may best be understood as congruence rather than convergence. Across Europe, firms have increasingly focused on costs and flexibility and are therefore more concerned with the internalization and localization of bargaining. States are also more concerned with active labor market policies, such as training initiatives and welfare reform, to promote work incentives. And at the supranational level the profound complexity introduced by the simultaneously 'wider' and 'deeper' European Union has prompted an employment policy based on 'soft regulation' in the form of benchmarking and monitoring around goals and minimum standards.

In the 1990s, Dølvik (2000, p.48) noted 'an ambiguous instance of institutional stabilization and qualitative transformation' in European industrial relations. While the transition to EMU lent some support to IR institutions (for example, through various employment 'pacts'), it also helped transform their functioning around competitiveness and wage restraint. It was always clear that the incomplete architecture of EMU (a monetary but not a political, fiscal or even a banking union), together with different levels of economic development and competitiveness amongst its constituent member states, would intensify competition and restructuring and ensure that any external shock would have severe asymmetric effects (Sisson et al. 1999). Less well-anticipated perhaps was the effect it would have on transferring power to large corporations (Crouch 2011; Nolan 2011). As a result, in the new millennium, institutional frameworks too began to change; Germany is the paradigm case where 'a severe erosion of the system of collective regulation' occurred not by full-frontal attack but through the incremental and cumulative effect of declining collective bargaining coverage, increased recourse to exemptions, changed works council functions and the like (Baccaro and Howell 2011, p.30).

Each of the contributions to this book take the broad processes of liberalization, deregulation and internationalization as the overarching context in which to identify the magnitude and significance of the transformations that have occurred in European employment relations in the last two decades. Though this might suggest some sort of general trend toward convergence, this is enacted less in terms of closer institutional similarities, or radical institutional change, than as a product of changing power relations and strategies. What emerges is a continuous process of fragmentation in employment relationships, which potentially elicits degradation of working conditions (e.g., wages, working time, quality of work and participation at work) and which is aggravated by changing European and national economic-driven policy discourses. A simple but effective expression of relative economic and political power is the wage share of gross domestic product. Since the formation of the EU, 'real wage growth has tended to fall continuously behind productivity increases and profits', and the wage share declined from 70 percent in 1992 to 65 percent in 2007 (Arpaia and Pichelmann 2008, p.29). Perhaps an even more fundamental indication of power resources is how the economic and political crises in Europe that followed the GFC hardly led to new and significant constraints on international capital; rather, it led to further assaults on labor through austerity and yet more corporate restructuring.

Thus, if there are convergent pressures and effects, the process is mediated by the differentiation of employment relations in Europe, within what remain highly diverse national economies and societies. Most EU workers, it should be remembered, reside in just six countries—Germany (17 percent), the UK (14 percent), France (12 percent), Italy (11 percent), Spain (9 percent) and Poland (8 percent)—each of which maintain highly distinctive systems of employment and labor market regulation. As our authors explain, the key to understanding the transformations that have occurred is to recognize the fundamental shift in the balance of power within the employment relationship. This has been driven by the internationalization and concentration of business and facilitated by various deregulatory state policies. Institutions have changed, but more important is the contribution of changed power relations and actors' strategies in reconfiguring the focus and function within those institutions toward a 'flexibility' agenda.

REFERENCES

Anderson, P. 2009. *The New Old World*. London: Verso.

Arpaia, A. and Pichelmann, K. 2008. Dimensions of Inequality in the EU. Proceedings of OeNB Workshops no.16, Sept.

Arrowsmith, J. and Marginson, P. 2006. 'The European cross-border dimension to collective bargaining in multi-national companies', *European Journal of Industrial Relations*, 12:3. 245–266.

Baccaro, L. and Howell, C. 2011. 'A common neoliberal trajectory: The transformation of industrial relations in advanced capitalism', *Politics & Society*, 39. 521–563.

Bosch, G., Lehndoff, S. and Rubery, J. 2009. (eds.) *European Employment Models in Flux*. London: Palgrave-MacMillan.

Clauwaert, S., Schömann, I. and Warneck, W. 2009. 'Has European social dialogue and social legislation supported the Lisbon strategy?' in *Benchmarking Working Europe 2009*. Brussels: ETUI. 67–76

Crouch, C. 2011. *The Strange Non-Death of Neoliberalism*. Cambridge: Polity Press.

Crouch, C. and Farrell, H. 2004. 'Breaking the path of institutional development? Alternatives to the New Determinism', *Rationality and Society*. 5–43.

Dølvik, J.-E. 2000. EMU: *Implications for Industrial Relations and Collective Bargaining in Europe*. Brussels: ETUI.

Esping-Andersen, G. 1999. *The Three Worlds of Welfare Capitalism*. Princeton: Princeton University Press.

European Commission 2011. 'Macro Economic Report to the Communication from the Commission to the European Parliament, the Council, the European and Social Committee and the Committee of Regions', *Annual Growth Survey 2012*, Brussels: European Commission.

Garnier, G. 2007. 'European integration from the perspective of M&A activity', *Mergers and Acquisitions Note, no. 4.* Brussels: European Commission. 11–23.

Heyes, J., Lewis, P. and Clark, I. 2012. 'Varieties of capitalism, neoliberalism and the economic crisis of 2008–?' *Industrial Relations Journal*, 43. 3.

Katz, H. 1993. 'The decentralization of collective bargaining: A literature review and comparative analysis', *Industrial and Labor Relations Review*, 47. 3–22.

———. 2005. 'The causes and consequences of increased within-country variance in employment practices', *British Journal of Industrial Relations*, 43. 577–583.

Katz, H. and Derbishire, O. 2000. *Converging Divergences: Worldwide Changes in Employment Systems*, Ithaca: Cornell University Press.

Marginson, P. and Sisson, K. 2004. *European Integration and Industrial Relations.* London: Palgrave-Macmillan.

Nolan, P. 2011. 'Money, markets, meltdown: The twenty-first century crisis of labour', *Industrial Relations Journal*, 42:1. 2–17.

Pontusson, J. 2005. 'Varieties and commonalities of capitalism', in D. Coates (ed.) *Varieties of Capitalism, Varieties of Approaches.* London: Palgrave. 163–188.

Sisson, K., Arrowsmith, J., Gilman, M. and Hall, M. 1999. *EMU and the Implications for Industrial Relations: A Select Bibliographic Review.* Luxembourg: Office for Official Publications of the European Union.

Soskice, D. and Hall, P. 2000. *Varieties of Capitalism.* Oxford: Oxford University Press.

Streeck, W. and Thelen, K. (eds.) 2005. *Beyond Continuity: Institutional Change in Advanced Political Economy.* Oxford: Oxford University Press.

Thelen, K. 2003. 'How institutions evolve: Insights from comparative historical analysis', in J. Mahoney and D. Reuschemeyer (eds.) *Comparative Historical Analysis in the Social Sciences.* Cambridge: Cambridge University Press.

2 Private Sector Employment Relations in Western Europe

Collective Bargaining Under Pressure?

Keith Sisson

INTRODUCTION

This chapter reviews collective bargaining developments in the private sector of the major European economies. Its primary focus is on the structure of collective bargaining—the level, units, scope and form—and the implications of recent developments. It is a measure of its significance that, historically, the main distinguishing feature of these countries when compared to Japan and the US has been an inclusive structure of multiemployer bargaining at sector and/or cross-sector level. Indeed, as the European Commission (2009) recognizes, such collective bargaining could be said to be one of the defining features of the European social model—it means that the benefits are not just reserved to the well-organized; legislation can be 'reflexive' and 'procedural', allowing social partners to 'tailor' legal measures to suit their specific circumstances; and it helps to maintain the status and membership of trade unions and employers' organizations, providing the platform for their greater involvement in and deliberation of economic and social policymaking, along with the networks for achieving greater social cohesion. Consistent with these benefits, the econometric evidence suggests that an inclusive structure of collective bargaining is a key factor in the greater equality of income and levels of trust or social capital in the wider society (for further details, see Panic 2007; Hutton 2008).

Even so, the future of multiemployer bargaining is in doubt. It has all but collapsed in one country (the UK). There have also been major changes in others, leading not just to an overall decline in collective bargaining coverage, but also contributing to substantial reductions in the membership of trade unions (see Table 2.1) and employers' organizations (EIRO 2010a). The possibility that the end of an era is being witnessed has to be seriously considered. Important to emphasize too is that this is not just because of the recession that swept throughout Europe following the banking and Euro crisis of recent years. Rather, it is because of underlying developments that have been taking place for more than two decades.

Under these circumstances, this chapter has several aims that are reflected in its structure: to better understand the origins and development

Table 2.1 Trade union density 1960–2010 (percent): OECD data

Year	Austria	Belgium	Denmark	Finland	France	Germany	Ireland	Italy	Neths	Portugal	Spain	Sweden	UK
1960	67.9	41.5	56.9	31.9	19.6	34.7	43.1	24.7	40.0	N/A	N/A	72.1	38.9
1970	62.8	42.1	60.3	51.3	21.7	32.0	50.6	37.0	36.5	N/A	N/A	67.7	43.0
1980	56.7	54.1	78.6	69.4	18.3	34.9	54.3	49.6	34.8	54.8	N/A	78.0	49.7
1990	46.9	53.9	75.3	72.5	9.9	31.2	48.5	38.8	24.3	32.0	12.5	80.0	38.2
2000	36.6	49.5	74.2	75.0	8.0	24.6	38.0	34.8	22.9	21.6	16.7	79.1	30.2
2010	28.1	(52.0)[1]	(68.8)[1]	70.0	(7.6)[1]	18.6	(33.7)[1]	35.1	(19.4)[1]	19.3	(15.9)[1]	68.4	26.5
Change													
60–70	-5.1	+0.6	+3.4	+19.4	+2.1	-2.7	+7.5	+12.3	-3.5	N/A	N/A	-4.4	+4.1
70–80	-6.1	+12.0	+18.3	+18.1	-3.4	+2.9	+3.7	+12.6	-1.7	N/A	N/A	+10.3	+6.7
80–90	-9.8	-0.2	-3.3	+3.1	-8.4	-3.7	-5.8	-10.8	-10.5	-22.8	N/A	+2.0	-11.5
90–20	-10.3	-4.4	-1.1	+2.5	-1.9	-6.6	-10.5	-4.0	-1.4	-10.4	+4.2	-0.9	-8.0
20–10	-8.5	(+2.5)[1]	(-5.4)[1]	-5.0	(-0.4)[1]	-6.0	(-4.3)[1]	+0.3	(-3.5)[1]	-2.3	(-0.8)[1]	-10.7	-3.7

[1] 2009

Source: Online OECD Employment database at www.oecd.org/employment/database.

of multiemployer bargaining; to appreciate the pressures for change—economic, organizational and ideological—and how these pressures work out in practice; to map the major changes taking place; and to consider prospects for the future.

THE STARTING POINT: NEVER A PERFECT EQUILIBRIUM?

The development of multiemployer bargaining had a common logic across countries (Sisson 1987; Traxler et al. 2001). The universalization of standard terms and conditions throughout a sector enabled trade unions to establish the 'common rule', at the same time giving them the opportunity to husband scarce resources by focusing on a single set of negotiations. Economies in transactions costs were also attractive to employers, especially in industries with a large number of small and medium-sized enterprises such as printing. For employers, however, the main benefits came from 'market' and 'managerial' regulation. Multiemployer bargaining not only provided a degree of market control by putting a floor under competition on wages and working time. It also pooled employers' strength *vis-à-vis* organized labor, enabling them to counter trade union 'whipsawing' or 'leapfrogging' tactics with the threat of lockouts that considerably raised the costs of industrial action. Significantly, too, it helped to further managerial concerns with the control of labor, containing trade union activities in the workplace by exhausting the scope for negotiations and/or limiting the role that unions could play at that level. In these circumstances, governments viewed sector agreements as a means of institutionalizing and containing industrial conflict, along with delivering other key policy goals, ranging from employment standards to price control.

That said, the precise form of the initial compromise was just that—a compromise contingent on circumstances, the crisis years following the two World Wars being especially critical. Whereas trade unions and employers might have had a common interest in exploiting multiemployer bargaining to achieve a measure of *market* regulation, their positions on *managerial* regulation always differed. For trade unions, the sector agreement was the beginning of the process of influence over the employment relationship; for employers it was the end—the neutralization of the workplace to uphold managerial prerogative.

PRESSURES FOR CHANGE

In discussing the widespread decline in trade union membership, much of the attention focuses on the changing patterns of employment—in particular, the decline of manufacturing and the growth of services, the increasing feminization of the workforce, the changing forms of contract (i.e., full-time/part-time and permanent/temporary) and so on (see, for example, Lesch

2004; Visser 2006). This by no means the whole story, however. Also important are developments in collective bargaining, which reflect not just trade union activities but more fundamentally the changing views of employers and their organizations, above all in large MNCs (EIRO 2009a).

Changes in Business Portfolios

In the 1970s many companies embarked on substantial programs of diversification in order to spread investment risks (Whittington and Mayer 2000). In the 1980s the fashion changed, with many drawing back to concentrate on 'core' activities or businesses. Movement around this axis has been more or less continuous ever since, with the recent period characterized by streamlining of portfolios around fewer lines of business as companies have sought to extend their geographical reach across markets, turning themselves into MNCs. In effect, 'breadth' across business activities has been traded for increased geographical reach across established international markets and those in rapidly emerging economies (van Tulder et al. 2001). Thus, the most recently available data suggest that home-based MNCs employ more workers than foreign-owned ones in most Western European countries—in Germany, Sweden and the UK the figure is around twice as much (EIRO 2009a, p.6).

Not only have both developments confirmed the company as the center of gravity, but they have also had considerable implications for the structure of collective bargaining. Diversification across established sector boundaries means a growing mismatch between the constituencies of employers' organizations and the activities of large companies. Provisions of agreements that may be appropriate in one sector may prove damaging to operations in others in which the company is involved. Alternatively, in blurring existing boundaries between sectors, these developments place a question mark over the continued viability of established sector structures. An example is the emergence of *bancassurance* groups that cut across traditional boundaries between banking and insurance, each of which had its own sector agreement in most countries. At the same time, the internationalization of markets for products and services and intensification of international competition within given territorial markets means that, for growing numbers of medium as well as most large MNCs, sector multiemployer bargaining within one country is increasingly anomalous. This is because, to return to one of the underlying logics, multiemployer bargaining within the nation state no longer provides a floor, taking wage costs out of competition.

Intensifying Competition

It has long been recognized that there is a close association between developments in collective bargaining and the nature and extent of the product market competition that companies experience—indeed, it was Commons (1909) who first drew attention to the link more than a century ago. Thus, as the previous section indicated, a major factor in the development of multiemployer bargaining was its ability to take wages out of competition. In recent years, however, the nature and extent of competition has changed dramatically, spreading beyond the boundaries of the national state with which such bargaining had come to be associated. Especially important is the rise of first Japanese, and then Chinese, manufacturers. A further consideration is the collapse of the former USSR and the incorporation of Bulgaria, the Czech Republic, Poland, Hungary, Romania and others into the EU: there are now many alternative, and much cheaper, locations for investment within Europe.

Intensifying competition means that employers increasingly find many of the provisions of multiemployer employer agreements restrictive. For example, those dealing with hours of work may make it difficult to extend working time to cope with longer opening/operating hours; there may be restrictions on the increased use of part-time or temporary work. Perhaps even more fundamentally, there are also much smaller 'rents' for employers to share with trade unions in the form of higher levels of wages. In emphasizing the importance of competitive product markets, a major study that draws on the UK's representative *Workplace Employment Relations Survey* puts it like this: 'The growth of collective bargaining in the twentieth century had been nurtured by imperfect competition. Tightening product market competition suffocated it' (Brown et al. 2009, p.47).

Intensifying competition is not just a product market phenomenon, however. The liberalization and deregulation of capital markets in the 1980s and 1990s have put greater emphasis on company financial performance. The emergence of much more active/aggressive investors such as hedge funds, private equity groups and sovereign wealth funds is important here. Coupled with the greater availability of capital to finance merger and acquisition activity, this has made for a redefinition of the nature of competition itself, which has come to be known as 'financialization'. In the 1970s and 1980s, to paraphrase Froud (2000) and her colleagues, competition was based on product and process, most notably in sectors such as cars and consumer electronics. By the late 1990s, the emphasis of competition shifted to financial results in the form of current and projected cash returns on investment using cross-sector league tables such as MVA (market value added) and EVA^{TM} (economic value added), with the returns on investment in one firm explicitly compared against all others regardless of product or sector; pressure was exerted through the capital market by shareholders via buy, sell and hold decisions; and the management challenge came to be represented in narrow financial terms. A key consequence of 'financialization' has been to intensify the pressure on managers to increase returns to shareholders.

The impact of 'financialization' differs from country to country, reflecting sources of business funding and the systems of corporate governance—the UK is the extreme case of so-called 'outsider' systems among EU member countries because of the dependence of business on the stock market and the priority accorded to shareholder interests (Marginson and Sisson 2004). Even so, there are key respects in which the developments in product and capital markets outlined above are relevant across the board. First, the application

Table 2.2   Changing emphases in industrial relations

The 'old' industrial relations	The 'new' industrial relations
Key assumptions	
stability	change
conflict	co-operation
social justice	continuous improvement
standardisation	diversity
a predominant level of activity	multiple levels of activity
centralisation	decentralisation (subsidiarity)
Subject matter	
claims/grievances	information/ benchmarking
rights/obligations	standards/targets
pay and conditions	employment and competitiveness
inputs	outputs
Processes	
distributive bargaining	integrative bargaining
agreement making	social dialogue
law making	benchmarking/target setting
vertical integration	horizontal co-ordination
enforcement/sanctions	monitoring/learning

Source: Sisson and Marginson (2001).

of market principles to decision making results in greater resort to 'competitive tendering', 'market testing' and the subcontracting or outsourcing of activities previously undertaken in-house. Second, and even before the recession, the agenda of collective bargaining has increasingly become oriented toward questions of competitiveness, adaptability and employment—a shift from 'productivity-oriented' to 'competition-oriented' collective bargaining (Schulten 2002). Third, and relatedly, as well as leading to more and more issues being decentralized for company or workplace determination, they are said to be encouraging the 'development of a "different paradigm" of industrial relations' (Léonard 2001, p.30). Table 2.2 tries to capture the essence of what is being suggested.

Multilevel Governance Issues

Paralleling developments in business portfolios and the nature and extent of competition have been changes in the wider governance framework of industrial relations that are calling into question the significance of the national sector. From inside companies come major changes in structure and organization reflecting and re-enforcing the greater pressure on performance. Notable here are 'divisionalization' and 'budgetary devolution'. Effectively, the company is divided into a number of semiautonomous businesses units that operate as individual profit and/or cost centers with considerable devolution of responsibility for operating management. Headquarters retains control over target setting and resource allocation, however—in effect operating as a 'central banker' shifting resources to and from the divisions depending on achievement of key performance indicators (KPIs) for strategic business units (SBUs) and for managers themselves. Especially important here is the microchip revolution and the accompanying development in computer software dealing with not just operational matters but also human resource management outcomes. More or less instant data on activity and costs are used both to monitor performance against targets and to make 'coercive comparisons' between individual units. The result is the more or less continuous stretching of targets. The possibility of transferring operations to lower cost countries in the light of such data is a potent factor as examples listed in Table 2.3 confirm.

Table 2.3   Cross-border comparisons involving manufacturing MNCs

---

Voest-Alpine has repeatedly threatened to relocate its Austrian steel manufacturing operations, because of labour costs and environmental regulations. The ongoing dialogue has involved the local public authorities as well as social partner representatives.

At VW's Forest plant in western Belgium, a reduction in pay levels and an increase in working time from 35 to 38 hours a week were negotiated in line with standards prevailing at the company's sites in Germany, thereby minimising the threat of relocation.

Negotiations at the Czeck aluminium producer Alcoa Fujikura resulted in lower wage increases than elsewhere because of threatened relocation. Nonetheless, in 2008, the company moved part of its production to a site in Romania, where labour costs are lower.

In 2004, Daimler announced that a new Mercedes model might have to be relocated if cost savings and longer actual working time could not be realised at its Sindelfingen plant in southwestern Germany. An agreement along these lines was reached, utilising a recent opening clause in the sector agreement.

The German Metalworkers' Union and the works council at VW agreed to a special package of measures for a new autonomous production unit, Auto 5000, in 2001. Levels of pay for the 5,000 employees are lower than those collectively agreed at the parent company, in order to avoid production of the model being moved to sites in Portugal or Slovakia.

In 2004, the electronics group Siemens concluded an agreement with IG Metall to increase weekly working time from 35 to 40 hours at two sites manufacturing mobile phones, in the face of the management's threat to relocate part of its production and jobs to two plants in Hungary.

(Continued)

Table 2.3   (Continued)

In 2004, the food producer Danish Crown threatened to shut down the Tulip Slaughterhouse on the island of Zealand: production would be moved to German operations with lower labour costs, if the 230 workers refused to accept a 15% wage cut. Initially, the employees accepted the cut, but after protests from the Food and Allied Workers' Union and widespread strikes at other Danish Crown slaughterhouses, they refused the measure. In the end, the Tulip Slaughterhouse was closed and production moved to Germany.

The dispute in Finland's paper industry in 2005 was accompanied by speculation of relocation of some operations of the MNCs dominating the sector to Russia and other countries, if the employers' demands on the use of sub-contract labour (on lower wages and conditions) were not met.

In 2004, an agreement was reached at the electronics engineering group Bosch's Vénissieux site in eastern France aimed at averting relocation to a site in the Czech Republic. The agreement consisted of concessions on pay and working time, including a shift from a 35-hour to a 36-hour week. Bosch subsequently pressed for similar agreements at its other French production sites.

The glass manufacturer Waterford Crystal regularly issued threats of relocation, as well as outsourcing, to influence the agenda and outcomes of company negotiations. This resulted in wage reductions and increased flexibility of working.

The international tobacco group British American Tobacco announced it was relocating its profitable Maltese production operation to eastern Europe, where costs were lower. Trade union attempts to retain production locally were unsuccessful, and enhanced redundancy packages were negotiated.

In a context where the agricultural equipment manufacturer Kværneland was considering moving production to sites elsewhere in Europe, the trade union agreed to a two-year wage freeze, along with new and more flexible working time arrangements. The agreement was reached as part of a major restructuring initiative, which maintained production and employment at the company's Norwegian operations.

Management at the VW subsidiary AutoEuropa systematically uses comparisons of costs and performance in local negotiations, with an implicit threat to relocate. This has resulted in agreements on extended and more flexible working time arrangements and on new practices seeking to reduce absenteeism.

In 2005, management at Opel in Azambuja in western Portugal demanded that the works councils sign agreements on working time aimed at implementing similar arrangements to those negotiated at AutoEuropa. Despite the threat of relocation, the works council did not accept the demands. Production ceased at the end of 2006, and was transferred to sites in Spain and Russia.

In the UK PSA Peugeot-Citroën's car manufacturing plant was unable to secure a mandate to produce new models, despite successive local agreements that had delivered rapid improvements in costs and flexibility; this was attributed to its inability to match the lower costs that investment in a new facility in Slovakia promised. The plant eventually closed in 2007.

Source: EIRO (2009a), Table 9.

Critically important for the present argument is that the logic of devolved budgetary responsibility associated with 'divisionalization' is at odds with traditional multiemployer agreements. The purpose of devolving operational and financial responsibility is to transmit the competitive pressures on companies to individual units and, in making them more responsive to these pressures, to enhance the adaptive capability of the wider company to changing market circumstances. This means that SBUs should, as far as possible, be in a position to determine their own costs and revenue. Moreover, the more management has become confident of engaging with employee representatives at company level, the more the role of multiemployer agreements in neutralizing the workplace becomes redundant.

Challenges from Above

Simultaneously, there are developments serving to undermine the national sector level from above. Economic and Monetary Union (EMU) unleashed widespread restructuring and rationalization as companies look to service one regional market, rather than a series of national markets. Combined with intensifying competition, handling this restructuring has not only prompted a reorientation of bargaining agenda, but it also compounded the pressures for decentralization. Furthermore, in promoting deregulation so as to extend the reach of the single market across a wider range of business activities, EMU led to the privatization of former state enterprises that are not part of established multiemployer bargaining arrangements.

There are other ways in which EU developments are complicating matters. The coming of EMU meant the spread across Europe of the German *Bundesbank's* 'nonaccommodating' monetary regime of targeting relatively low rates of inflation with corresponding borrowing rates. The intention and effect has been not only to help bring down the rate of inflation—a major consideration in sector pay bargaining—but also to make pay bargainers recognize that attempts to reach above-inflation settlements would now result in unemployment. In practice, trade unions have had to adjust the point of resistance to the prevailing level of inflation in the attempt to maintain living standards, while employers have done everything they can to minimize the impact on unit costs by insisting on major changes in working practices. The effect has been something of a convergence of pay settlements around the level of inflation—a 'European going rate' (Hassel 2002b)— which has taken some of the meaning out of national sector bargaining, at the same time as encouraging further decentralization to secure off-setting productivity increases (see Marginson and Sisson 2004, pp.252–261).

EMU also helped to strengthen the cross-sector level in many countries, encouraging governments to seek national-level understandings with the social partners—so-called 'social pacts'—on wage moderation, greater labor market flexibility and reform of social protection systems. With rare exceptions, such as the UK, national level concertation is to be found across the EU member states. In many, but not all instances, such concertation led to the conclusion of successive multiannual social pacts: in Belgium, Denmark, Finland, Greece, Ireland, Italy, the Netherlands, Portugal, Spain and Sweden. In Austria and Norway, existing centralized structures have been utilized for concertation. The phenomenon also spread to the accession countries, with Bulgaria and Hungary concluding a national tripartite agreement on recommendations for wage increases at sector and company levels in the context of the economic pressures surrounding accession. More recently, the recession following the banking crisis has given further impetus to national level understandings.

There are strong grounds for suggesting that, far from being merely a response to an immediate crisis, cross-sector concertation will be a permanent feature for the foreseeable future. The external constraint remains in terms of ensuring compatibility between the outcomes of national wage bargaining and the macroeconomic parameters of EMU. Social protection and labor market reforms are also long-term agenda items, with pension arrangements having to be aligned with the implications of demographic developments. Bearing in mind that the proportion of older people's incomes coming from public sources is well more than half in countries such as France (85 percent), Germany (73 percent) and Sweden (68 percent) (OECD 2009), the cross-sector level can hardly be avoided.

Complicating matters even further is that EU developments have also encouraged forms of transnational coordination, embracing 'benchmarking' and 'pattern bargaining' as well as the more obvious 'social dialogue' and 'framework agreements'. Moreover, this is not only true of the sector level, where there have been significant developments but also at the company level, where European Works Councils have become negotiating forums (EIRO 2009a). In principle, there need not be a conflict between national sector bargaining that is freestanding or coordinated (see, for example, Léonard et al. 2007). Indeed, coordination is necessary to avoid a process of 'regime competition', where one country competes to undercut another (Schulten 2002; Dølvik 2001). Even so, time and energy are limited resources. As well as a variety of options, the parties are confronted with Scharpf's (1988) so-called 'joint decision trap'—the more successful an activity is at one level in handling the situation, the more difficult it is to involve others.

Ideological Considerations

The view that multiemployer bargaining is a public 'good' has also come under challenge. Its role in institutionalizing and containing industrial conflict is increasingly forgotten as the incidence of strikes has declined (which itself reflects reduced trade union membership and collective bargaining coverage). Since the 1980s the 'new ideological hegemony of neoliberalism' in Europe has challenged both the goals and institutions associated with 'political correction of market outcomes' (Schulten 2002, pp.177–178). In as much as multiemployer bargaining sets nonmarket wages, it is held to result in unemployment, thereby generating inequality in the labor market: too little wage differentiation favors 'insiders' at the expense of 'outsiders'.

Debates over the connections between bargaining structure and economic performance are relevant too. A prevailing consensus developed amongst economic opinion that the relationship involved is nonlinear (Calmfors and Driffill 1988). Highly centralized bargaining structures, such as those characterizing the Nordic area at the time, apparently performed better in terms of key economic outcomes because the scope for externalizing the wider economic effects of wage decisions was minimized; the same was true of highly decentralized ones because they were disciplined by the market. The worst performing structures were those that were neither fully centralized nor decentralized (i.e., those based on the sector). Although this received economic wisdom has been subject to a thorough reappraisal by Traxler and his colleagues (2001), it continues to hold sway in many policy-making circles.

New ways of thinking about managing the employment relationship associated with 'human resource management' (HRM) are also relevant. Controversy continues to surround the 'rhetoric' and 'reality' of HRM, but definitions usually embrace a number of common elements (Bach 2005 pp.11–16): the view that employees are a strategic resource for achieving competitive advantage; an emphasis on the coherence of personnel policies and their integration with business strategy; an approach to managing employees which is proactive rather than reactive; a shift in emphasis from management–trade union to management-employee relations; stress on individual commitment; and the development of individual-based pay and performance control mechanisms. If employees really are an asset crucial to securing competitive advantage, then it is difficult to justify the company relinquishing control of wages and major conditions to external employers' organizations.

The significance of the links between changing business strategies, management structures and HRM practices is illustrated by the decision of the three major Dutch financial services groups, ABN-AMRO, ING and RABO, to withdraw from their sector agreements in banking and insurance in 1999. As representatives of the Dutch unions explained to their colleagues from other countries, one consideration is a greater willingness on the part of the Dutch groups to compete with one another.

Simply put, the groups are fighting for (the best) employees, and HRM is believed a powerful tool to engage in this continuous fight (pulling employees in and binding them). Not surprisingly, on the reward side, employee benefits as part of the integrated HRM play an increasingly important role. The groups all state that they would like to meet the demands of their (potential) employees by offering the individual more flexibility within the package of remuneration. The groups concede that individualization and differences in the personal situations of the increasingly heterogeneous employee population lead to different wishes (UNI-Europa 2000).

Another factor is that, despite the European Commission's (2009) continuing strong support, the European 'social model' can no longer unequivocally be presented as one characterized by strong interest associations, regulating the labor market through inclusive agreements. A significant group of member states in the enlarged EU have little or no tradition of multiemployer bargaining. Indeed, Meardi (2002) has gone so far to argue that the Central and Eastern Europe accession countries could turn out to be the 'Trojan horse' for the 'Americanization' of industrial relations across the wider EU.

The Dynamics of Change

It is not enough, however, to list the factors linking changes to trade union membership and collective bargaining coverage with a range of variables. It is also necessary to appreciate the dynamics of change. Take, for example, the very considerable reduction in the coverage of collective bargaining in the UK between 1984 and 1998, along with a halving of TU density. Very rarely was this a consequence of active and aggressive acts of derecognition. Rather it reflected a process of withering on the vine—in some cases, managers were not bothered to recognize trade unions in newly established workplaces; in others, the demise of the multiemployer agreement or the breakup of the company (multisite) agreement similarly meant that some workplaces fell through the net. There was also a great deal of 'implicit derecognition' (i.e., a gradual reduction in the range and intensity of issues subject to negotiation)—with the balance shifting in favor of consultation or communications. Put simply, managers found that they could function perfectly adequately without trade unions (Brown et al. 2009).

Similarly, to begin with, the decentralization of collective bargaining and the 'hollowing out' of multiemployer agreements in other countries (discussed below) rarely reflected a deliberate strategy. Rather employers found it increasingly difficult to meet trade union aspirations for annual cost of living wage increases without any quid pro quo in the form of a reduction in labor costs and/or improved performance. But it is difficult to do this on an industry basis. Also, many of the 'new' issues of flexibility that negotiators have to confront, such as the freedom given to employers to vary working hours, do not lend themselves to 'hard' regulation in the same way that wages do.

Complicating matters is the increasing difference of interest between large and smaller employers, many of which are in close (low-cost) subcontracting relationships with one another. In the words of Hornung-Draus (2001, p.7), who was an official of the German Employers' Confederation:

> The big global players which were exposed to international competition were interested above all in avoiding industrial disputes, particularly strikes, which would lead to a loss of international clients for their companies. At the same time they imposed cost reductions on their

small supplier companies, which were sitting at the same negotiating table, and were therefore interested above all in avoiding cost increases imposed by collective agreements. The result of this was a situation of increasing tension on the employers' side with a number of smaller companies either leaving the employer organisations or not respecting contractual obligations arising from the collective agreements.

THE NATURE AND EXTENT OF CHANGE

A Changing Agenda

Traditionally, collective bargaining is associated with trade union demands for a 'common rule' for wages, hours of work and other terms and conditions of employment. Increasingly, however, as the previous section suggested, there has been a shift towards a 'competition-oriented' agenda with a much wider range of topics on the table. Significantly, too, it is management taking the initiative in raising them. Table 2.4 gives an idea of the issues that were typically involved in the negotiation of 'pacts for employment and competitiveness' in the second half of the 1990s. More recently, similar issues have loomed large in the light of the global financial crisis. For example, there have been major restructuring exercises involving companies such as Daimler (Germany), Škoda Auto (Czech Republic), Hewlett-Packard (Spain), Axa (Ireland), Electrolux (Italy), Volvo (Sweden), and Jaguar Land Rover and JCB (UK). Typically, redundancies and skill loss have been avoided. In return, however, there have been pay freezes and short-time working (EIRO 2009a). More difficult to determine is whether there has been a fundamental change in management–trade union relations (as depicted in Table 2.2). Skeptics might say that much of what is happening largely boils down to 'concession bargaining'—managers need the legitimation of employees and their representatives for very difficult decisions such as job cuts and major changes in terms and conditions.

A changing structure. So far there is just one case where the pressures discussed above have led to the demise of multiemployer bargaining in most sectors. This is the UK. In 1968, the Donovan Royal Commission on Trade Unions and Employers' Associations referred to multiemployer bargaining as the 'formal' system of industrial relations. By the end of the 1980s, this was no longer true, and by 1998, no more than three percent of workplaces had wages set at this level (Brown et al. 2009). Multiemployer bargaining may remain dominant in other countries, but there are important changes underway concerning its scope and substance.

Fraying at the edges. In Germany, the process Hornung-Draus describes above means that multiemployer agreements are shrinking in their coverage of firms. In the key metalworking sector, the membership density of *Gesamtmetall*, the employers' association, has declined steadily since 1980, when it stood at 58 percent, to 44 percent in the western part of the country

Table 2.4   Pacts for employment and competitiveness

Employment

guarantees of employment and/or no compulsory redundancy

investment for particular establishments

transformation of precarious into more stable jobs

additional employment for groups such as the young and unemployed

the relocation of the workforce within the company

introduction of 'work foundations' to improve the employment prospects of redundant workers

Pay

reduction in pay levels and associated benefits

lower starter rates for new employees

commitments to moderate pay demands

increases linked to indicators such as prices, productivity, exchange rates

share ownership

Working time

temporary or long-term reduction in the working week

greater variability in working hours without overtime premium

increased use of part-time work

extension of operating hours (e.g. weekend work)

new conditions for using fixed-term contracts, temporary work and outsourcing

Work organisation and human capital

new forms of work organisation such as team work

training and development

Source: Based on Sisson and Artiles (2000).

in 1993 and 34 percent in 1998. In the eastern part of the country, it stood at only 17 percent in 1998, having fallen from 35 percent in 1993 (Hassel 1999, p.494; 2002a, p.312). In Hassel's words (2002a, p.312), '[B]ig companies tend to remain members of the employers' associations while small companies tend to resign'. More recent data suggest that the coverage of collective bargaining is continuing to shrink. More than half of the establishments in Western Germany and approximately three quarters of Eastern German companies are not bound by collective agreements (EIRO 2010b). A further significant development is the establishment by German employers' associations of separate 'Ohne-Tarif' ('without collective agreement') organizations. 'OT' members receive the same services from the employers' association, but have considerable flexibility in determining levels and systems of pay and working time.

Decentralization. With the increasing orientation of the bargaining agenda toward questions of competitiveness, adaptability and work organization, more and more issues are being decentralized to the company level because of the detail involved in their negotiation. Indeed, sometimes they cannot even be dealt with at the overall company level. Many company agreements take the form of 'framework agreements', leaving detailed implementation to individual business units, and reflecting also the need to legitimate change with those involved.

The devolution of bargaining is not just a 'top-down' process under the control of higher levels, however. It also reflects a 'bottom-up' dynamic in which higher-level agreements are periodically adjusted to take account of autonomous developments at company level. For example, this dynamic has long been a feature of the relationship between sector- and company-level bargaining in Italy. It is also becoming apparent in other countries. In Germany, for example, much of the decentralization is 'unauthorised' (Hassel and Rehder 2001); in other words, company agreements are in open breach of sector-level standards and agreements or deal with issues on which the sector agreement is silent.

Hollowing out. Historically, sector agreements tended to be relatively 'hard' in their application. Basically, this means two things: first, they are consistent with the principle of universal standards; and, second, they tend to be 'complete' in that they prescribe the parameters of local outcomes. In recent years, however, a number of devices have been used to introduce scope for company-level variation within the framework of sector agreements that mean they are becoming increasingly 'soft' in their application. These vary in the degree of the 'softness' introduced. At one end of the continuum are agreements that are little more than 'frameworks'—they may specify minimum standards, but the nature of the 'opening' (sometimes known as 'hardship') clauses means that the scope for company variation is virtually limitless. At the other end are agreements that continue to specify standard conditions—any 'opening' clauses limit company variation to very few issues within strict parameters. The further toward the 'softer' end of this continuum, the more the substantive content of agreements tends to become 'hollowed-out' and the more they assume a procedural character (for further details, see Marginson and Sisson 2004, chapter 6).

Even wages and working time, which provided the core of sector agreements' standards, are affected. In the case of wages, for example, the amount of the increase may be decided in the sector agreement, but distribution of the settlement and the precise ways in which the money is actually paid may be delegated for decision at the company level. In the case of working time, the same is true of any reductions in working hours: the decision as to whether these are to be taken in the form of fewer weekly hours or additional holidays can be left to the parties to decide locally.

'Opening' clauses have become a more or less universal feature of sector agreements across Europe, with their nature and extent proving to be controversial in some countries. In France, for example, the 'loi Fillon' of 2004 was introduced despite trade union opposition. Previously, a collective agreement at company (or workplace) level could only improve on the employees' rights laid down in a sector-level agreement. Under the new law, collective agreements may deviate from the provisions of higher-level ones unless such derogation is expressly forbidden (EIRO, 2004). The favorability principle remains in force in respect of four themes: minimum wages; job classifications; supplementary social protection measures; and multicompany and cross-sector vocational training funds.

In Italy, a not dissimilar controversy surrounded the negotiation of the cross-sector agreement of January 2009, to which the government was a party. Among a raft of proposals designed to build on a July 1993 protocol and modernize the Italian system of industrial relations, there is provision for introducing 'opening clauses' to cope with restructuring or to foster economic growth and employment creation. Crucially too, these deal not just with wages but also with the normative parts of sector agreements dealing with issues such as working time. Supporters say the agreement will help to strengthen the national-level and decentralized bargaining at the same time: in the view of the vice president of Confindustria, the broader scope for decentralized bargaining is essential, as 'at company level it is possible to respond more directly to the needs of workers and employers, thereby improving productivity and competitiveness, two crucial elements in this phase to cope with the economic situation' (EIRO 2009b). The main trade union confederation, CGIL (*Confederazione Generale Italiana del Lavoro*), refused to sign the accord, however, arguing that it would make it easier to weaken worker protection, while at the same time being too vague and weak to promote decentralized bargaining (for further details, see EIRO 2009b).

Developments in Denmark and the Netherlands also suggest that the company level is far from being the endpoint of the decentralization process. In Denmark, innovative agreements in the banking, insurance and important slaughterhouse sectors concluded in early 2003 effectively introduced *à la carte* provisions. A proportion of the wage package is left open for individual employees to make annual choices between more money and other items including more time off and (in the case of slaughterhouses) increased occupational pension contributions. In financial services, the choices available will be specified by 'catalogues' to be drawn up between the parties at company level (EIRO 2003a and 2003b). In the Netherlands, the Foundation of Labour (the joint body responsible for advising the government on socioeconomic decision making) reached an agreement promoting 'tailored employment conditions' in 1999. Referred to as a 'multiple-choice model' (van der Meer 2001), the understanding encourages negotiators at lower levels to introduce, within the framework of the collective agreement, scope for greater individual choice with regard to certain employment conditions.

There might be a tradeoff, for example, between 'time and money' or current and deferred remuneration (for further details, see Marginson and Sisson 2004).

FUTURE PROSPECTS

It is extremely unlikely that the pressures on inclusive forms of multiemployer collective bargaining will diminish. Indeed, they are likely to intensify. It does not necessarily mean that other countries will follow the UK, however, in witnessing the demise of such bargaining. This is above all true because of long-standing differences in the legal status of collective agreements. In the UK, collective agreements are grounded in procedural rules and are voluntary in status. In most other countries, they are rooted in substantive rules and are legally enforceable contracts and codes; in many cases, too, statutory provisions for trade union recognition are national rather than workplace-based.

Arguably, however, the outcome of such bargaining is unlikely, except in rare situations, to take the form of the comprehensive contracts of old. There is a number of possible directions in which arrangements might go. A first possibility is that the scope for company-level negotiation is progressively widened as 'organized decentralization' is taken further and sector agreements increasingly become 'framework' agreements, as many employers' organizations have argued for. A tradeoff here might be the incorporation into the sector agreement of additional issues such as work-life balance—especially where highly skilled or 'knowledge' workers are involved. A second possibility is that twin-track arrangements emerge: large employers may abandon sector multiemployer bargaining and establish their own company agreements, leaving the sector agreement to regulate the terms and conditions for medium- and small-sized companies. A third possibility is what might be described as the 'Irish' solution: in smaller countries sector bargaining finds itself squeezed between the national and the company level. Each of these possibilities could occur either by design or, as was the case with the UK's 'unorganized decentralization', by default—with both 'authorized' and 'unauthorized' decentralization encouraging employers to behave opportunistically.

Conceivably, the emphasis could shift from the national sector to the EU sector (Arrowsmith and Marginson 2006). In many respects, this would be wholly consistent with the historical trend in which collective bargaining follows the product market. Yet it is unlikely even if there are further moves towards fiscal union: the more decentralized bargaining becomes within countries and the more globalized product markets become for large companies, the less significant will be the national sector level.

Perhaps the most critical point to make is that, such is the significance of an inclusive structure of collective bargaining, these and other options are not matters just for individual trade unions and employers' organizations to decide. Much will and should be decided in the political domain. If policy makers (both at national and EU levels) want inclusive forms of collective bargaining to continue—and, to return to what said at the very beginning, there are very good reasons why they should—they need to understand the pressures that it faces. In particular, they need to appreciate that the crisis decisions they take can exaggerate the multilevel governance threats that have been highlighted. More positively, they need to think about what actions they should be taking to secure their future. For example, legislative initiatives could be tailored to ensure implementation by inclusive collective agreements. Much more could also be made of provisions for the legal extension of collective agreements. The same goes for minimum wage legislation. EU social dialogue could also be used to encourage the negotiation of agreements at country and/or sector level. In any event, if policy makers do not take action, the decline of collective bargaining is likely to continue with significant negative implications for the European 'social model'.

REFERENCES

Arrowsmith, J. and Marginson, P. 2006. 'The European cross-border dimension to collective bargaining in multinational companies'. *European Journal of Industrial Relations*, 12:3. 245–266.

Brown, W., Bryson, A. and Forth, J. 2009. 'Competition and the retreat from collective bargaining', in W. Brown, A. Bryson, J. Forth and K. Whitfield (eds.) *The Evolution of the Modern Workplace*. Cambridge: Cambridge University Press. 22–47.

Calmfors, L. and Driffill, J. 1988. 'Bargaining structure, corporatism and macroeconomic performance', *Economic Policy*, 6. 13–61.

Commons, J. 1909. 'American shoemakers 1648–1895: A sketch of industrial evolution', *Quarterly Journal of Economics*, 24. 38–83. Reprinted 1968, in R. L. Rowan and H. R. Northrup (eds.) *Readings in Labor Economics and Labor Relations*. Homewood: Irwin. 60–76.

Dølvik, J. 2001. 'Industrial relations in EMU: Re-nationalization and Europeanization: Two Sides of the Same Coin?'. Paper presented to the IIRA 6th European Congress, Oslo, June 25–29.

EIRO 2003a. 'New collective agreements signed in banking'. [online] Ref: DE0301202N. Available at <www.eurofound.europa.eu/eiro/2003/01/inbrief/de0301202n.htm>

EIRO 2003b. 'New agreements introduce "individual options" for employees'. [online] Ref: DK0302102F. Available at <www.eu.eurofound.ie>

EIRO 2004. 'Collective bargaining reform law passed'. [online] Ref: FR0404105F. Available at <www.eu.eurofound.ie>

EIRO 2009a. 'Multinational companies and collective bargaining'. [online] European Foundation for the Improvement of Living and Working Conditions. Available at <www.eu.eurofound.ie>

EIRO 2009b. 'CGIL refuses to sign agreement on collective bargaining reform'. [online] Ref: IT090205591. Available at <www.eu.eurofound.ie>

EIRO 2010a. 'Developments in social partner organisations—employer organisations'. [online] Ref: TN0910049S. Available at <www.eu.eurofound.ie>

EIRO 2010b. 'Germany: Industrial relations profile'. [online] Available at <www. eu.eurofound.ie>

European Commission 2009. *Industrial Relations in Europe 2008*. Brussels: Directorate-General for Employment, Social Affairs and Equal Opportunities Unit F.1.

Froud, J., Haslam, C., Johal, S. and Williams, K. 2000. 'Shareholder value and financialisation: Consultancy promise, management moves', *Economy and Society*, 29:1. 80–111.

———. 1999. 'The erosion of the German industrial relations system', *British Journal of Industrial Relations*, 37:3. 484–505.

———. 2002a. 'The erosion continues: Reply', *British Journal of Industrial Relations*, 40:2. 309–317.

———. 2002b. 'A new going rate? Co-ordinated wage bargaining in Europe', in P. Pochet (ed.) *Wage Policy in the Eurozone*. Brussels: PIE-Peter Lang S.A. 149–173.

Hassel, A. and Rehder, B. 2001. 'Institutional Change in the German Wage Bargaining System—The Role of Big Companies'. *MPIfG Working Paper* 01/9 Cologne: Max-Planck-Institut für Gesellschaftsforschung.

Hornung-Draus, R. 2001. 'Between E-economy, Euro and Enlargement: Where Are Employer Organisations in Europe Heading?' Plenary paper presented to the 6th IIRA European Congress. Oslo, June 25–29.

Hutton, W. 2008. 'The fallacy of the fix. Reform just won't cut it. We need nothing less than an overhaul of the way we do capitalism', *The Guardian*. 19 November. Available at <www.guardian.co.uk/commentisfree/2008/nov/19/g20-economic-reform-capitalism-budget>

Léonard, E. 2001. 'Industrial relations and the regulation of employment in Europe', *European Journal of Industrial Relations*, 7:1. 27–47.

Léonard, E., Erne, R., Marginson, P. and Smismans, S. 2007. *New Structures, Forms and Processes of Governance in European Industrial Relations* Dublin: European Foundation for the Improvement of Living and Working Conditions.

Lesch, H. 2004. 'Trade Union Density in International Comparison'. *CESifo Forum*, 5:4. 12–18.

Marginson P. and Sisson, K. 2004. *European Integration and Industrial Relations*. Basingstoke: Palgrave-Macmillan.

Meardi, G. 2002. 'The trojan horse for the Americanization of Europe? Polish industrial relations towards the EU', *European Journal of Industrial Relations*, 8:1. 77–99.

van de Meer, M. 2001. 'From Taylor-made to tailor-made'. Paper presented at the Conference on the Netherlands HRM Network, Nijmegen. 15 November.

OECD 2009. *Pensions at a Glance: Current Trends and Policy Topics in Retirement-Income Systems in OECD Countries*. Paris: OECD.

Panic, M. 2007. 'Does Europe need neoliberal reforms?' *Cambridge Journal of Economics*, 31. 159.

Scharpf, F. 1988. 'The joint-decision trap: Lessons from German federalism and European integration', *Public Administration*, 66. 239–278.

Schulten, T. 2002. 'A European solidaristic wage policy?' *European Journal of Industrial Relations*, 8:2. 173–196.

Sisson, K. 1987. *The Management of Collective Bargaining: An International Comparison*. Oxford: Blackwell.

Sisson, K. and Artiles, A. M. 2000. *Handling Restructuring: A study of Collective Agreements on Employment and Competitiveness*. Luxembourg: Office for the Official Publications of the European Communities.

Sisson, K. and Marginson, P. 2001. '"Soft regulation"'—travesty of the real thing or new dimension?' *One Europe or Several? Working Paper* 32/01. Falmer (Brighton): University of Sussex.

Traxler, F., Blaschke, S. and Kittel, B. 2001. *National Labour Relations in Internationalized Markets*. Oxford: OUP.

UNI-Europa 2000. *Pay benchmarking and the Euro—How should UNI-Europa respond?* Geneva: UNI-Europa.

Van Tulder, R., van den Berghe, D. and Muller, A. 2001. *Erasmus (S)coreboard of Core Companies: The World's Largest Firms and Internationalization.* Rotterdam: Rotterdam School of Management.

Visser, J. 2006. 'Union Membership statistics in 24 countries', *Monthly Labor Review*, January. 38–49.

Whittington, R. and Mayer, M. 2000. *The European Corporation: Strategy, Structure And Social Science.* Oxford: OUP.

3 Worker Voice Under Pressure

Collective Workplace Representation and the Challenge of Multiplying Spaces and Actors

Miguel Martínez Lucio and Maria González Menéndez

INTRODUCTION

Modes of representation within the firm and the workplace have developed through a variety of forms in EU countries, and are related to the process of collective bargaining in various ways (see chapter 2, this volume). First, worker representation can be established with varying degrees of independence of the employer and management. That is to say, worker representatives may be imposed, selected or elected by a variety of means. However, within the EU it is generally accepted that worker representatives within workplaces and their forums for discussing issues with management should be independent of employer interests. Second, channels for workers' voices can be established through a body of formal legislation. In some cases custom and practice remains very important, as in the UK, but in most European countries there is some form of constitutional underpinning. Third, bodies such as works councils, which we discuss below, are often consultative but in some countries bargain collectively with management. The fourth characteristic is the relation with trade unions, which in the EU is significant. Workers' collective representation is tied into the broader networks and structures of trade unions by virtue of the nature of the representatives (their affiliation and allegiances) at works councils and similar bodies. Each of these characteristics have, for the second half of the twentieth century at least, underpinned the nature of worker voice within the European workplace.

However, across these four dimensions—the extent of independence *vis-à-vis* management, the link with the state, the relationship with collective bargaining activities and the role of trade unions—there are variations in terms of depth. This presents us with a dilemma in that gaps may emerge across these dimensions, and the argument is that in the past twenty years these gaps have become more significant. They are primarily a challenge to the issue of coordination and occur across various dimensions: the link between sector and company representation, the link between works councils/company forums and trade unions, the link between collective and direct/individual representation and the link between different units of the firm in the context of subcontracting and other forms of decentralization. Fracturing processes within representation occur through these different spaces and gaps such that we see a problem of multiplicity of sites and relations being the main challenge to worker representation.

This chapter first explains the context and background of the mechanisms for workers' collective representation within the (Western) EU workplace and then proceeds to focus on the forces for change that are widening the gaps outlined above. The chapter discusses a series of national experiences that vary according to the activities and structures of bodies such as works councils. It shows how we are seeing changes across various national contexts even if the basic features of such bodies and their roles appear to remain in place. The chapter argues thus that while change does not appear to be so extensive when observing these bodies from a formal and descriptive perspective, there are subtle shifts that suggest that the pattern of workplace representation is fragmenting. This argument is further elaborated through a discussion of how workers' direct participation has emerged as a counterpoint and challenge to established forms of worker representation of a collective nature. The conclusion is that we need to be increasingly sensitive to the pressures that workers' representation is under.

CONTEXT AND BACKGROUND: HOW COLLECTIVE REPRESENTATION WAS MADE

The modern tradition of organized industrial relations, for the large part of the latter twentieth century, was linked to various regulatory practices within Western Europe. A body of collective legal rights and formalized structures of representation at different levels of the economy and the firm (with varying points of emphasis) underpinned the role of voice within the industrial relations systems of Europe. Increasingly, liberal-democratic industrial relations emphasized and focused on creating a 'social dialogue' through mechanisms of representation, which had a specific presence at the level of the firm and sometimes even the workplace.

Thus, alongside the practice of collective bargaining and macrolevel political representation there was a general commitment to ongoing social dialogue within the firm. According to Hyman and Mason (1995), the development of worker representation, and participation more generally, was not solely the outcome of economic development and new forms of state intervention in the mid-twentieth century. Extending the logic of representation within the workplace was also inspired by the democratic context after the war, and by broad social and intellectual concerns about the importance of voice and welfare at work (Kaufman 2008). However, it was also the outcome of a political tension, the changing balance of forces between labor and capital (Ramsay 1983), and the growing importance of legal norms structuring management prerogative—showing the manner in which specific views and understandings of participation and representation emerge at particular times and in different country contexts (Marchington and Wilkinson 2000; Knudsen 1995).

One of the enduring reasons for the stability of workers' workplace collective representation in many of the more organized and unionized systems of industrial relations in Western Europe since the 1950s is that it brought benefits to the different social partners, albeit not always similar. Knudsen (1995) outlines how, for unions, the benefits concern being able to influence the social and economic agenda of firms; for the employer, there are perceived benefits in terms of efficiency; and for the state, there is the prospect of greater social cohesion. Hence, it is not simply a case of there being a strong social-democratic consensus or realization of mutual gains that underpins workers' workplace participation but also of there being a set of interests that can be balanced through structured dialogue within the firm. However, it is this balance that began to destabilize from the 1970s onward. Knudsen (1995) also points out—as the cases below will further reveal—that participation at the level of the firm within different countries is structured around very different traditions of dialogue and power resources such that the outcome of dialogue is reflects quite different inputs and expectations.

At the heart of the concept of workplace voice representation is the *works council* and similar bodies. For some, this is the quintessential instrument of European bargaining and/or consultation. It is the space around which class compromise is institutionalized on a routine and ongoing basis. It is also a space that can become an active agent in its own right, intervening in the array of private and public spheres of the organization. This entity forms one of the major dimensions of Western European industrial relations and has become a focus point for discussion (Rogers and Streeck 1995). Whilst their relation with collective bargaining varies across countries, these institutions carry a representative logic by being subject to electoral processes. Their relations with unions vary also, with some contexts having a very close relation whilst in others they may be more ambivalent, even if works councilors are normally trade union members or even activists themselves (Müller-Jentsch, 1995).

FORCES FOR CHANGE: CHANGING MARKET AND SOCIAL FORCES AND THEIR ROLE IN UNCOUPLING THE POSTWAR MODEL

Understanding the forces that have reshaped workers' workplace voice representation since the 1970s raises some challenges for constructing a clear narrative of historical development. There is a tendency to focus on the changing nature of market forces, the impact of globalization and the less supportive attitude of the state as factors 'undermining' representation. However, this dominant approach to the issue—driven by managerial proponents of change and, ironically, their critics who seem to emphasize the downward trajectory of indirect representation under neoliberalism—ignores many of the contradictory and highly diverse forces driving such change. Just as the construction of a system of workplace participation was complex and contested—with the emergence of a set of varieties on a generally common model—so the pressures for change are equally complex and even contradictory. The pressures may indeed be seen to emerge in the wake of the economic crisis of the 1970s and the emergence of the New Right and its early neoliberal agenda, yet this is a not wholly convincing account. First, increasing competitive pressures on private and public sector employers actually made the issue of worker representation more salient, notwithstanding the range of social pressures and political discourses/policies propagating greater investment in workers' representation and industrial democracy. Second, it followed, in the 1960s, a moment when worker activists and networks were beginning to challenge the perceived passivity of institutions such as works councils and even trade union officials and leadership. The steady erosion of the 'social democratic consensus', and its vested interest in structured dialogue around specific elements of the employment relation such as wages, opened a debate on 'worker control' in broad and perhaps loose terms within countries as diverse as the UK and Italy.

In the economic and political dimensions, it is argued that the increasing pressures placed on employers as a consequence of the economic crisis of the 1970s (partially through increasing material and labor costs), coupled with the early opening of national markets, created a need to focus on containing wage costs for competitive reasons. This placed pressure on wage bargaining and general labor costs within industrial relations systems (Lash and Urry 1987). Certainly, from the early 1980s onward, with the emergence of the New Right in the UK and the US, the consensus around collective bargaining and the utility of workers' representation at the workplace was challenged in an overt manner (MacInnes 1987). The presence of trade unions and their forums within the firm became an object of political scrutiny—although as noted above one could argue that this political concern had its origins in the 1960s due to increasing conflict within the workplace. Yet added to this economic and political context of the 1980s were significant developments in the structure of the firm. Increasing use of subcontracting and outsourcing, temporary and agency work and the growth of smaller and medium-sized employers meant that in many European countries a new decentralized logic emerged to challenge organization and 'centered' decision making (MacKenzie and Forde 2006).

To these structural changes one can add the strategic changes identified in relation to the conduct of management. The emergence of innovative forms of communication such as quality circles, the use of team leaders, the development of surveys, and the use of nonunion representatives in an informal and even formal manner contributed to a new link between management and the workforce (Martínez Lucio and Weston 1992; Bacon and Storey 1993). In the UK, these initiatives attracted the attention of management as it became enamored—at least rhetorically—with American and Japanese models of 'human resource management' (Stewart 1996; Klikauer 2007). That these developments were not as systematic as portrayed is another matter, as we discuss later, but they formed part of a new 'armory' in challenging workers' voice representation through trade union and independently elected representatives. At a time when trade union membership was declining or remained at a low threshold in major countries such as the UK, France and Spain, these developments represented a potential turn in the form of industrial relations away from macrolevel corporatism and more structured forms of representation (see Stuart and Martínez Lucio 2005).

However, the response by employers and management were driven not solely by economic pressures and new 'supportive' market-leaning political contexts. The 1980s and 1990s began to see a new wave of interest in the question of representation and social rights, a theme rarely picked up in the debate on workers' workplace representation. We see new dynamics in the space of representation with the firm, with greater contestation not solely concerning employment relations (e.g., wages and working hours) but also the broader employment needs of individuals and their status. First, the emergence of a greater emphasis on equality in countries such as the UK, the Netherlands, and more recently, Spain, started to widen the dialogue between labor and management. Second, this is paralleled by an increasing employer engagement with information and consultation, partly driven by the regulatory apparatus of the EU (Broughton 2005), but also by the increasing intensity of organizational change and the role that participation can play with regards to efficiency and value (Storey 2005a and 2005b). Hence, we see that the *pull* for workers' workplace participation and representation remains, forcing employers and unions to start contesting its future forms, especially as 'communicative relationships' have become increasingly central to the organization (Klikauer 2007).

These developments are also increasingly linked to changes taking place in technology, which reinforces pressure for change. Some argue that this places traditional forms of representation such as works councils in a difficult position: communication is not clearly directed through established channels but can be restructured through management emails, video links, and so forth. These can be used to provide information more directly and 'out-flank' the formal trade union communication with the workforce. However, there is an argument that trade unions have not been slow to respond to these developments and have used the Internet to set up their own direct links to the workforce as observed with European works councilors in key European companies (Pulignano 2009). In addition, it cannot be assumed that the sheer deluge of information may not saturate the space of representation (Walker and Creanor 2000), thus complicating representation spaces even further.

NATIONAL DYNAMICS AND CONTRADICTORY
DEVELOPMENTS IN EUROPE: VARIETIES IN TERMS OF
THE NEW FISSURES WITHIN COLLECTIVE REPRESENTATION

The recent dynamics of workers' representation is best understood through discussion of a series of national cases. First, though European approaches to collective voice may share much in common, there are also very different experiences and trajectories as we stated above. Moreover, the factors that are driving change are diverse and cannot simply be read in terms of the *marketization* or 'Americanization' of industrial relations. It is important to consider (i) the way workplace representation has been constructed to start with, (ii) the relationship between workplace and sector levels of regulation, and (iii) the general structure of trade unionism. We select three national case studies that reflect different approaches to collective representation. The UK case allows us to discuss the context of a dramatic decline in (private sector) worker representation. This is also prescient in Spain, where representation is formally underpinned in legal and regulatory terms but is challenged by a logic of decentering within the system of industrial relations, and even Germany where in a context of robust worker representation, there are serious issues in terms of fragmentation.

The UK: Markets, Individuals and Disorganization

The UK represents one of the most advanced cases of decentralization and fragmentation. The emergence of large swathes of nonunionized areas of the economy, and the role played by nonunion employee representatives, provides trade unions with a serious challenge in terms of their ability to organize and represent the workforce. Historically, the question of representation was based on a system of employer recognition of trade unions that has not been significantly changed for most of the past hundred years. Legislation in the late 1990s focused mainly on establishing a series of trigger mechanisms for employers to have to recognize trade unions for the purpose of bargaining, but these are generally considered minimalist and ineffective in underpinning trade union representation (Perrett 2007). There is no legal mechanism providing for ongoing workplace representation, and there is no legislation that binds collective agreements. In the past few years only 30 percent of workplaces with ten or more employees had a recognized trade union, and the majority of the workforce is not covered by a collective agreement (Kersley et al. 2005). This means that workers' voice representation is at its most advanced state of decline compared to most European countries.

The absence of legislative support for representation was endorsed, or at least not seriously questioned, by the trade union movement for most of the twentieth century due to its distrust of the state and judiciary and thus a preference for immunities from prosecution with regard to matters such as collective action (Phelps Brown 1983). Trade unions' recognition for the purpose of collective bargaining has been mainly voluntary in nature for the employer, with custom and practice (and tradition) dictating the presence of a specific trade union in any one firm or body of workers. Even when the custom was to have a 'closed shop' (a situation where all workers had to be a trade union member in order to be employed in a specific workplace), these rules were not governed by state legislation but by the balance of power between trade unions and employers. Furthermore, competition between trade unions for membership was covered by a range of rules overseen by the Trades Union Congress (TUC) to prohibit or limit—with varying degrees of success—the ability of a union to engage in recruitment activities of a workforce or occupation linked to another union organization. A final characteristic worth noting of the UK labor movement is that it has had a strong workplace presence in many sectors. The bargaining and trade union role of the workplace representative, commonly known as 'the shop steward', was much broader in comparison to European counterparts (Batstone et al. 1978).

The historical strength of trade unions and the character of industrial relations were based on a series of consultative committees and parallel structures—somewhat more formalized in the public sector—as bases of workers' representation. Both at workplace level and at higher levels in the organization, there traditionally was no statutory structure for employee representation (Fulton 2011). Workers' representation has been seriously affected by a series of factors facilitated by this historical failure to systematically regulate industrial relations, especially since a decline in trade union membership from 55 percent in 1979 to just over 20 percent in 2011, which means that organized labor has a low coverage, especially in the private sector (Arrowsmith 2010). This gives rise to capacity issues and problems related to staffing. Further, many firms have installed management-led consultative committees with very little trade union independence (Charlwood and Terry 2007). Nonunionized employers have bypassed trade unions, used direct forms of participation to control the space of representation, or gone so far as to establish forms of representation that appear to be collective but which are based on individual and management-dependent representatives (Dundon and Rollinson 2004). Employers and management have therefore attempted to *occupy* the workplace space with a variety of individual and collective strategies. Whilst many sectors still have strong traditions of union representation, there is now a significant area that has created a parallel industrial relations system—albeit one that is by no means coherent in form and content (Dundon and Rollinson 2004).

Furthermore, developments in subcontracting and interfirm collaboration means that, in the context of a lack of sector-level regulatory arrangements, many different patterns of workers' representation may coexist. It is important to note that the UK model is therefore incoherent and in many respects is not a simple 'Americanized' counter to the more coordinated models and deeper systems of regulation that exist elsewhere in Europe; indeed, employer advocates argue that diversity in representation and consultation is more the 'UK approach' (Yeandle 2005). The future is less a marketized and individualized system and more a parallel set of practices which coexist due to an absence of an overarching regulatory logic. Recent interventions in terms of information and consultation—driven by the EU and implemented reluctantly by the UK—have not reversed this trend (Hall et al. 2011).

Spain: Declining Coordination, Resource Challenges and Decentralization

Workers' workplace representation in Spain is based on works councils, which exist at the company and office/plant level depending on employment size. They emerged from those constructed during the Francoist dictatorship (1939–1975), which was dominated by management and did not involve independent representatives and trade unions—although an electoral logic did emerge in the latter years. The number of councilors varies according to the size of the workplace, with councilors elected every four years by the entire workforce. Since 1978 a significant majority of the Spanish workforce has voted in these events and the two main left-wing trade unions—Comisiones Obreras (CCOO) and Unión General de Trabajadores (UGT)—have dominated the results. Works councils are therefore closely linked to trade unions and are an integral part of labor activists' work. Smaller companies (more than five and less than 50 employees) tend to participate in the trade union elections, but the outcome is a smaller number of workers' representatives participating in a less formal representative body.

According to Escobar (1995), works councils in Spain have played an active role across three important dimensions. First, they have a legal right to negotiate at the firm level, and agreements struck by the majority of the representatives with management are binding for all workers. Many of these negotiations are held at the plant level as well and can cover a range of issues from wages to social conditions, so long as they do not undermine any higher-tier agreement related to the firm, although this is changing (see below). Second, such bodies also play a significant role in regulating the decisions of management and can influence promotions and other internal labor market issues. Third, they also cooperate with management in many instances with regard to restructuring and other questions of organizational change. Large companies with works councils normally try to sign relevant agreements; significant examples include the Peugeot plant in Madrid (Martínez Lucio 1988) or the General Motors plant in Zaragoza (Ortiz 1998), where the works councils cooperated with management on various aspects of organizational change and workplace reform during the 1980s and 1990s. The relationship between works councils and management can thus be symbiotic in some cases in which a more proactive dialogue has been able to flourish. There are also various subcommittees, on health and safety, for example, that bring the works councils close to a range of specific employment issues.

Hence, workers' representation is highly formalized in many medium to large workplaces and companies.

Notwithstanding this, there have been various challenges in recent decades. Works councils are rarely dominated by one trade union, meaning that there are two stages of negotiation and discussion: one between the different trade unions represented and then one between the unions and management. Part of the problem in the 1980s was the manner in which a third dimension of negotiation existed between individual trade unions and management. The UGT in some cases was known for a more conciliatory and 'realistic' tone in the 1980s and would sometimes maintain direct communications and links with management (Martínez Lucio 1998). It was also not unknown for the two majority unions to close off discussions to some of the minority unions. Management attempts to divide the works councils were also common and partly reflected the nature of worker representation in Spain, and partly the differing levels of ability amongst workplace trade unionists. Escobar (1995) also outlined how management and employers could sometimes isolate works councils with reference to a sector agreement, promote collaborationist trade unions and associations as in retailing, and develop a more business-oriented relation. Retailing and fast-food industry employers and management often interfered in the elections for representatives with the objective of undermining more radical currents (Ortiz and Royle 2009). In addition, in many smaller firms and workplaces, trade union representatives once elected with the purpose of representing the entire workforce would become isolated and sometimes even marginalized, as they did not have as much support from unions and their organizations as representatives in larger firms. Trade union elections are therefore significant events, but there are serious issues related to organizational support and coordination between the trade unions and their representatives in small and medium-sized firms.

In addition to these structural (organizational and political) problems, compounded by the recent economic crisis, the legal framework was recently changed in terms of the link between local and sectoral agreements. Since 2010, with the Law 35/2010 on urgent measures for the labor market reform, an agreement between a works council and management will be sufficient to opt out of the terms of a sectoral collective bargaining agreement. These conditions are applicable to wage modifications and also a wide set of working conditions concerning areas of working time and the structure of remuneration. Sector-level agreements now prevail only in three areas: maximum yearly hours of work, professional classifications, and social improvements at work. In many smaller and medium-sized workplaces this may have a broad deleterious effect as negotiations on wider issues may be undermined.

Formally speaking, the Spanish system is highly regulated but in practice there is much fragmentation. Right-wing and neoliberal currents within Spanish politics have in the past ten years become more focused on undermining the sector-level bargaining frameworks of the country in the knowledge—or belief—that what lies beneath is a disjointed system of workers' representation that will edge closer to market considerations in the absence of such regulatory supports. Hence, the major threat to representation is not solely the emergence of microcorporatist logics or a more insular and less solidarity-based approach to worker representation. The fractured manner in which workplace representation emerged and developed, and its reliance on political agreement between the different factions of the labor movement for there to be coherent strategies toward management, means that employers can exploit differences and fissures within the established system of worker representation. The question of change in Spain with regard to collective representation is therefore less related to new forms of decentralization and fragmentation and more to the way in which the fissures within the system are intensified by changing political and social dynamics.

Germany: Separation and Dualism within Market-Facing Solidarity

German works councils are elected by the workforce of establishments with five or more workers every four years, and possess a series of rights on social and personnel matters (Müller-Jentsch, 1995). As in Spain, most works councils are dominated by trade union representatives of the affiliated unions of the main confederation, the DGB, along with others. The system is supported by an elaborate structure of industrial democracy—'codetermination'—which, whilst not as robust as some would want, does provide the works council with extensive and significant corporate information. The restrictions placed on works councils' collective action have also played a part in developing this approach. This facilitated the development of forms of comanagement within many larger works councils and the role of the head of a works council such as that of Ford, Volkswagen, and BMW in Germany is analogous to that of a national politician or spokesperson. Hence relations between works council representatives and management can be symbiotic and mutually supportive in many cases with an orientation toward forming consensus.

In the 1980s and 1990s, works councils and trade unions in Germany were seen to play an important part in adjusting their workplaces and members to the 'needs' of new forms of management practices such as team-working and quality circles (Murakami 1997). However, this was done within an overarching set of union strategies that attempted to 'humanize' these new approaches and link them to concerns with worker engagement and worker health. Many German trade unionists and works councilors embraced such new forms of participation and work organization within a framework of partnership with management and with a concern with workplace humanization. To this extent workers' workplace representation in Germany was fused with strategic and discursive initiatives that allowed its structures to mediate organizational change and the manner in which new forms of work organization were developed. This ideological or informational aspect is very often missing in discussions on workers' voice representation.

Yet there is a range of concerns with the direction of workers' workplace representation in Germany. Over a decade ago, Hassel (2002) pointed out that only 15 percent of German workplaces were actually covered by a collective agreement and a works council, and that there was an ongoing threat of decentralization. More recently, Doellgast and Greer (2007) have argued that the growth of subcontracting and the increasing use of temporary agencies has created a sphere of the labor market that is much harder to regulate by core workers through their established systems of representation. A myriad of sector agreements and practices are giving rise to real coordination issues, compounded by the use by employers of immigrant workers in sectors such as construction (Lillie and Greer 2007). The basic structures and remits of works councils are intact, but there is a parallel space of industrial relations emerging beyond any effective regulatory control.

It could be argued that such developments are part of a tradeoff between unions and employers to permit a greater degree of flexibility within the employment system that does not undermine the basic tenets of regulation for the majority. Thus, Bosch (2003) has argued that the pressures brought about by German unification and economic change led to a new relationship between the centralized and coordinated features of collective bargaining and regulation and the increasing role of works councils in terms of bargaining, by means of the opening clauses. Also, the current crisis illustrates that solidaristic arrangements such as using short-time working as opposed to job cuts indicates that dialogue and negotiation remain at the heart of the German system. Yet there are concerns that such tradeoffs may weaken rather than strengthen management commitment to the culture of regulation and dialogue in an ever more fragmented context, especially when German organizations are beyond the regulatory constraints of German regulation abroad (Ferner and Varul 2002). Furthermore, greater decentralization of collective bargaining could create serious coordination issues, as explored below.

THE QUESTION OF DIRECT REPRESENTATION: FRACTURING THE WORKFORCE THROUGH INDIVIDUALISM

Reliable comparative data on the extension and growth of direct participation in EU countries is scant. National and European employee surveys rarely address specific schemes other than teamwork, focusing instead on workers' perceptions of consultation and information, autonomy at work or satisfaction with current levels of participation. Yet, such evidence suggests that much of the last decades' expansion of direct participation in the EU workplace has been uneven both across national frontiers and in time (see González 2009 for a review of available survey data). Further, the nature and significance of direct representation much depends on how new regimes of work organization are linked to and mediated by traditional forms of representation.

The industrial relations literature has long been concerned with the potential threats to representative participation posed by direct participation between management and individual workers (Pateman 1970; Ramsay 1983), and although some saw room for a positive interaction between the two (IDE 1981), they were far from representing the dominant view in the field. The ambivalent European policy on workers' participation at the workplace—increasingly referred to as *workers' involvement* and portrayed as a productive factor or, at best, an element of job quality, rather than a right—together with mixed results as to its impact on workers' well-being (Gonzalez 2010) did not help make direct participation attractive to most observers though the debate may be moving toward a complementarity view (Poutsma and Veersma 2010).

Since it is generally accepted that direct participation has been management-led in all European countries (Knudsen et al. 2011), there are various explanations for its overall (if often timid) expansion within the EU. Following Knudsen's (1995) Durkheimian approach, direct participation may prove to be increasingly acceptable to workers and trade unions (i.e., that some social compromises may be crystallizing from the last decades of struggles with direct participation). Whether this means that workers and their representatives have accepted direct participation on workplace efficiency or diminished power grounds, or see it as even creating new spaces for contestation and workers' solidarity (Danford 2005; Tuckman and Whittall 2010; Martínez Lucio 2010) remains a moot point. Certainly, much depends on management motivations. For example, the HRM drive for direct participation has been felt deeply in the UK, France and Italy, if not necessarily with the same results: while in the UK union presence suffers (Pollert 2010), in France it has been enhanced (Amossé and Coutrot 2011), and the jury is out in Italy (Telljohann 2010). Union power, and concerns with quality of working life are also relevant (Gallie 2007), as has been shown by studies of regions with powerful unions in Italy (Antonioli et al. 2010) and Spain (González Menéndez 2011). The nature of direct participation in a workplace with union presence also depends on how the common interest and actor legitimacy is defined by the parties; in this sense Regini's (1993) reflection on employers' opportunism as to being more cooperative with business-aware unions could as easily be made concerning trade unions' pragmatism as to being more cooperative with union-aware employers.

That the workplace context is still important even in the often-idealized Nordic world of work has been highlighted by Knudsen et al. (2011). They identified four types of Danish workplaces depending on the depth and scope of participation: 'bipartite participation' (representative participation marked by its framework of regulation paired with a marginal direct participation linked to productivity and job satisfaction), 'HRM' (intense direct participation and weak representative participation), 'hybrid' (both present, none being very intense and direct participation strictly linked to productivity) and 'democratic' (intense representative participation beyond the regulatory boundaries and intense direct participation not primarily management-driven and not limited to operational matters). The latter workplaces had the best quality of work environment; they also were in the minority. Consistent with this, quantitative research in France (Amossé and Coutrot 2011) and Spain (González Menéndez 2011) shows that direct participation was increasingly used since the 1990s essentially as an *add-on* to Taylorism and, perhaps more importantly, that such neo-Taylorism may have become the predominant socioproductive model in both countries up to the mid-2000s. A similar concern is reported for Germany by Kratzer et al. (2010).

Returning to the question of the consequences for representative participation of the growth of direct forms, a negative effect was found in small German firms (Helfen and Schuessler 2009), although on the whole German works councils may be much more effective at blocking direct participation than their French and Spanish counterparts (Gallie 2007). However, while Amossé and Coutrot (2011) point to collective conflict and union presence in France as being increased by employer-led introduction of direct participation, González Menéndez (2011) finds workplace representative participation fosters direct participation in Spain. Such divergent results as to the link between direct and representative participation in these two countries call for a closer look.

Both countries share key industrial relations features such as the *erga omnes* principle of the application of collective bargaining, an extensive coverage of industry agreements, a strong legal protection of representative participation at firm level (less oriented to building a consensus than defensive of workers' interests *vis-à-vis* management), and a state policy fostering dialogue between the social actors, paired with a low level of union membership. But there are also important differences. First, the Spanish system of worker representation at firm level through a works council empowered to bargain and to call strikes fosters worker solidarity and encourages unity of action, despite low union density (Rigby and Marco Aledo 2001). Second, workplace elections are the only path to trade unions' representativeness in Spain, which makes them much more keen on firm-level bargaining than their French counterparts. Also, engaging with production issues has been an important element of the strategy for renewal of Spanish trade unions to increase trade union membership (Beneyto 2011). Third, Spanish employers' traditional low trust in the capabilities of workers, paired with a zealous containment of collective bargaining contents, could make them less interested in promoting direct participation than their French counterparts (González Menéndez 2011). Thus, while the low levels of direct participation found in Spain essentially maintains the *status quo* in the balance of power between managers and unions at the workplace (González Menéndez 2011), in a way consistent with the model of 'social partnership at a distance' (Rigby 2002), it poses a distinct threat to the balance of power in the French workplace that rallies a collective response consistent with its model of institutionalized contestation.

The first implication of this is that, despite similar levels of workplace union power *vis-à-vis* employers based on broadly similar representation structures, both employers' and trade union workplace participation strategies may differ significantly. There is thus a connection between macro- and micro-regulation and strategies around direct participation that is essentially political (Martínez Lucio 2010). The second implication is that different union strategies (negotiation or contestation) concerning management-led direct participation may be differently suited to enhancing established political dynamics of industrial relations, participation and even trade union power in different contexts.

CONCLUSION AND FUTURE SCENARIOS

On the face of it, one would be hard pressed to accept that the tradition of workers' collective representation at the workplace within European industrial relations has been substantially altered, especially in those countries with strongly established traditions. The basic workings of bargaining, consultation and dialogue appear to be in place apart from the liberal-market economies of the EU and the Eastern European context where they are relatively marginalized. However, what we are beginning to see is a greater degree of fragmentation in terms of representation. This is happening in various ways.

First, there are greater challenges to the ability of sector-level bargaining to cover and regulate the main features of the employment relationship, with the UK representing an extreme example of this. In addition, there are sectors that are beginning to see a greater degree of employment 'downgrading' through subcontracting and agency-based employment, which is visible even in contexts such as Germany. The cases we have discussed suggest that this fragmentation in representation works through the fissures that exist within the way the systems of industrial relations were established. The nature of worker representation and the structure of the union movement appear to be a focus point for employer business and competitiveness strategies. Hence, we need to become alert to what we mean by fragmentation and how it develops.

Second, another issue is the question of coordination and use of resources between and within trade unions. That is to say that a more fragmented system of representation brings forth the need for greater monitoring and benchmarking if worker voice is to be sustained. Trade unions face either a disorganized workforce or an organized workforce that is more diverse in terms of workplaces and spatial terms. The pressures on trade unionists in monitoring the activities and outcome of workers' representation at the workplace are a major challenge. In this respect, as elements break away or become autonomous, even if they are unionized and 'organized', we will see real organizational and structural challenges in sustaining common reference points and effective worker representative roles. This is exacerbated by ever increasing forms of direct representation, which, while not always part of a coherent 'countersystem', even in the UK with its incoherent developments and continuities, does challenge the communication reach of trade unionists (Martínez Lucio and Weston 1992). Even if direct participation does provide possibilities in the search for ways to bridge the democratic deficit within the workplace—and can indeed be linked and controlled or mediated through forms of collective representation (as seen in parts of the German system)—it does present an organizational and logistical challenge to worker representatives. In fact, it presents management with similar dilemmas as well, even as the supposed initiators of such developments.

REFERENCES

Amossé, T. and Coutrot, T. 2011. 'Socioproductive models in France: An empirical dynamic overview, 1992–2004', *Industrial and Labor Relations Review*, 64:4. 786–817.

Antonioli, D., Mazzanti, M. and Pini, P. 2010. 'Innovation, industrial relations and working conditions—evidence from two Italian productive systems', in F. Garibaldo and V. Telljohann (eds.) *The Ambivalent Character of Participation*. Frankfurt: Peter Lang. 375–400.

Arrowsmith, J. 2010. 'Industrial relations in the private sector', in T. Colling and M. Terry (eds.) *Industrial Relations: Theory and Practice*. West Sussex: John Wiley. 178–206.

Bacon, N. and Storey, J. 1993. 'Individualization of the employment relationship and the implications for trade unions', *Employee Relations*, 15:1. 1–17.

Beneyto, P. 2011. 'Sindicatos, relaciones laborales y gestión de RRHH', in M. González Menéndez, R. Gutiérrez Palacios and M. Martínez Lucio (eds.) *Gestión de Recursos Humanos. Contexto y Políticas*. Pamplona: Thomson-Cívitas. 343–364.

Bosch, G. 2003. 'La evolución de la negociación colectiva en Alemania: Una descentralización coordinada', *Cuadernos de Relaciones Laborales*, 21:3. 179–214.

Broughton, A. 2005. 'European comparative practice in information and consultation', in J. Storey (ed.) *Adding Value through Information and Consultation*. Basingstoke: Palgrave. 200–218.

Charlwood, A. and Terry, M. 2007. '21st-century models of employee representation: Structures, processes and outcomes', *Industrial Relations Journal*, 38:4. 320–337.

Danford, A. 2005. 'New union strategies and forms of work organisation in UK manufacturing', in B. Harley, J. Hyman and P. Thompson (eds.) *Participation and Democracy at Work*. London: Palgrave. 166–185.

Doellgast, V. and Greer, I. 2007. 'Vertical disintegration and the disorganisation of German industrial relations', *British Journal of Industrial Relations*, 45:1. 45–76.

Dundon, T. and Rollinson, D. 2004. *Employment Relations in Non-Union Firms*. London: Routledge.

Escobar, M. 1995. 'Spain: Works councils or unions?' in J. Rogers and W. Streeck (eds.) *Works Councils*. Chicago: CUP. 153–188.

Ferner, A. and Varul, M. 2002. '"Vanguard" subsidiaries and the diffusion of new practices: A case study of German multinationals', *British Journal of Industrial Relations*, 38:1. 115–140.

Fulton, L. 2011. *Workplace Representation*. [online] Available at <http://www.worker-participation.eu/National-Industrial-Relations/Countries/United-Kingdom/Workplace-Representation>

Gallie, D. 2007. 'Production regimes and the quality of employment in Europe', *Annual Review of Sociology*, 33. 85–104.

González, M. 2009. 'The multidimensional impact of workplace direct participation in European jobs', in A. Guillén and S.-A. Dahl (eds.) *Quality of Work in the European Union*. Brussels: P.I.E. Peter Lang. 187–210.

———. 2010. 'Workers' direct participation at the workplace and job quality in Europe', *Journal of European Social Policy*, 20:2. 160–168.

González Menéndez, M. C. 2011. 'The determinants of workplace direct participation: Evidence from a regional survey', *Work, Employment & Society*, 25:3. 397–416.

Hall, M., Hutchinson, S. Purcell, J., Terry, M. and Parker, J. 2011. 'Promoting effective consultation? Assessing the impact of the ICE regulations', *British Journal of Industrial Relations*, June. doi: 10.1111/j.1467-8543.2011.00870.x.

Helfen, M. and Schuessler, E. S. 2009. 'Uncovering divergence: Management attitudes towards HRM practice and works council presence in German SMEs', *Economic and Industrial Democracy*, 30:2. 207–240.

Hyman, J. and Mason, B. 1995. *Managing Employee Involvement and Participation*. London: Sage.

IDE 1981. *Industrial Democracy in Europe*. Oxford: OUP.

Kaufman, B. 2008. *Managing the Human Factor: The Early Years of Human Resource Management in American Industry*. Cornell: Cornell University Press.

Kersley, B. A., Alpin, C., Forth, J., Bryson, A., Bewley, H., Dix, G. and Oxenbridge, S. 2005. *Inside the Workplace: First Findings from the 2004 Workplace Employment Relations Survey (WERS 2004)*. London: DTI/ACAS/ESRC/PSI.

Klikauer, T. 2007. *Communication and Management at Work*. Basingstoke: Palgrave.

Knudsen, H. 1995. *Employee Participation in Europe*. London: Sage.

Knudsen, H., Busck, O. and Lind, J. 2011. 'Work environment quality: The role of workplace participation and democracy', *Work, Employment & Society*, 25:3. 379–397.

Kratzer, N., Dunkel, W. and Menz, W. 2010. 'Employee participation in new forms of organization and control', in F. Garibaldo and V. Telljohann (eds.) *The Ambivalent Character of Participation*. Frankfurt: Peter Lang. 91–112.

Lash, S. and Urry, J. 1987. *The End of Organised Capitalism*. London: Polity.

Lillie, N. and Greer, I. 2007. 'Industrial relations, migration and neo-liberal politics: The case of the European construction sector', *Politics and Society*, 35:4. 551–581.

MacInnes, J. 1987. *Thatcherism at Work*. Buckinghamshire: OUP.

MacKenzie, R. and Forde, C. 2006. 'The myth of decentralisation and the New Labour market', in L. E. Alonso and M. Martínez Lucio (eds.) *Employment Relations in a Changing Society*. London: Palgrave. 69–85.

Marchington, M. and Wilkinson, A. 2000. 'Direct participation' in S. Bach and K. Sisson (eds.). *Personnel Management, 3rd edition*. Oxford: Blackwell. 340–364.

Martínez Lucio, M. 1998. 'Spain: Regulating employment and social fragmentation', in A. Ferner and R. Hyman (eds.) *Changing Industrial Relations in Europe, 2nd edition*. Oxford: Basil Blackwell. 426–458.

———. 2010 'Labour process and Marxist perspectives on employee participation', in A. Wilkinson, P. J. Gollan, M. Marchington and D. Lewin (eds.) *The Oxford Handbook of Participation in Organizations*. Oxford: OUP. 105–130.

Martínez Lucio, M. and Weston, S. 1992. 'Trade union responses to human resource management: Bringing the politics of the workplace back into the debate', in P. Blyton and P. Turnbull (eds.) *Reassessing Human Resource Management*. London: Sage. 215–232.

Müller-Jentsch, W. 1995. 'Germany: From collective voice to co-management', in J. Rogers and W. Streeck (eds.) *Works Councils*. Chicago: CUP. 53–78.

Murakami, T. 1997. 'The autonomy of teams in the car industry—A cross-national comparison', *Work, Employment, and Society*, 11:4. 749–758.

Ortiz, L. 1998. 'Union response to teamwork: The case of Opel Spain', *Industrial Relations Journal*, 29:1. 42–57.

Ortiz, L. and Royle, T. 2009. 'Dominance effects from local competitors: Setting institutional parameters for employment relations in multinational subsidiaries; a case from the Spanish supermarket sector', *British Journal of Industrial Relations*, 57:4. 653–674.

Pateman, C. 1970. *Participation and Democratic Theory*. Cambridge: Cambridge University Press.

Perrett, R. 2007. 'Worker voice in the context of the re-regulation of employment: Employer tactics and statutory union recognition in the UK', *Work, Employment and Society*, 21:4. 617–634.

Phelps Brown, H. 1983. *The Origins of Trade Union Power*. Oxford: OUP.

Pollert, A. 2010. 'The non-unionised worker and workplace problems: Forms of individual and collective voice at work', in F. Garibaldo and V. Telljohann (eds.) *The Ambivalent Character of Participation*. Frankfurt: Peter Lang. 223–250.

Poutsma, E. and Veersma, U. 2010. 'Direct and indirect participation: reconcilable voices?' in F. Garibaldo and V. Telljohann (eds.) *The ambivalent character of participation*. Frankfurt: Peter Lang. 23–32.

Pulignano, V. 2009. 'International cooperation, transnational restructuring and virtual networking in Europe', *European Journal of Industrial Relations*, 15:2. 187–205.

Ramsay, H. 1983. 'Evolution or cycle? Worker participation in the 1970s and 1980s', in C. Crouch and F. Heller (eds.) *International Yearbook of Organizational Democracy: Organizational Democracy and Political Processes*. Chichester: Wiley. 203–226.

Regini, M. 1993. 'Human resource management and industrial relations in European companies', *International Journal of Human Resource Management*, 43. 555–568.

Rigby, M. 2002. 'Spanish trade unions and the provision of continuous training: Partnership at a distance', *Employee Relations*, 24:5. 500–515.

Rigby, M. and Marco Aledo, M. L. 2001. 'The worst record in Europe? A comparative analysis of industrial conflict in Spain', *European Journal of Industrial Relations*, 7:3. 287–305.

Rogers, J. and Streeck, W. 1995. 'The study of works councils: Concepts and problems', in J. Rogers and W. Streeck (eds.) *Works Councils*. Chicago: CUP. 3–26.

Stewart, P. 1996. *Beyond Japanese Management*. London: Frank Cass.

Storey, J. 2005a. 'Employee information and consultation: An overview of theory and practice', in J. Storey (ed.) *Adding Value through Information and Consultation*. Basingstoke: Palgrave. 2–20.

Storey, J. 2005b. 'Conclusion' in J. Storey (ed.) *Adding Value through Information and Consultation*. Basingstoke: Palgrave. 272–274.

Stuart, M. and Martínez Lucio, M. 2005. *Partnership and the Modernisation of Employment Relations*. London: Palgrave.

Telljohann, V. 2010. 'Work organisation, workers' participation and the role of EU legislation in Italy', in F. Garibaldo and V. Telljohann (eds.) *The Ambivalent Character of Participation*. Frankfurt: Peter Lang. 131–148.

Tuckman, A. and Whittall, M. 2010. 'Giving employees a voice? Lessons from the new employee forums in the UK', in F. Garibaldo and V. Telljohann (eds.) *The Ambivalent Character of Participation*. Frankfurt: Peter Lang. 269–284.

Walker, S. and Creanor, L. 2000. 'European trade union distance education: Potential and problems', in M. Asensio, J. Foster, V. Hodgson and D. McConnell (eds.) *Networked Learning 2000: Proceedings of the Second International Conference*. Lancaster: Lancaster University and University of Sheffield. 341–353.

Yeandle, D. 2005. 'An employers' organisation perspective', in J. Storey (ed.) *Adding Value through Information and Consultation*. Basingstoke: Palgrave. 29–37.

4 Employment Relations in the Public Services
Between Hierarchy and Contract

Giuseppe Della Rocca

INTRODUCTION

The second half of the last century saw a growth in public-sector union membership and in collective bargaining in many European countries. Among the main issues for the unions was to establish collective bargaining rights in a context where the state often determined working conditions unilaterally. This phenomenon is a relevant factor in the transformation of the European scenario of industrial relations. In the last five decades, in most European countries, unions organizing public employees have also played a significant role in defining strategies in national industrial relations and have increased their membership as a countertendency to the decline of union membership in industry.

In general, union density has been and remains higher in the public than the private sector, even if in some countries it is difficult to measure membership, due to the fact that the same unions organize both private and public sector employees. The expansion of professional occupations (often female-dominated) within the growing service economy, and the relative decline of industrial employment, has effected a change in the social composition of the workforce and union representation, along with the rise of white-collar unionism (Ebbinghaus and Visser 2000). Only in Belgium is union density not higher in the public sector than in the total economy, though public-sector figures range from close to 90 percent in Denmark, Finland, Sweden and Cyprus, to between 20 percent and 30 percent in Germany, Spain, Portugal, Hungary and Estonia, and below 20 percent in Czech Republic, Lithuania, and France (Glassner 2010).

The diffusion of collective bargaining and trade union membership developed largely out of traditions of relatively consensual relations and in a framework of unilateral decision making by governments. Unilateral practices were the rule because public-sector employees were considered to work for the general interest of the nation, and the pursuit of sectional occupational interests was not considered as legitimate as in the profit-making sectors. Hence unions were recognized but free collective bargaining and the right to strike were generally not acknowledged; on the other hand, public-sector workers benefited from a special status and better terms and conditions of employment than those offered in the private sector. This represented an informal exchange, involving acceptance of a hierarchical regulation of working conditions on one side and, on the other, relatively beneficial outcomes in terms of employment security, pensions, compensation and disciplinary regime.

In this context, collective action and negotiation machinery, where they existed, were usually embedded in some form of legal regulations. This involved joint unions' and employers' committees, or some other formal or informal procedure of consultation or participation of employees or their union representatives in decision making. The development and diffusion of collective bargaining in such a context served to improve wages and working conditions further while at the same time preserving the special employment status that served as the foundation of relatively privileged conditions. This diffusion of collective bargaining became increasingly controversial, not just because unilateral practices remained in force in many countries, but also because by the 1980s the economic and political context had altered, placing restrictions on public expenditure and collective bargaining practices. The general acceptance of the need for more efficient and effective public services (taking into account growing criticism of the quality of public service provision) motivated governments to improve flexibility in pay negotiations and enhance the power of managerial roles.

This change was labeled the 'New Public Management' (NPM) approach as it embraced private-sector 'best practices' and professional management (Hood 1991). Privatization, management by performance, flexibility in employment and wages were the main issues of NPM (Bach and Della Rocca 2001). Most recently, since the economic crisis that began in 2008, cost considerations have come to the fore. Under this economic pressure governments were compelled not only to adopt private-sector management practices, but also to enforce unilateral practices with the intent of reducing public sector deficits, including through the restriction of wages, collective bargaining and consultative procedure with unions (Glassner 2010). Many governments have attempted to reduce public expenditure and labor costs in the public sector.

This chapter addresses the transformation of public-sector employment in Europe since the late 1980s. Key questions include the following: How far do macroeconomic constraints and the NPM template lead to a greater convergence between the public and private sectors, and between countries, taking into account significant differences in the structure and legacy of national institutions? What is the space (or the future) of collective bargaining given continuous restructuring and more recent unilateral interventions by the state? In short, in what ways has transformation proceeded in the organization of public services, and in union and employer relations, in the last decades? In this context *transformation* implies a purposeful, intensive and sustained attempt to alter the basic organizational principles of public sector employment relations (Bach 1999).

EMPLOYMENT AND COLLECTIVE BARGAINING COVERAGE

The size, scope and role of the public sector vary between its different branches; that is, core functions of the state (administrative government); education and science; health care and social services; public utilities; transport; and communications. The core public services, better known as public administration, may be centralized at national government level, or decentralized at regional and local government levels with, in some cases, such as the UK and the Scandinavian countries, a degree of decentralized autonomy through the constitution of central agencies. Education and health services may be public or private, centralized or decentralized. Teachers, doctors and nurses may be part of the regional or local municipality government (such as in Sweden) or employed under the central jurisdiction of the ministry, like teachers in Italy and France. Public enterprises in sectors such as water, gas, electricity, transport and communications have greater autonomy because they are also usually under market regulations and open to privatization (see Hemerijck, Huistamp, de Boer 2002).

The chapter is focused on the public services, i.e., central and local administration and welfare services such as education, health care and social assistance, excluding public enterprise). It is in the public services where, since the Second World War, there has been significant transformation in structures and employment. A large increase in the range of occupations (namely in health care and social assistance and education) has had important effects on the occupational profile of public employees, with a shift from the traditional administrative concept to a more professional one based on performance. It was in the public services too, where, during the period after the Second World War, governments assisted in establishing bilateral negotiations, partly in response to the increase of union power.

Employment statistics of the International Labor Organization (ILO), used in two reports of the European Commission, provide an indication of the relative importance of public service employment in the European countries (Ziller 2010). With the caveat that sector definitions and data are not always consistent, public-sector employment as a proportion of total employment varies from 12 percent to 33 percent of the total work force with around a third in Sweden (33.9 percent), Lithuania (33.3 percent), Denmark (32.3 percent), Latvia (31.9 percent), Slovenia 31.1 percent and Malta 30.7 percent. Excluding public enterprise, the Scandinavian countries (Sweden, Denmark and Finland), plus France, Lithuania, and Malta have above 25 percent of the total work force in the public sector; and only six countries are below 15 percent (Spain, Italy, Germany, Portugal, Luxembourg and Austria). This high percentage in many countries gives an indication of the shift from Weber's conception of the state to the modern welfare state. The Weberian understanding was one of civil servants, or 'bureaucracy', concerned with defense, internal order, taxation, justice, treasury, foreign affairs and employment in the municipalities.

Prior to the great expansion of the welfare state in Europe, the percentage of public service employment was much lower than it currently is. The culture of the 'public servant' was mainly an administrative one, based on the notion that such employees work for the general interest of the nation and are located in the main on hierarchical regulation and trust. This gave rise to special arrangements in labor relations and conditions of employment. The arrival of the welfare state meant that most public employees are no longer considered to be civil servants but professional workers, like teachers, nurses, doctors, social workers and others, with a direct commitment to the community and the individual user of the service—and to their professional occupation—more than to the state as employer. The increase in the number of employees and the change in professional commitment from the state to the community and the individual may be considered one of the reasons for the diffusion and increased power of professional associations and trade unions, and the spread of collective bargaining in the public sector.

Yet, there remain limits to public-sector collective bargaining. One useful data source is a European Foundation report which provides an overview of industrial relations in central government and in the public services in European Union Member States (with the exception of Sweden) and Norway up to 2005 (Bordogna, 2007). Bilateral negotiations over wages took place for all, or most, public employees in less than half of the twenty-seven countries (Cyprus, Denmark, Finland, Ireland, Italy, Malta, the Netherlands, Norway, Slovakia, Slovenia and the UK). Also pertinent are recent reports from the EPSU (European Federation of Public Service Unions) and ETUI (European Trade Union Institute), which identify a number of limitations concerning rights to freedom of association, information and consultation, collective bargaining and collective action in the public services (Clauwaert and Warneck, 2008; Warneck and Clauwaert, 2009).

These trade union reports also consider the situation in regard to the application or signature and ratification of relevant European Union directives, and the Social Charter of the European Council and ILO conventions. The states that signed Convention 151 on labor relations in 1978 and 154 on collective bargaining in 1981 along with several recommendations by the ILO (159/71–163/81) are those which, taking into account the national legal framework, in a direct and formal way, recognized collective agreements. Such information does not mean that in some other countries informal practices relating to union rights is not occurring, but it does provide a picture of the extent of a plain, formal recognition of collective bargaining in the public services. Essentially, freedom of association is recognized all over Europe with the ratification of ILO Convention 87 on freedom of association and protection of the right to organize (with the exception of Liechtenstein), while for Convention 154, concerning the extension of collective bargaining, countries signing the convention were (until 2008) only fourteen: Belgium, Cyprus, Finland, Greece, Hungary, Latvia, Lithuania, the Netherlands, Romania, Spain, Slovenia, Sweden and Norway (not in the European Union). However, more countries have signed and ratified ILO Convention 151, which states that the only categories that can be excluded from the right of collective bargaining are the armed forces and police, and public servants employed in government ministries. These states consist of, in addition to the above group, Denmark, Italy, Luxembourg, Poland, Portugal, the UK and Turkey (not an EU member). It might also be noted that only Austria, Bulgaria, the Czech Republic, Estonia, France, Germany, Ireland, Malta, and Slovakia, plus Croatia and Iceland (not an EU member), have signed ILO Convention 98. In this convention several articles guarantee adequate protection against antiunion discrimination and state a 'general preference for measures, appropriate to national conditions, to be taken, where necessary' to encourage and promote the full development and utilization of machinery for negotiations.

THE PRESSURE TO CHANGE

During the 1980s the metaphor of 'growth to limits' reflected an institutional diagnosis of the difficulty for OECD countries in maintaining the program of social policies that had developed during the 'long boom' or *'trente glorieuses'* from 1945–1975 (see Flora 1986). An increase of social expenditure intended to deliver real advantage to the large part of the population was replaced in more difficult economic circumstances by an agenda dictated by increased public deficit and debts. Such a syndrome, with other important transformations such as the demographics of aging and the globalization of the economy, came to create a climate of 'permanent austerity' (Pierson 2001).

Besides this macroeconomic constraint, the agenda of public debate was increasingly framed by a demand for better quality and efficacy in delivering services, reflecting growing attention to the welfare of the individual and quality of life, progressive interest in decision making in the area of public goods and increasing dissatisfaction with the burden of taxation. Governments struggled, on the one hand, to try to reduce public spending, initiate policies of privatization and competition in the public services and, in the meantime, try to maintain, or increase, the social dimension of collective services.

New policies associated with NPM therefore came to prominence, in which the traditional bureaucratic organization was challenged by the idea of reforms introducing a movement from hierarchy to contractual relations—indeed, *Management by Contract* was the very guideline for NPM

(OECD 1995). Despite the heterogeneous and doctrinal nature of NPM, there is widespread agreement that the main goal was to eliminate differences between the public and the private sector and to shift from legal and administrative accountability to accountability for results (Hood 1991). The most important dimensions have been the following: structural reorganization to break down monolithic organizations; decentralization of management responsibility; contracting out and quasi-market relations between public agencies and private services; and new budget and assessment procedures.

In employment relations the general concern was to re-enforce managerial prerogative and limit union power, mimicking private-sector techniques in Human Resource Management (HRM). These included high levels of reward to attract the 'best and brightest' from outside; fast career tracks for best performance; replacing seniority principles with performance assessment for pay increases and careers; greater mobility among jobs, departments and agencies; and more fixed-term employment contracts, part-time and flexible working hours.

The backbone of such changes was performance management (that is, setting targets for and appraising administration inputs, outputs and outcomes with the intention of replacing traditional controls on the fulfillment of administrative procedures). Performance management and measurement was especially linked to the purpose of regulating new personnel relations with the workforce. It responds first to the idea of endowing managers with more responsibility concerning objectives, programs and resources utilized, as well as an emphasis on overall improvements in the provision of services. The idea of performance management strongly influenced employment practices through targets, appraisal and monetary incentives. Such a process was important for settling decentralized pay determination, with decisions concerning the allocation of resources and the selection of incentives prior to the start of negotiations.

However, this did not lead to an all-inclusive policy of quasi-market–oriented approaches, as many countries in Europe adopted a selective policy concerning NPM issues and instruments. Governments were largely pragmatic in their approach, preferring 'selective shopping' that led more to a 'modernization' than to a marketization of public services (Ibsen et al. 2011). Such innovation programs did not aim to abolish collective bargaining but to change the structure of public services and the procedures of union-employer relations. Indeed, in itself NPM may have facilitated collective bargaining in replacing, in some countries, employees' public status and unilateral regulation of working conditions. Even decisions to decentralize the system of industrial relations and procedures for PBR may provide scope for negotiations at the local level. In general, the question of the effects of centralized or decentralized systems in public collective bargaining is ambivalent. On the one hand, decentralization of the structure of employment relations is intended to make pay more responsive to local labor market conditions and organizational needs. It may also mean for governments and managers a more confrontational relation to unions in a perspective of strengthening managerial prerogative. But in a context of high union density and with strong administrative and legal union rights, decentralization was, for the unions, not necessarily a threat but an opportunity to establish a firmer control of working conditions and work organization (Clegg 1976; Batstone, Boraston and Frankel 1977).

Arguably, this scenario worked until recent years but, as Braudel (1966) said, in history, in the short period, there is more than one conjuncture that can give rise to different fluctuations in the behavior of collective actors. The financial crisis in the banking sector, which started in the US in the middle of 2008, had a bigger impact on the world economy than the crash of 1929 and placed public budgets under great strain (European Commission 2010). Hence, the political and bargaining climate in the public sector profoundly changed, with heavy employment cuts in several countries (notably in Greece, Romania, Lithuania and Latvia) and widespread cuts in wages and benefits, including pensions (Glassner, 2010). These were usually implemented unilaterally by governments and were met with union opposition that included mobilization of public discontent as well as industrial action. Only in a few cases were wages settled by concession agreements as in Ireland, Slovenia and Hungary.

As a result, the structural change in state organization and personnel relations, from 2008 until today remains conducted inside a context of heavy administrative intervention by the state. Decisions on resources are more centralized, with a revival of traditional bureaucratic organization, but this time directed toward a further shakeup of traditional public sector 'privileges'. Yet this does not represent a return to hierarchy from contractual relations, as the objectives remain similar: flexibility of organizational structure and internal labor markets, management by objectives and major control over expenditure.

CONVERGENCE IN INDUSTRIAL RELATIONS: FROM PUBLIC TO PRIVATE AND AMONG EUROPEAN COUNTRIES?

The founding prescription of NPM is convergence between the public and private sectors, and between countries, in management practices and employment relations (OECD 1995). In general terms the research literature is skeptical about a move toward a common NPM template (Bach and Bordogna 2011). However two common trends may be noted: decentralization of the structure of employer-union relations, along with differentiation in pay including PRP.

Decentralization

The term 'decentralization' is multifaceted. Much depends, for example, on whether the local level is the single (or the main) level of decision making and whether collective negotiations are voluntary-based, even if the central government closely monitors costs and budgets. When there are two levels (national and local negotiations) decentralization may take the form of devolution, in which there is a transfer of competence and responsibility to the local level, or 'delegation' in which the central authority retains ultimate responsibility and authority (Rexed et al. 2007). Differences in meaning can also be found in relation to 'voluntary' and 'mandatory' decentralized negotiations. In the case of a full or quasi-mandatory decentralization, results can be just the opposite of flexibility; local administrations must negotiate with union representatives and the differences from private experience, where mandatory local negotiation does not exist, are significant.

The UK is the country in Western Europe where decentralization has gone furthest in the central government agencies, while in education and health, the 'pay review body' system determines national arrangements without formally involving collective bargaining. The Conservative governments of the 1980s introduced radical reforms; the civil service unions had to contend with department and agency agreements, while for local authorities, for instance, the national job evaluation scheme became optional and authorities were allowed to move away from national grades and modify scales through local negotiations (Bach and Winchester 1999).

Other significant examples include Spain, for service workers (*laboral*) and Sweden. In Spain service workers have a different status from civil servants and different procedures of collective bargaining. While for civil servants negotiations are centralized and restricted for service workers, mainly employed in the local government and services, employers and unions have by law the possibility to choose at which level to reach an agreement. Within this legal framework, it is possible to have single agency agreement (municipality, country, ministry), single occupational agreement, multiagency or cross-sector agreement (De Giovanni and Calindro 2007).

In Sweden central employer associations and national unions remain the backbone of the system, though there was substantial collective-bargaining decentralization from the 1990s. The national contract now provides for the possibility in a first stage of having two levels of negotiations (national and local) and further, in the last decade, provides for the possibility, if local social parties agree, of only one local level of negotiations (Ibsen et al. 2011). In 2007 about 32 percent of employees in central government agencies and 28 percent in local administrations were covered only by local agreements (Aurilio 2007). At the same time, negotiations at a national or local level take place in a framework in which the average index of public wage increases are linked to that of the private sector. Other Scandinavian countries also have the dual level system, but, whereas in Sweden there is a devolution of competency and responsibility, in, for example, Denmark and Finland it is more accurate to describe a delegation as at a local level since competences and responsibility will revert to the central parties if local efforts to reach agreement fail (Rexed et al. 2007).

In other Continental countries having the two levels of negotiations is common practice, but this does not necessarily mean convergence with the private sector. Devolution to local parties from the national contract is the trait of the Italian system, for example, but the statutory right to local negotiation in the public sector means that labor costs and wages increase more than in the private sector. In the Italian private sector, local collective agreements take place only in about 30 percent of enterprises; in the majority of the others (mainly small firms) the minimum, national wage standard coexists with substantial unilateral and discretionary payment of bonuses (Dell'Aringa and Della Rocca 2007).

There are also signs of decentralized bargaining developing in countries that until recently were rather immune to these trends, notably due to the drive for performance-based pay. In Germany, which maintains a formally centralized and uniform system, there has also been a partial process of decentralization because the diversification of economic conditions across the country means that municipalities experience problems in maintaining unified national employer coalitions (Keller 2011). In France too, where wage bonuses or PRP was introduced in 1990 only for senior civil servants at central government levels, such negotiations now involve a large part of the workforce.

Differentiation of Pay Structures and PRP

Pay flexibility in the public sector has involved two main related changes. First was the introduction of a Broad Banding System (BBS), adopted most extensively in the UK, Sweden, Italy and France. The BBS system groups wage levels within skill bands, with increases inside of each band often based on performance assessment by supervisors. The growth of PRP is also marked. In the 1990s, this was still rare in France, Germany and Denmark, though used in Sweden, Italy, Spain, Finland, Ireland, the Netherlands and especially the UK (Dell'Aringa and Lanfranchi 1999). More recently, a study of central government found PRP to be implemented in Denmark, Estonia, Finland, France, Germany, Hungary, Ireland, Italy, Latvia, the Netherlands, Slovenia, the UK and Malta (Bordogna 2007).

However the implications of both BBS and PRP for wage dispersion appear to be moderate. Limited financial resources delivered by governments were one important reason for the inadequacy of local pay bargaining. A possible explanation for the perseverance with PRP in these circumstances may be found in the procedures of goal setting that it involves. Goal setting in performance pay enables management to redefine the working norms of the organization and to obtain compliance with those norms with the explicit or tacit agreement of as many employees as possible (Marsden 2004). At the same time, fixed-term contracts and negotiations over working time seem to improve flexibility more than PRP. Local bargaining initiatives, in the early 1990s, on working time, in particular over shift patterns, part-time and flexible working, were found to be much more effective than pay initiatives in the UK (Arrowsmith and Sisson 2002). The diffusion of part-time work and flexible employment are also well documented in several other European countries in recent years (Derlien and Peters 2008).

After more than two decades of reform, the question of performance management is still open, though in effect it did not satisfy the objectives of increasing productivity and employees' motivation. In addition to limited financial resources is the difficulty of measuring performance in organizational or individual terms (de Bruijn 2002). Financial performance is everywhere an expanding concept, but it has acquired multidimensionality, incorporating different meanings, and nonfinancial measures are still in second place (Pollitt 2006). In professional service institutions (like health and education) individual performance measurement is intrinsically complex and problematic, and efforts to limit the autonomy and the independence of the professions mean that individual performance management systems can have perverse results (Ackroyd, Kirkpatrick and Walker 2007). Indeed, distortions introduced by targets in the public services have encouraged management to concentrate on reducing labor costs, rather than meeting the needs of service users (Crouch 2003).

Cross-National Convergence

National institutional contexts explain differences in employment relations in the public services, and four different trajectories of change may be identified. The first corresponds closely to a market-oriented system of governance placing a premium on cost-effectiveness criteria. In Europe the prime case is the UK, where administrative and legal regulations are easy to modify whether to allow for managerial autonomy, break down structures into autonomous units, or promote contracting out and practices such as 'fast-track' careers, fixed-term contracts and flexibility in pay structures and outcomes. Vital personnel policies governing the selection, development and remuneration of employees are not necessarily carried out according to administrative rules but according to assessment of performance. The focus on outcomes means the implications for collective bargaining are mixed. Conversely from the private sector (see chapter 2, this volume), whereas voluntary collective bargaining to single decentralized levels is in force in areas such as the central government agencies, in other public services, practices of centralized bargaining exist. In any case, broad-banding classification of wages and payment by results are widespread, and wage increases are strictly controlled by the Treasury linked to financial, productivity and quality targets in a context of often adversarial employer-union relations.

The second trajectory corresponds to a sovereign administrative system of government typical of Continental Europe. The paradigm case here is Germany. Changes take place in a context of the supremacy of law and an administrative regulation, separate from the private sphere—in contrast to the UK, where common law traditions predominate (Knill 1999). This leads to a stronger institutional path dependency in which this Continental group of sovereign administrative governments tries to adapt rather than change the existing systems of governance. Consequently, the reform process is less intensive but more protracted. Contracting out is practiced, but quasi-market competition amongst the various administration units and private agencies is a less urgent strategy. Increased labor flexibility is achieved through part-time jobs, fixed-term contracts for newly hired employees and by use of temporary work under a regime of coordinated employment relations. In countries like Austria, Belgium, Germany, France, Luxembourg, Spain, the Netherlands and Greece, wages may be generally negotiated by unions and employers, but collective agreements are implemented by a formal decision of the government and within still robust administrative rules regulating public employment (Hemerijck, Huiskamp, de Boer 2002; Glassner 2010). Similarly, in countries such as Austria, France, Germany and Italy, personnel practices concerning recruitment and internal careers are under administrative regulation rather than driven by HRM policies. Bargaining structures are again mixed; centralized or regional collective bargaining prevail in France, Germany, and the Netherlands, while in Italy, Belgium, and Spain, a dual level (national and local) is much more formally established and implemented. Different procedures exist for union involvement in information, consultation and decision making.

The third trajectory involves decentralization within a strong system of social partnership and a robust and compact welfare-social system. That is the case in the Scandinavian countries (Denmark, Finland, Norway, and Sweden) where the structure of the state corresponds to the Continental model of administration but is strongly tempered by a significant vertical decentralization (via agencies) and a territorial one through the counties and municipalities. The vast majority of public employees are employed at the local level (Derlien and Peters 2008), and counties and municipalities have a high degree of autonomy concerning taxation and resource management. The basic idea is the governance of 'welfare communes' (Premfors 1998) in which the efficiency and effectiveness of welfare is emphasized, and citizens' involvement is important in demanding lower cost, better services and high standards of professional performance.

Within this framework, decentralization of public budgeting gives autonomy to managers in managing resources. Contracting out and customer choice in welfare services are stressed, but there is also strong cooperation between public and private agencies and central and local levels in terms of quality control and skills development (Peters 2010). A strong emphasis is also placed on cooperation between trade unions and employers in monitoring innovation processes, results and resources (Ibsen et al. 2011). In effect, high union density allows for a managed and coordinated form of decentralization, though there are differences between the countries. For example, collective agreements are the principal form of employment regulation in

Sweden and Finland, whereas in Denmark (for civil servants), if agreement is not reached, then the state, as employer, can use legislation. In Sweden too the two levels of negotiation (central and local) encourage local agreements and thereby the greater diffusion of arrangements such as PRP and BBS than in the other countries.

The fourth trajectory can be found in the former communist countries of Central and Eastern Europe. Here, the context is largely shaped by privatization and decentralization in a context of sovereign administrative systems of government resembling those of Continental Europe. The main concern is the supremacy of the state and a special administrative regulation in managing public organizations and employment. In general the pay of public-sector employees is implemented by government decree. Performance-related pay has also grown in a context of weak union density and underdeveloped institutions of collective bargaining (Glassner 2010). In Romania unilateral decision making is the practice, while in Poland collective bargaining is free, but union power and density is very low (Clauwaert and Warneck 2008). Several countries (e.g., Bulgaria and the Czech Republic) have not signed ILO Conventions 151 or 154. Formal restrictions on negotiations and the right to strike are common, and there is a lower involvement of unions, with the exception of Slovenia, in the coordination of collective bargaining (Glassner 2010).

BETWEEN HIERARCHY AND CONTRACT—AND THE CRISIS

Despite the growth in collective bargaining in recent decades, bilateral negotiations over wages took place in nearly half of European countries as EPSU reports have documented (Clauwaert and Warneck, 2008; Warneck and Clauwaert, 2009). The determination of pay and working conditions by unilateral legal procedures remains the rule for large groups of public employees even in countries where collective bargaining has been adopted for a long time.

A number of patterns may be observed. Germany is one case in which employees are divided in two main groups, *Beamte* who do not have the right to collective bargaining and *Angestellte-Arbeiter* who do. A distinction between civil servants and the majority of public employees can be found in other countries; but what is peculiar to Germany is that the area of *Beamte* is quite large, about 40 percent of public employees. It covers not only officials of the central and local government but also a wide group of workers like teachers (Derlien 2008.

In other cases the demarcation is not between occupations covered by collective agreements or not but by the ultimate power of the government to unilaterally determine pay and working conditions. France is a good example; unions have the right to conduct negotiations, but the agreement is not legally binding for the government itself. The government is free to decide whether to start negotiations, whether to reach an agreement and whether or not to observe an agreement. Hence there is a system of free collective bargaining subject to unilateral veto by the government. Similar procedures apply to many other countries including Austria, Belgium, Greece, Luxembourg, and Spain and in most of Central and Eastern Europe.

The UK differs from this despite being considered as the case in which there is a large diffusion of voluntary and decentralized collective bargaining practices. In fact, the determination of pay for more than a quarter of all public-sector employees is based on recommendations of independent Pay Review Bodies (PRBs), rather than by means of collective bargaining. The PRB was introduced for the first time in 1971 for senior officials in the state civil service, for the military and for magistrates, but it was extended to doctors and nurses in 1983 and schoolteachers in 1991, both years when NPM policies were being vigorously pursued by Conservative governments. The formal exclusion of these groups from collective bargaining does not mean that pay determination is a direct matter of unilateral decision by the government; the PRBs receive detailed evidence from trade unions, employers and ministers, which is made public along with its recommendations. The government has the power to refuse PRB recommendations, but this has never been exercised. Equally, however, if it is not a unilateral practice, the review body is not equivalent to collective bargaining. Even if the nominal power of the government is not explicitly considered, the way that unions and employers try to influence the independent body is different from direct negotiations (Bordogna and Winchester 2001).

As a final outline three basic procedures of public-sector collective bargaining can be distinguished: 1) the determination of working conditions and wages may rely formally, as in the private sector, on collective bargaining for a significant part of employees; 2) working conditions and wages are settled in negotiations between union and government, but the final application is formally decided by a parliament or by the government or other public agencies; 3) working conditions and wages are settled by unilateral state decision, and the role of unions is limited to a type of participation procedure without formal negotiations or the possibility of collective action (Traxler et al. 2001). In many countries these different procedures coexist for different groups of public-sector employees.

An important effect of the recent financial-economic crisis, from 2008 until today, has been to increase the space for unilateral and centralized decision making in public-sector employment relations. The priority is to use top-down procedures in order to reduce public expenditure, rather than utilizing NPM instruments similar to market-oriented practices involving decentralization of collective bargaining and flexible pay agreements. Essentially, budgetary austerity changed the mode of pay determination; wage cuts and freezes were imposed even in countries like Ireland, Portugal, Spain, Italy and the UK, where collective bargaining was well established. In the Baltic countries and Bulgaria and Romania, where the state traditionally has a stronger role, unions' demands and recommendations were even less likely to be considered.

Budget reductions were often huge. Official figures, from the EPSU report at the end of 2010, show that the cuts over two years (2008–2010) ranged from 5.2 percent in Lithuania to 37.1 percent in Romania. In Estonia (for local government), the reduction was 6 percent, and in Hungary 7.1 percent. Figures of 15 percent for Greece and 13 percent for Ireland and Spain have been estimated for one year. For four states—Latvia, Hungary, Romania and Greece—a cut in public-sector pay was the condition for financial support by the IMF and other international financial institutions. In Bulgaria and the Czech Republic, despite a low ratio of public debt, governments also adopted austerity programs that extended to wages. In Bulgaria the government demanded a 10 percent reduction in labor costs for 2009–2011 through job reductions and a wage freeze. The Czech government decided upon a pay cut of 4 percent for senior officers in 2010 and for 2011 further wage cuts, of around 10 percent were planned (Labour Research Department 2010). The approach to cuts differs from country to country, from reductions in additional payments and bonuses to unpaid leave, but commonly there were repeated cuts because the first round was judged insufficient (Spain was the only country to have a single round). Except in Ireland and Spain, PBR and other additional bonuses were the first to be cut.

In other countries governments unilaterally adopted a policy of wage freezes: in Portugal for civil servants and employees in public companies and in Italy for a three-year period in the public services. In the UK the Local Government Association unilaterally imposed a wage freeze for 2010–2011. In Germany the government presented an austerity package, effective until 2014, which included the termination of public-sector employees' Christmas bonuses (Glassner 2010).

Only in Lithuania, Hungary and Slovenia have negotiations taken place, though the focus remains on cuts. In Lithuania a wage cut was introduced for civil servants; in Hungary the negotiations concerned cutting the thir-teenth month of salary; and in Slovenia the government and public sector unions agreed on an austerity package from early 2009 in order to avoid exceeding the government goal of 3 percent of GDP deficit. The Stability and Growth Pact includes the reduction of jobs and freezes on pay during 2010 and 2011 for public employees in order to reduce public spending on wages.

These wage cuts and freezes were often accompanied by pay system reforms, such as the introduction of new regulations for the remuneration of central government employees in Bulgaria and Lithuania, or new arrange-ments for teachers in Latvia. A significant element of such reforms was to limit and reduce the highest pay grades and in some cases to increase that of the lower pay groups, a trend which was observed across the public sector as a whole in many countries (Glassner 2010). Efforts to protect the lower paid were made to a greater or lesser extent in Greece, Latvia, Ireland, Hungary, Lithuania and Spain (EPSU 2010).

CONCLUDING REMARKS

It is not easy to answer the question of how far union and employer relations have been transformed in recent decades, notwithstanding heavy macroeconomic constraints and changes in public service organization and personnel policies. Neither has there been convergence between the public and private sectors in spite of the aspirations of the NPM template. The same holds for convergence between countries with different institutional contexts. Transformation, in the sense of a purposeful, intensive and sustained attempt to alter the basic organizational principles of the public sector and its employment relations, is perhaps too strong a label to describe its fragmented and fluctuating nature in Europe. While there has been a widespread dissemination of NPM techniques, in many countries modernization of the organizational structure and collective bargaining is a better description than transformation. Yet, continuity with the past, as seen in the unilateral setting of employment conditions, is intensified in the context of severe economic crisis.

Policies of monetary incentive were implemented in many countries but were largely hampered by limited financial resources delivered by the government and difficulties in defining individual goal setting, performance and appraisal systems. Public-sector wage dispersion thus remains relatively moderate in most countries. As for market procedures like contracting, these practices seem to work best in countries, like the Scandinavian ones, where they are embedded in a context of strong community involvement, open to the collective participation of different type of institutions and voluntary associations (Peters 2010).

Some moves along the trajectory from public regulation to arrangements resembling the private sector may be discerned in the decentralization of collective bargaining, in the introduction of PRP and BBS and in the flexibilization of working time even if decentralization does not introduce significant flexibility in pay. Employers have more leeway over areas such as working time than pay, where funding levels as well as structures are primarily controlled by the state. Usually it is the central state and the national contract that set the parameters and final responsibility for pay determination even with formal decentralization of bargaining competencies (Dell'Aringa 2001).

A more recent development is the growth of industrial conflict in many countries. Prior to 2008 the evolution of NPM often proceeded incrementally and via consultation and even joint decision making. In the years since, this scenario has changed rapidly with governments imposing wage reductions or freezes and job cuts. This led to a rise of adversarial relations as well as a shift back from bilateral to unilateral, and from decentralized to centralized systems of management and employment relations, which reduced the scope and impact of collective bargaining. Is this a relatively short-lived legacy of the crisis, or does it signify something more fundamental? This is difficult to say, but most of these provisions are the opposite of the NPM template.

Certainly, measures such as the decentralization of decision making and collective bargaining and flexibility in pay and careers, or PRP, are less high on the governmental agenda. On the other hand, the NPM prescriptions concerning performance management and flexibility have not been superseded. Governments continue to emphasize performance assessment, the use of fixed-term contracts, flexible working time and reduced costs, and collective negotiations are increasingly linked to concession bargaining and productivity increases.

In conclusion, in most countries unilateral practice seems to be the preferred way for the state to govern employment and wage systems in the public services. Unilateral practices seem now to coexist with bilateral ones, a hybridization of employment regulation that suggests an uneasy relationship between collective bargaining and unilateral practice. The financial crisis has, perhaps, permitted governments to adapt NPM, recognizing its limitations in terms of variable pay and collective bargaining, while continuing to drive its performance agenda through greater accountability, cost containment and contractual flexibility through outsourcing and more variable working time arrangements.

REFERENCES

Ackroyd, S., Kirkpatric, I., and Walker, R. 2007. 'Public management reform in the UK and its consequences for professional organization: A comparative analysis', *Public Administration*, 85:1. 9–26.

Arrowsmith, J. and Sisson, K. 2002. 'Decentralization in the public sector, the case of the UK National Health Service', *Industrial Relations*, 57. 354–380.

Aurilio, A. 2007. 'Svezia' in A. Simeoli (ed.), *Le relazioni sindacali nel pubblico impiego in Europa*. Roma: Formez.

Bach, S. 1999. 'Europe, changing public service employment in S. Bach, L. Bordogna, G. Della Rocca, and D. Winchester D (eds.) *Public Service Employment Relation in Europe: Transformation, Modernization or Inertia?* London and New York: Routledge. 1–17.

Bach, S. and Bordogna, L. 2011. 'Varieties of new public management or alternative models? The reform of public service employment relations in industrialized democracies' in *International Journal of Human Resource Management*, 22:11.2281–2294.

Bach, S. and Della Rocca, G. 2001. 'The new public management in Europe' in C. Dell'Aringa, G. Della Rocca, and B. Keller (eds.) *Strategic Choices in Reforming Public Service Employment: An International Handbook*. London: Palgrave. 24–47.

Bach, S. and Winchester, D. 1999. 'Britain, the transformation of public services employment relations' in S. Bach, L. Bordogna, G. Della Rocca, and D. Winchester D (eds.) *Public Service Employment Relation in Europe: Transformation, Modernization or Inertia?* London and New York: Routledge. 18–44.

Batstone, E, Boraston, I. and Frenkel, S. 1977. *Shop Stewards in Action*. Oxford: Basil Blackwell.

Bordogna, L. 2007. *Industrial Relations in the Public Sector*. Dublin: European Foundation for the Improvement of Living and Working Conditions.

Bordogna, L., and Winchester, D. 2001. 'Collective bargaining in Western Europe' in C. Dell'Aringa, G. Della Rocca, and B. Keller (eds.) *Strategic Choicse in Reforming Public Service Employment: An International Handbook*. London. Palgrave. 48–70.

Braudel, F. 1966. *Le Mediterranée et le Monde Méditerranéen à l'Époque de Philppe II*. Paris: Libraire Armand Colin.

Clauwaert, S. and Warneck, W. (eds.) 2008. *Better Defending and Promoting Trade Unions Right in the Public Sector: Part 1: Summary of Available Tools and Actions Points*. Brussels: European Federation of Public Services Union—European Trade Union Institute—Research Education Health Safety.

Clegg, H. 1976. *Trade Unions under Collective Bargaining*. Oxford: Basil Blackwell.

Crouch, C. 2003. *Commercialisation or Citizenship Education policy and the Future of Public Services*. Fabian Ideas no. 606. London: Fabian Society.

De Bruijn, H. 2002. *Managing Performance in the Public Sector*. London and New York: Routledge.

De Giovanni, E. and Calindro, L. 2007. 'Spagna' in A. Simeoli (ed.) *Le relazioni sindacali nel pubblico impiego in Europa*. Roma: Formez.

Dell'Aringa, C. 2001. 'Reforming public sector labor relations' in C. Dell'Aringa, G. Della Rocca and B. Keller (eds.) *Strategic Choice in Reforming Public Service Employment: An International Handbook*. London. Palgrave.

Dell'Aringa, C. and Della Rocca G. 2007. *Pubblici Dipendenti, una Nuova Riforma?* Soveria Mannelli, Rubettino.

Dell'Aringa, C. and Lanfranchi, N. 1999. 'Pay determination in the public service: An international comparison' in R. Elliott, C. Lucifora and D. Meurs (eds.) *Public Sector Pay Determination in the European Union*. London: Macmillan Press LTD.

Derlien, H. U. 2008. 'The German public service: Between tradition and transformation' in H. U. Derlien and B. G. Peters (eds.) *The State at Work, Public Sector Employment in Ten Countries: Volume 1*. Cheltenham: Elgar. 170–196.

Derlien, H. U. and Peters, B. G. (eds.) 2008. *The State at Work, Public Sector Employment in Ten Countries: Volume 1*. Cheltenham: Elgar.

Ebbinghaus, B. and Visser, J. 2000. *Trade Unions in Western Europe since 1945*. Basingstoke: Macmillan.

European Commission 2010. *European Economic Forecast*. Brussels: European Commission Directorate-General for Economic and Financial Affairs.

Flora, P. (ed.) 1986. *Growth to Limit: The West European Welfare State since World War II*. Berlin, New York: de Gruyter.

Glassner, V. 2010. 'The public sector in the crisis', Working Paper 2010.07 Brussels: European Trade Union Institute.

Hemerijck, A., Huiskamp, R. and de Boer, R. 2002. *Public Sector Reform under EMU*. Dublin: European Foundation for the Improvement of Living and Working Conditions.

Hood, C. 1991. 'A public management for all seasons?' *Public Administration*, LXIX. 1.

Ibsen, C. L., Larsen, T. P., Mardsen, J. S. and Due, J. 2011. 'Challenging Scandinavian employment relations: The effect of new public management reforms' in *International Journal of Human resource Management*, 22:11.2295–2310.

Keller, B. 2011. 'After the stability: Recent trends in the public sector of Germany' in *International Journal of Human resource Management*, 22:11.2331–2348.

Knill, C. 1999. 'Explaining cross national variance in administrative reform: Autonomous versus instrumental bureaucracy'. *Journal of Public Policy*, 19: 2. 113–139.

Labour Research Department (LRD) 2010. *The Wrong Target—How Government Are Making Public Sector Workers Pay for the Crisis*. London: LRD.

Marsden, D. 2004. 'The role of performance related pay in renegotiating the "effort bargain": The case of the British public service', *Industrial and Labor Relation Review*, 57:3. 350–370.

OECD 1995. *Governance in Transition: Public Management Reforms in OECD Countries*. Paris: OECD.

Peters, G. 2010. *The Politics of Bureaucracy, an Introduction to Comparative Public Administration*. London and New York, Routledge.

Pierson, P. 2001. 'Coping with permanent austerity: The welfare state restructuring in affluent democracies' in P. Pierson (ed.) *New Politics of the Welfare State*. Oxford: Oxford University Press.

Pollitt, C. 2006. 'Performance management in practice, a comparative study of executive agencies', *Journal of Public Administration Research and Theory*, 16. 1.

Premfors, R. 1998. 'Reshaping the democratic state: Swedish experience in a comparative perspective', *Public Administration*, 76:1. 141–159.

Rexed, K., Moll, C., Manning, N. and Allain, J. 2007. 'Governance of decentralised pay setting in selected OECD countries'. Working Paper on Public Governance. Paris: OECD.

Traxler, F., Blaschke, S. and Kittel, B. 2001. *National Labour Relations in Internationalized Markets*. Oxford: Oxford University Press.

Warneck, W and Clauwaert, S. 2009. (eds.) *Better Defending and Promoting Trade Unions Right in the Public Sector: Part 2: Country-by-country overview*. Brussels: European Federation of Public Services Union—European Trade Union Institute.

Ziller, J. 2010. 'Free movement of European Union citizens and employment in the public sector, current issues and state of play'. *Part 1: General Report* and *Part II: Countries Report*. Brussels: European Commission.

5 Emerging Systems of Employment Relations in Central Eastern European Countries

Guglielmo Meardi

INTRODUCTION

With relatively young industrial relations structures and high dependence on foreign direct investment, Central Eastern Europe has emerged as a battlefield for change in European industrial relations, whether through multinational companies' (MNCs) 'coercive comparisons' and 'best practice' dissemination, or through political reforms. It constitutes a unique test bed for the study of the development of industrial relations in industrialized economies that have 'bypassed' the crucial period in the development of Western European industrial relations (the 1940s–1970s) or US industrial relations (the 1930s).

Industrial relations in Central Eastern Europe are not only of local interest: the EU accession of 100 million citizens with different labor and social standards modifies the industrial relations balance for the whole of the EU and raises questions concerning the enduring suitability of the so-called 'European Social Model'. In this regard, the new member states (NMS) have the potential of being 'Trojan horses' for the 'Americanization' of European industrial relations (Meardi 2002). EU enlargement may be considered a 'microcase' of the effects of internationalization on industrial relations, whereby competition and interactions between richer and poorer areas of the world is strongly intensified.

This chapter analyzes these issues in two parts. The first reviews the emerging industrial relations systems in the NMS, focusing on the weakness of institutional arrangements with regard to information and consultation of employees, tripartite relations between employers, trade unions and the state, and collective bargaining. The second part discusses the dynamics of labor market integration with Western Europe, and especially the effects of increased East-West migration (for further elaboration, see Meardi 2012).

THE 'EUROPEANIZATION' OF INDUSTRIAL RELATIONS IN CENTRAL EASTERN EUROPE

An Emerging Employment Regime

The employment regime that emerged in the NMS after the postcommunist transition and EU integration differs from the Western European one and continues to develop in a different direction. Its main feature is the weakness of institutions for employee participation and representation. The crisis of European trade unionism is not exclusive to the NMS, of course, but it is in these countries where it is most pervasive and least compensated by other institutions, be they works councils, state-supported collective bargaining or centralized social negotiations. Take Poland, the first mover in postcommunist transformation and a frequently mentioned neoliberal model. In 2000, when negotiations on EU accession were coming to a close, only 10 percent of owners and managers agreed that there should be union representation in private companies—something then being ratified as a fundamental right in the European Union (Gardawski 2001).

The outcome (Table 5.1) is a clear gap between the new and old member states in terms of industrial relations. Importantly, the gap is not narrowing with EU integration (whether measured from 1998, the start of the accession negotiation, or from 2003, the last year before accession). The European Commission's Industrial Relations in Europe Report of 2008 noted that in 2004–2006 in the NMS (weighted average according to country population) union density was only slightly below the old member states (22 percent against 25.8 percent), but collective bargaining coverage was much lower (42.5 percent against 68.8 percent), wage coordination was poorer, strikes were rarer and works councils had fewer rights (EC 2008a). In addition, even more than in Western Europe, union membership and collective bargaining are concentrated in the public sector. In summary, in the NMS, compared to Western Europe, unions are weaker and less encompassing, are declining faster, negotiate fewer agreements and have less capacity to challenge this situation through industrial action. And the trend is divergence, not convergence with the West.

Equally, the state does not compensate for this weakness of associational industrial relations, as Kohl and Platzer (2007) or Bluhm (2006) had hoped. Table 5.1 also shows that employment protection is generally poorer in the NMS—without even considering the problems of actual enforcement. If on this dimension there is some convergence with the old member states, it is because some of these (especially Italy, Germany and Sweden) have recently moved toward 'Eastern European' standards through labor market reforms, rather than the other way around. Reflecting this combined effect of weak industrial relations and state regulations, the last columns of Table 5.1 report the enthusiastic assessment of the conservative Fraser Institute, which evaluates employers' 'freedom' worldwide. The Fraser index for labor market regulation is, like its OECD counterpart, based on the legal rather than the actual situation on six dimensions, and gives a maximum of ten in the case of absolute employer freedom. Not only do the NMS generally provide employers with more discretion than the old ones (except the UK), but this freedom was increased particularly generously between 2000 and 2007. EU accession has been a great present for employers but not necessarily for employees who, for instance, in the European Working Conditions Survey, keep expressing their dissatisfaction.

Table 5.1 Industrial relations in new and (selected) old member states

	Union density			Collective bargaining coverage			Employment protection legislation			Labour market regulation freedom	
	2006	±from '03	±from '98	2007	±from 2003	±from 1998	2008	±from 2003	±from 1998	2007	±from 2000
Estonia	13.2	-4.4	-5.7	22.0	+1.0	+2.0				5.04	+0.30
Lithuania	14.4	-2.4	-12.6	12.0	-2.0					5.00	+0.77
Poland	14.4	-4.8	-14.2	35.0	-5.0	-8.0	1.90	+0.25	+0.50	5.73	+1.53
Latvia	16.1	-1.8	-13.2	20.0	=					6.84	+2.31
Hungary	17.8	-0.7	-10.4	35.0	=	-17.0	1.65	+0.13	+0.38	5.87	+0.28
Czech R.	21.0	-0.7	-28.7	44.0	-2.7	-11.0	1.96	+0.06	+0.06	6.20	+0.98
Slovakia	23.6	-6.3	-17.0	35.0	-5.0	-13.0	1.44	+0.10	-0.36	6.47	+1.93
Slovenia	41.0	-0.3	-1.8	100.0	=	=				5.90	+2.30
Bulgaria	21.3	-0.6	-3.4	25.0	=					7.07	+2.15
Romania	33.7	-4.8								6.41	+0.13
France	8.0	-0.2	-0.5	95.0	=	-1.4	3.05	=	+0.07	5.61	+0.67
Spain	14.6	-1.2	-1.7	80.0	-1.5	+0.4	2.98	=	+0.05	5.07	+1.15
Germany	20.7	-2.3	-5.2	63.0	=	-2.0	2.34	=	-0.22	3.96	+1.11
UK	28.7	-1.0	-2.0	34.8	-1.1	+2.5	0.75	=	+0.15	7.17	+0.25
Italy	33.2	-0.3	-2.5	80.0	=	-1.0	1.89	+0.07	-0.81	5.72	+2.19
Sweden	75.0	-2.2	-7.3	92.0	=	+1.0	1.87	-0.37	-0.37	4.67	+1.29

Data in italic are from the previous year.

Source: Union density and collective bargaining coverage: Institutional Characteristics of Trade Unions, Wage Setting, State Intervention and Social Pacts (ICTWSS) Database, Amsterdam Institute for Advanced Labour Studies (AIAS), Amsterdam (except for Slovenia 2005: ETUI estimate); Employment protection legislation: OECD database; labour market freedom: Fraser Institute.

There are differences among NMS, of course. The Baltic states present the biggest challenges to those who hope for an assimilation to Western European standards: Soviet Union legacies, ethnic divides, and very dependent economies combine in creating much worse employment regimes than in the so-called Visegrád group (Poland, Czech Republic, Hungary and Slovakia). There is then the exception of Slovenia, which belongs to a different tradition. In fact Yugoslavian and even Austro-Hungarian traditions, cohesive 'valley' communities, national creation myths and a strong export economy have combined in making Slovenia one of the best, rather than worst, EU countries in terms of social development (Grdešić 2008). However, even in its uniqueness, it is a telling confirmation of the general trend: Europeanization has involved very serious strains on Ljubljana's welfare state and corporatist institutions.

The weakness of employee representation is an aspect of a broader weakening of labor. The new employment regimes imply not only poor representation rights, but poor social rights altogether. This is particularly apparent in the welfare state. According to data from Eurostat, social expenditure is lower than in Western Europe, ranging from 10.7 percent in Latvia to 21.9 percent in Hungary, against a 25.9 percent average for the EU15. Moreover, whereas the latter figure has been constant in recent years, in the NMS it has been declining: again, the trend is divergent rather than convergent.

An additional distinctive feature of social protection in the NMS is its very unbalanced structure, which focuses on the older population, through old-age pensions, incapacity benefits and healthcare. The welfare state of the NMS (in particular, that of Poland and Hungary) is largely a 'residual welfare state', combining legacies from communist times with social programs introduced at the time of transition to limit mass unemployment and protest from core workforces (Vanhuysse 2006). Beneficiaries from such welfare states are mostly the older generations, who inherited virtually free housing, had enjoyed employment security, and received relatively generous early retirement or incapacity benefits. On the other side, those who are at work today in the NMS are in a more vulnerable position than their counterparts in Western Europe. They have no access to public housing; have inadequate employment security, due to the liberalization of labor law; are only offered expensive and unsecure contribution-based pensions; and are faced with increasingly privatized health and education services and worsening childcare for their children (except in Hungary). If they become unemployed or poorly paid, they receive extremely poor benefits, generally below subsistence levels, and suffer from a regressive tax system that includes in many countries a 'flat tax' on income, low corporate tax, high employee social contributions and high indirect taxes. The effect is clearly visible if one disaggregates the rates of poverty by age: according to Eurostat data, unlike in Western Europe, in Hungary, Poland and former Czechoslovakia, the younger the person, the higher the risk of poverty. In the Baltic states, Romania and Bulgaria, which have a worse welfare state, the poverty risk is also high for the elderly. The implications for employment relations are that employees have very little social security, and the state, instead of partially 'decommodifying' labor as in Western Europe (Esping-Andersen 1990), fosters its extreme commodification (i.e., dependence on the market).

Information and Consultation of Employees

Accession to the EU exacerbated these characteristics rather than correcting them, in spite of the transposition of the *acquis communautaire* and of the promotion of social dialogue (see chapter 9, this volume). Within the *acquis*, the most important directive for industrial relations should have been the Information and Consultation (I&C) of Employees (2002/14/EC), which was meant to set a minimum floor of representation rights for employees in the EU. The directive was expected to affect the NMS because (with the exception of Hungary and Slovenia) they had no works councils. However, the transfer of Western-style employee representation has not occurred. Several NMS governments (Poland, Slovakia, Estonia) were actually quick to exploit the opportunity given by the directive transposition to undermine, rather than reinforce, employee prerogatives. Governments' initial proposals tried to replace the single-channel (union-only) representation with a dual-channel system in which the establishment of a works council could have made the unions disposable. These proposed laws would have opened an avenue for union-avoidance techniques and 'yellow', or at least ineffective, works councils. Only after strong union opposition were such proposals amended and replaced by systems of 'residual' works councils, which give priority to unions as employee representatives (of all employees, not just union members) in workplaces (Carley and Hall 2008). Only Bulgaria and Estonia introduced a dual channel that guarantees union presence but still raises the risk of union marginalisation. Yet, the legal framework recently changed in Poland and the Czech Republic following decisions of the Constitutional Courts.[1] These rule that a works council can be established at an employer's business and can also operate alongside a trade union (thereby introducing a dual channel), which reintroduces the threat to trade unions. In the short term, the unions are maintaining their dominance of the already-established works councils, but for the future the option for nonunion representation and thereby undermining of independent employee organization is now open.

The implementation of the new I&C bodies is in any case proceeding slowly. In the Baltic states, it is reported that employees lack the assertiveness and information to take action demanding I&C rights (Woolfson, Calite and Kalliste 2008). In Slovakia and Poland few companies have introduced I&C bodies (Gładoch 2008). In Poland 90 percent of them are simply ratifications of previously existing union bodies, and the remainder appear to be relatively weak and inactive (Surdykowska 2008). In February 2008, a review of the directive's implementation by the European Commission (EC 2008b) reported no, or no problematic, impact in Bulgaria, Czech Republic, Estonia, Lithuania, Poland and Romania—and the positive impact reported in Latvia, Hungary and Slovakia was generic and subjective, with no real evidence of any kind, possibly stemming from governments' interest in reporting success rather than lack of it. In the meanwhile, not only union membership, but also the perception of union rights, keeps falling. In 2007, for example, the Polish survey 'Working Poles' found that only 41.4 percent of all employees believed that the right of unionizing is respected—a fall of 18.3 points in comparison to the same survey two years earlier (Męcina 2009, p.280).

One positive effect of EU accession for I&C is the extension of European Works Councils, but these institutions only cover multinational companies (MNCs) and therefore a small minority of the workforces in the NMS. Indeed, not only have MNCs failed to transfer indirect participation practices from Western Europe (Meardi et al. 2009), they have exerted pressure on domestic industrial relations systems by increasing competition for investment between sites and countries to further promote disorganized decentralization. As Rugraff (2006, p.455) put it, 'by their weight in the economy and their determinant role in the coordination of these countries' economies, MNCs impede the emergence of organized industrial relations.'

National-Level Social Dialogue

In Central Eastern Europe tripartite institutions were universally established in the early 1990s, under influence from the ILO, but their functioning was often dismissed as 'illusory corporatism' (Ost 2000) aimed at defusing potential trade union opposition. EU accession was seen as an opportunity to strengthen social dialogue, part of the so-called 'soft' *acquis communautaire*, and more specifically to promote the practice of 'social pacts'. Social pacts (tripartite agreements on income policies and the welfare state) were popular in Western Europe in the 1990s, associated with the path to Economic and Monetary Union (EMU) in countries such as Italy, Spain, Portugal, Ireland and Finland. They are not part of the *acquis* and are not formally required by the EU, but they appear to have been frequently recommended during 'peer reviews' at multiple levels (Ghellab and Vaughan-Whitehead 2003). A comparative study by the European Foundation for the Improvement of Working and Living Conditions in 2004 suggested that social pacts could be the most socially acceptable way to meet the Maastricht criteria (Tóth and Neumann 2004), an opinion also expressed by academic observers (Donaghey and Teague 2005).

These arguments have not convinced many local policy makers, however. First, in the Baltic states, macroeconomic convergence was not so compelling an issue because these young nations did not inherit high debt. In these countries, the Maastricht criteria were practically already met (Lithuania had expected to enter the EMU in 2007; Estonia in 2011). At the time, policy makers perceived no need for social pacts because (as an Estonian official put it to me in 2007) there was no social problem. Yet when the Baltic bubble—which was caused by low-interest credit in foreign currency, dumped by foreign-owned banks thanks to the free movement of capital—eventually burst in 2008, governments started to need social pacts very much, to manage protest and negotiate the drastic reforms requested by the International Monetary Fund and the EU (to take one example, Latvia, in the summer of 2009, cut state-sector wages by 15–27 percent, and shut down 10 percent of state schools).

Social pacts were thus signed in the three Baltic states in 2009, in a situation of emergency and protest, but, not having established the necessary organizational capacities and dialogue culture before, they were characterized by very poor governability capacity. These cross-sector agreements were not generally respected by sector-level employers and trade unions. Therefore, in the public sectors hit by cuts, protests and strikes went on, while in the private sector wages were not controlled. The 2009 social pacts amounted to no more than concession bargaining, but in an ineffective way: they did not provide unions with any guarantees that concessions would be sufficient, and governments soon started planning even harsher reforms and cuts. Given such poor governability, a political crisis emerged to accompany the economic one in Lithuania and Latvia—though their respective governments were replaced by even more neoliberal ones.

In the Visegrád countries, by contrast, public debt (and to a lesser extent inflation) is an open problem, but governments have opted, rather than for social pacts, for two opposite strategies: unilateral enforcement of macroeconomic convergence, at the cost of electoral defeat (Slovakia, Poland and Czech Republic) or a Maastricht-ignoring Euro deferral in order to ensure political survival (Hungary). Even more than in the West, then, EMU entry and sociopolitical stability are mutually irreconcilable: you cannot satisfy at the same time the electorate on one side, and international financial institutions on the other—unless you have an instrument to involve society in the reforms, and make the latter more acceptable. This is what social pacts were meant to offer, and why governments should have been able to look for support from the social partners. This has not happened. Social pacts did not occur, or they occurred in one-sided, ineffective ways.

Poland made some attempts at social pacts in 2002–2005, when the then center-left government felt it was too weak to pass reforms unilaterally. But even in this case, which presented striking analogies with some Western European situations, no success was achieved, mostly because of political divisions among trade unions and the noncooperation of employers and of the Central Bank (Meardi 2006; Gardawski and Meardi 2010). Among the Visegrád countries, only in Hungary did the government prioritize social consent to Maastricht. The socialist-liberal coalition that narrowly won the 2002 elections engaged in populist concessions and especially wage increases in the public sector, disregarding the financial implication. It also experimented, in November 2005, with a sort of tripartite social pact, including a three-year minimum wage agreement and pay policy guidelines. However, this pact responded to internal political considerations only (the imminent elections) rather than EMU constraints. As a result, the government did, with an exceptional recovery of popularity, manage to win the elections of April 2006, but immediately after, it was punished by the international markets for an excessive budget deficit (7 percent). A financial crisis followed, with the Fiorint's value falling. A few months later, when, under direct international and EU financial pressure, the same government had to introduce a real economic program of monetary convergence, social dialogue was promptly abandoned. While the unions were left to protest against the government's unilateral and hard proposals, and employers considered terminating the 2005 agreement, the president referred the draft laws on social dialogue to the Constitutional Court with the aim of setting policy free from corporatist constraints, and riots exploded in the streets of Budapest. A new national wage agreement was concluded in January 2007 only with much difficulty after the trade unions were threatened with the end of national negotiations. In 2008, public sector strikes hit the country and the populist opposition called and won a 'social referendum' against some of the reforms, paving the way for its electoral triumph in 2010.

Slovakia's path was the opposite of the Hungarian case, but it also illustrates the symmetric consequences of the lack of social dialogue. In fact, EU accession was immediately followed by the deterioration of social dialogue: the conservative Dzurinda government in November 2004 repealed the act on tripartism and replaced the Council for Economic and Social Concertation with a watered-down, consultation-only Economic and Social Partnership Council. Socioeconomic reforms pleased Brussels and foreign investors, the Slovak 'flat tax' of 19 percent for VAT, income tax and capital tax became the flagship of liberal reformers across the whole region, and the country met the Maastricht criteria, allowing it to enter the EMU in 2009. However, those reforms, involving drastic cuts to social expenditure, caused social discontent, from riots in 2004 to healthcare strikes in 2006, that led to Dzurinda's defeat in the 2006 elections (Bohle and Greskovits 2010). A coalition of populist parties from the Right and the Left then came to power—to be replaced by liberals in 2010.

That under EMU macroeconomic social dialogue remains no more than a disposable option is confirmed by the fact that in the only NMS where it flourished in the 1990s and continued until 2004, it has subsequently weakened. In Slovenia, a social pact on the EMU was signed in 2003, but a new right-wing government elected in 2004 while making EMU accession an urgent priority (the country became the thirteenth EMU member in 2007), disposed of social dialogue in favour of unilateral neoliberal and monetarist proposals. The EU had a direct impact on the deregulation of the previously corporatist Slovenia by requiring the separation of the Employer Confederation from the all-encompassing Chambers of Commerce and challenging state control of large firms, undermining in this way two important pillars of the Slovenian social model. Increased competition for foreign investment in the single market achieved the rest. The Slovenian unions were left with no other option than protesting, organizing the largest demonstration since independence in December 2005 and successfully opposing the introduction of a 'flat tax' in 2006. A new social pact was signed after EMU accession, in 2007, but under a strict subordination of social aims to the Maastricht criteria and international competitiveness considerations (especially inflation); this was in contrast to the pre-2004 social pacts that contained payoffs for labor as well as, notably, generous pension reforms (Stanojević 2010). Interestingly, the one-sided pact of 2007 was not enough for the government to avoid electoral defeat the following year. With the arrival of the crisis, and a new center-left government, Slovenian social partners negotiated hard over a new social pact in 2009, but the negotiations broke down and the employers left the Economic and Social Council in protest. Europeanization might thus imply the end of the Slovenian brand of corporatism.

The real EMU effects are on wage growth and public expenditure controls. Their implementation through social dialogue may have been a reasonable strategy for Western unions with large loyalty reserves, but it is dangerous for unions in the NMS, as they risk losing the little popularity they have—also because the euro has lost much of its attractiveness in the meanwhile. Symbolic tripartism has allowed unions in the NMS to survive as organizations, but nothing more. Hence, EU accession—and Europeanization in general in the whole of the EU—may have fostered the 'expressive' functions of concertation, and thereby guaranteed the survival of tripartism despite its apparent lack of results (Traxler 2010). But this has happened at the cost of concertation's instrumental functions in the actual regulation of labor, and therefore the content is increasingly nebulous. In this way, while tripartite social dialogue may have contributed to limit the 'legitimation crisis' of the state in the region, this has happened at the cost of deepening the 'legitimation crisis' of trade unions—increasingly associated to obscure central negotiation with the elites and thereby perceived as far away from the workplaces. Social dialogue after EU accession has thus reinforced the power unbalance between employers and employees, preempting real negotiations.

Disorganized Collective Bargaining

At least as far as wages are concerned, a precondition of coordinated social dialogue is the existence of multiemployer collective bargaining, which in Western Europe tends to occur at the sector level. In the NMS, with the exception of Slovenia, it has long been observed that this important prerequisite is nonexistent. Slovakia has a relatively large number of sector agreements, but they are of very little substance, and even they were drastically weakened by reforms of the conservative government in 2010 (Cziria

2010). On the eve of EU enlargement, ILO experts labeled the sector as 'the weakest link' in social dialogue in the region, and pointed at the meager content, low coverage and poor enforcement of collective agreements in general (Ghellab and Vaughan-Whitehead 2003). As explanations for this dire situation, the weakness of the social partners, the ambiguous role of the state (at the same time too interventionist and too little facilitating) and the unfavorable economic environment were mentioned.

As far as the social partners are concerned, it is employer organizations that constitute the crucial pillar of multiemployer bargaining: in some Western countries such as Germany, it is the strength of employer organizations that allows sectoral-level collective bargaining to survive in spite of the rapid weakening of trade unions. In the NMS, until recently the weakness of employer organizations was blamed on, more generically, employers' organizational weakness due to their (post-1989) emergence as autonomous economic actors. For instance, in her study of Polish employer organization, Kozek argued that Polish business was not strongly organized because it was still 'in a developmental state', 'fighting for survival', faced with 'the challenges of the European market and globalization', still in search of its 'ethos', and 'social identity' (Kozek 1999, p.102). Such an interpretation requires a fundamental revision: business in the NMS is not weak at all and its disorganization is not a fate but a choice. Collective organization is, technically, simpler for employers than for employees. And in the NMS, it is not the weakest employers, such as small and medium enterprises, which hold back organization: it is, from the beginning (Ghellab and Vaughan-Whitehead 2003), the multinational companies, which are neither weak nor unused to employer organizations. Moreover, employer associations actually exist, and are highly efficient in other activities than social dialogue, and especially in political lobbying—as in the case of the Polish Private Employers' Confederation (Behrens 2004).

The point is therefore not the capacity of employers to organize, but their choice of not doing it—and the failure of the EU to set up any incentive in the opposite direction. Collective bargaining in the NMS has actually declined with EU accession, at company as well as at sector level. In Poland, for instance, the decrease in registered company-level agreements has been constant: from 1,389 in 1996, to 405 in 2004, to 199 in 2008 (data provided from the State Labour Inspectorate). Moreover, according to the State Labour Inspectorate, there is a tendency toward the reduction of provisions that are advantageous to employees, and an increase in detrimental provisions, which have been allowed by incremental liberalization of the Labour Code during the 2000s. The decline is partly associated with the privatization of the economy, something the EU has encouraged without setting effective safeguards to maintain employee representation rights (despite the Directive on the Transfer of Undertakings). In the same way, sector-level bargaining has declined with the retrenchment of previously state-controlled sectors: in Poland in 2000 there were still six significant (i.e., without including small subsectors) sector-level agreements in the private sector. By 2008, half of them had disappeared due to employer withdrawal: road transport, cereal processing, and steel—all sectors where major privatization took place. Only one case followed the opposite trend, where railway workers managed to keep a sector-level agreement despite privatization. As a result all four surviving private-sector agreements have their roots in public ones: railways, energy, mining and the military industry.

Private employers' active disinterest in coordinated bargaining is clear. In Poland, employer association representatives from the private sector explicitly exclude relations with the trade unions from their functions, and some business organizations have gone as far as to forbid agreements with trade unions (Anacik et al. 2009). Gardawski (2009, pp.487–488) reports the telling cases of Polish foundry, automotive and retail sectors, in which, despite union pressure and advanced negotiations, eventually employers decided to withdraw or even, to avoid any risk of having to sign anything, to dissolve their own employer associations. It was not the lack of organization, but the explicit choice to disorganize that prevented collective agreements.

In the NMS there were some institutional preconditions to collective bargaining, such as the discussion of minimum wages in tripartite institutions (Hassel 2009). However, collective bargaining has been rejected by employer organizations. Joining the EU has not helped: industrywide wage negotiations were not seen as a part of the European social model but as an infringement of entrepreneurial freedom and barrier to competitiveness, for example, by the Klaus government in the Czech Republic from 1992 to 1997 (Bluhm 2006). Multinational companies, thanks to their 'systemic power' (Bohle and Greskovits 2007), have been the main actors behind this decision to avoid sector-level collective bargaining. Those operating in the export sectors, in particular, set their wage references cross-nationally and they are largely uninterested in national developments. But even in the sheltered sectors, such as services (e.g., retail), competition on wages is, rather than avoided, actively promoted by private companies—which betrays a focus on short-term predatory profit opportunities, rather than longer-term sustainable investment and competition on the basis of quality and efficiency.

If we look inside the companies, the rejection of coordinated social relations and social dialogue actually goes still further. For not only is wage setting decentralized toward the enterprise and the establishment, but also very often toward the individual, especially in the extreme case of the Baltic states. Woolfson, Calite and Kalliste (2008, p.328) describe the informal individualistic approach to salary issues in Estonia, Latvia and Lithuania, which leads to a drastic reappraisal of the real impact of collective bargaining even in those companies where it occurs. The widespread practice of 'envelope wages', whereby employers declare only part of the wage to reduce social security and tax contributions, constitutes a barrier against formal negotiations of wages (Woolfson 2007; Williams 2009). Wage secrecy is a very common company policy, even if it meets resistance on the employee side. Competition from the large informal sector is also a major obstacle to effective formal collective bargaining. According to the most trustworthy estimates, in 2004 the informal sector accounted for between 17 percent (Slovakia) and 39 percent (Latvia) of the economy, all above the OECD High Income average of 15 percent (Schneider and Buehn 2007). There is little evidence that this has declined: actually, according to Schneider and Buehn, if there is a trend at all, it is toward increasing informality. In Poland, the Central Statistical Office estimates that the number of workers in the informal sector increased from 900,000 to 1.2 million between 2002 and 2008, with a further increase expected for 2009 due to the slowdown in the formal economy (data from GUS). In Romania, a link has also been noted between emigration and informality, as circular migrants have a preference for short, informal jobs and tend to develop a 'culture of evasion' (Parlevliet and Xenogiani 2008).

MIGRATION AND THE SHIFT IN LABOR MARKET POWER

Movement of workers from the NMS to the old member states was, at about 2 million workers excluding short-term movement since accession, about twice the European Commission's forecast to 2008. The evidence indicates that the majority of these mobile workers are not simply attracted by higher pay elsewhere but pushed by dissatisfaction with working conditions at home. Surveys reviewed by Kahanec et al. (2009) show that workers in the NMS are generally more unhappy with their lives, dissatisfied with their salaries and working conditions, and concerned about the availability of good jobs and insecure about their current jobs, and that these are the factors pushing them to move abroad. Essentially, EU accession and freedom of movement have brought to the surface, via migration, the dissatisfaction and anger which thus far largely had remained hidden.

There is an important association between what has happened in terms of migration and what has happened to trade union membership. Increase in the former has gone side-by-side with a decrease of the latter. In 2003–2008, while about 2 million workers left the NMS for the EU15, trade unions in the region lost about 1 million members (while membership in the EU15 remained constant, confirming the further divergence between old and new member states). Table 5.2 shows that the countries with the highest number of emigrants have been those with the strongest fall in union membership, especially Slovakia and Lithuania, while those with the lowest migration have also lost fewer union members, especially the 'deviant' Slovenia, but also Hungary and the Czech Republic. The only important exception is Romania, because relatively strong unions and collective bargaining have survived despite a major loss of population (Trif 2008). This can be explained by the functional conservatism of Romanian unions (offering services rather than 'voice', especially at company level), and by the large and very mobile Roma

Table 5.2 Emigration and fall in union membership, 2003–2008

Country	A – Union membership change, 2003–08 (%)	B – Emigration as % of population, 2003–07	C – Union membership change, 2003–08 (000)	D – Population change to emigration, 2003–07 (000)
Lithuania	−34.1	2.3	−62	−75
Slovakia	−34.1	2.0	−196	−88
Estonia	−18.4	0.8	−8	−10
Bulgaria	−16.2	1.9	−94	−144
Poland	−16.1	1.9	−340	−721
Latvia	−15.8	0.8	−27	−18
Czech Rep.	−14.9	0.3	−77	−33
Hungary	−9.3	0.4	−80	−41
Slovenia	+2.6	0.0	+9	0
Romania	+4.2	4.6	+85	−1,000

Correlation between A and B: $r = -0.717$.

Source: Own elaborations on Carley (2009), EIC (2009).

minority. Once Romania is removed from the analysis, correlation between union membership change and emigration in population percentage terms is very high ($r = -0.80$).

Data on migration and union membership are heterogeneous, as the former refer to the whole population and the latter only to the workforce. It is important to note that the association between the two series does not necessarily indicate that those who leave the unions and those who leave the country are the same people. It indicates that (with the notable exception of Romania) union crisis is strongest where emigration is strongest, which suggests a tradeoff, so far, between 'exit' (emigration) and 'voice' (institutional collective representation) for employees.

In sending countries, migration has some positive economic effects: according to Brücker et al. (2009), GDP declines, but there are gains for real wages, productivity and GDP per capita. Migration numbers as a percentage of the population are much higher in sending than host countries, and effects are therefore more visible, while in the West, the influx of workers from the NMS, according to official sources, has had no significant effect on employment or wages, although it may have contributed to an increasing wage gap between skilled and unskilled workers in manufacturing (Brücker et al. 2009). A precise assessment is impossible because official data from LFS and the European Commission tend to grossly underestimate flows by missing all short-term movement. In the first three years after EU accession,

2.5 percent of active Poles, 2.4 percent of active Slovaks, 3.1 percent of active Latvians and 4 percent of active Lithuanians had registered for work in the UK alone, though numbers were much lower for the other NMS (Home Office 2009). If one includes similar data from other countries with high immigration flows (Ireland, Norway, Spain), the total share of workers who have chosen to 'exit' their countries, at least temporarily, after 2004 may be over 10 percent in the case of the Baltic States and Romania, and only slightly less in Poland and Slovakia.

Such exit patterns affect the balance of power in employment relations in the home countries. Both real and potential worker mobility (the right to legal employment in other EU states) after 2004 is less disruptive than capital mobility because capital remains inherently more mobile than labor. Still, by 2007 labor shortages were complained of in all NMS, and employer organizations were requesting the easing of migration barriers to workers from their eastern neighbors (Belarus, Russia and Ukraine). The exit threat also forced employers and governments to make concessions they had been unwilling to make before. Wages increased quickly between 2004 and 2006, even if less than productivity and therefore without damaging the competitiveness of these countries: according to Eurostat data, by 50.6 percent in Poland, 59.3 percent in Lithuania, 60.4 percent in the Czech Republic, 88.9 percent in Slovakia, 97.8 percent in Hungary, 100.4 percent in Estonia and 118.3 percent in Latvia, as against 26.3 percent in the Euro area. However, inflation and above all productivity growth were higher in the NMS, meaning that, in terms of unit labor costs, there was much more wage moderation in the NMS than in Western Europe (Van Gyes et al. 2007). Interestingly, these figures are roughly inversely correlated to collective bargaining coverage, which is higher in Poland and Slovakia than in the Baltic countries. Also, wage drift (the difference between actual pay and collectively agreed pay) is greater than in Western Europe. This means that formal industrial relations were not the driving force behind wage increases: these were granted not because of union power, but because of exit threats and labor scarcity. Not surprisingly, they were most generous in sectors such as construction and transport, where employees are most mobile.

An extreme case is that of Latvia, from which perhaps 50,000–100,000 people emigrated in the two years immediately following EU accession. Sommers and Woolfson (2008, p.65) report a Latvian State Employment Agency representative confirming that it is employment conditions in their countries that push workers to leave: '[E]mployers in Latvia are not ready to motivate their employees and give them good working conditions. This is the main reason why our citizens are looking for jobs in other European countries'. Latvia is also a country that followed the neoliberal creed most closely, introducing the flat tax already in 1995 (one year after Estonia). When eventually the financial crisis hit the Latvian bubble in 2008, sending the country into near-bankruptcy and the heaviest recession in Europe (with an estimated GDP shrinkage of 18 percent in 2009), a further market experiment followed. The government and national bank refused to devalue the lat, prioritizing a fixed exchange rate with the euro, and opted for major cuts in nominal wages—thereby concentrating all losses on labor rather than spreading them to the whole of the economy, including foreign banks. While real wages happen to fall quite often around the world, cuts in nominal wages are very rare and even neoclassical economists accept that, for social and psychological reasons, wages are too 'sticky' to be elastic downward. The Baltic states are different: already during the Russian crisis of 1998 they had demonstrated their peculiar allowance for downward flexibility of nominal wages, with major cuts in construction, fishing, agriculture, hotels and restaurants (Philips and Eamets 2009). In 2009, the Latvian government, with the active support of the IMF, confirmed its commitment to the elasticity of any price, including labor, by cutting state-sector wages by 15–27 percent. As mentioned in the previous section, the weakness of trade unions allowed this to happen despite public protests, but the effect was a new boost to emigration. The global economic crisis, which hit the favored host countries of the UK and Ireland particularly hard, served to reduce the propensity to move in the NMS, but the opposite occurred to Latvians. In the first quarter of 2009, the number of Latvians registering for work in the UK increased by 24 percent in comparison to the first quarter of 2008, while numbers declined sharply for all other NMS—by 54 percent for the total of EU8 countries. Interestingly, Latvia was then presented by international financial institutions like the IMF as an example to follow for old member states in crisis, such as Greece, Ireland and Portugal.

Chances for Increased Employee Assertiveness?

One can ask if the general deterioration in labor market conditions after EU accession might lead to increased opportunities for trade unions to organize and mobilize workers. So far, trade unions have not reversed their membership fall (Table 5.2). However, there are signs of increased mobilization. International statistics on strikes collected by the ILO (available at the LABORISTA database), however incomplete, indicate that some countries (Slovakia, Lithuania, Latvia, Romania) have persisted in the virtually strike-free status that characterized the region before EU accession. In Hungary and Poland, on the other side, there has been a clear increase in strike volume. While in Hungary this is probably due to the economic and political crisis, in Poland it appears to be due to changed labor market conditions. Polish strike figures from the General Statistical Office show that the number of days lost in strikes increased from 400 in 2004, to 3,300 in 2005, to 31,400 in 2006, to 186,200 in 2007, to 275,800 in 2008. Interestingly, this contrasts with trends in Western Europe, where according to ILO data, days lost due to strikes per 1,000 employees constantly declined. On protest at least, workers are starting to bridge the gap between old and new member states, with Poland already reaching the EU average.

Qualitative information points to the same direction (Meardi 2007). For instance, the successful union organizing of the Suzuki factory in Hungary in 2006 came after over ten years of failed attempts. Analysis of the variety and spread of the events indicate that while pay is the dominant issue, union rights, working time, restructuring and employment conditions also figure prominently. While the public sector (education, health, railways and civil service) is over-represented, all emerging private sectors with the exception of banking and finance have seen innovative developments as well—for instance, in retail. These occurrences of voice are heterogeneous, ranging from strikes to social partnership agreements, but mostly involve efforts in grassroots organizing. The unions are, however, aware of their own limits and one important way in which they are trying, with some success in Czech Republic, Hungary and Slovakia, to expand social regulation of employment is through extension procedures for collective agreements. Where there is no extension procedure, 'copycat' initiatives fulfill a similar function in socializing collective bargaining gains, as for instance in the wave of actions in the various transport companies in Tallinn in 2006–2007. Public demonstrations, political lobbying, warning strikes and stoppages are also more frequent than official strikes, which are subject to strict procedural regulations.

CONCLUSIONS

Our review of industrial relations change in the NMS reveals that accession to the EU in 2004/2007 has not involved convergence toward Western European patterns of industrial relations and social security because the accession has been dominated by economic competitiveness rationales rather than by social concerns. As a result, employment regimes are particularly market-oriented, distinctively decentralized and largely disorganized, with little scope for collective arrangements.

A major labor market development has been migration. On one side, migration follows and perpetuates the pattern of individualization and disorganization of industrial relations, revealing a 'low-commitment' employment regime. On the other side, it modifies the power balance between employers and employees, notably by causing labor shortages and therefore increasing the bargaining power of employees in the departure countries. This, in turn, has the potential to create opportunities for union organizing and to convince employers of the need for more stable social compromises and industrial relations arrangements. The economic crisis that started in 2008 stalled the increased assertiveness of labor and reduced the attractiveness of emigration, but has not appeared to lead to major changes in the main industrial relations patterns. It has, though, revealed major imbalances in countries that were previously heralded as neoliberal successes (Latvia) or economic tigers (Hungary).

To conclude, the analysis is consistent with a view of the EU as a mostly neoliberal project with disruptive effects on industrial relations, not compensated by its declared 'social dimension'. It is, however, disputable whether such a neoliberal experiment, which is most extreme in the NMS, is socially sustainable. High employee turnover, emigration, and the emergence of employee protest within and without the workplace means that even in regions where the traditions of the Western labor movement have no roots, a need exists for developing institutions of collective voice for employees in order to avoid social disruption and, from the employers' points of view, the emergence of low-commitment employment relations and wage 'leapfrogging' involving disorderly increases that distort competition.

NOTE

1. In the Czech Republic, judgment 83/06 of 12th March 2008; in Poland, judgment 23/07 of 1st July 2008.

REFERENCES

Anacik, A., Krupink, S., 'Otręba, A., Skrzyńska, J., Szklarczyk, D. and Uhi, H. 2009. *Diagnoza Stanu Rozwoju Sektorowego Dialogu Społecznego w Skali Ogólnopolskiej.* Krakow: Wyższa Szkoła Europejska im. ks. Józefa Tischnera.

Behrens, M. 2004. 'New forms of employers' collective interest representation', *Industrielle Beziehungen,* 11. 77–91.

Bluhm, K. 2006. 'Auflösung des liberalisierungsdilemmas—Arbeitsbeziehungen mittelosteuropas im kontext des EU-Beitritts', *Berliner Journal für Soziologie,* 16:2. 171–186.

Bohle, D. and Greskovits, B. 2010. 'Slovakia and Hungary: Successful and failed euro entry without social pacts' in P. Pochet, M. Keune and D. Natali (eds.) *After the Euro and the Enlargement: Social Pacts in the European Union.* Brussels: European Trade Union Institute. 345–370.

Brücker, H., Baas, T., Bertoli, S. and Hauptmann, A. 2009. *Labour Mobility within the EU in the Context of Enlargement and the Functioning of the Transitional Arrangements.* Nürnberg: European Integration Consortium.

Carley, M. 2009. *Trade union membership 2003–2008.* Dublin: European Industrial relations Observatory.

Carley, M. and Hall, M. 2008. *Impact of the Information and Consultation Directive on Industrial Relations.* [online] Available at <http://www.eurofound.europa.eu/eiro/studies/tn0710029s/tn0710029s.htm>

Cziria, L. 2010. *Government Plans Changes to Collective Bargaining Laws.* [online] Available at <http://www.eurofound.europa.eu/eiro/2010/10/articles/SK1010029I.htm>

Donaghey, J. and Teague, P. 2006. 'The free movement of workers and social Europe: Maintaining the European ideal', *Industrial Relations Journal,* 37:6. 652–666.

EC 2008a. *Industrial Relations in Europe Report.* Brussels: European Commission.

EC 2008b. *Employment in Europe Report 2008.* Brussels: European Commission.

Esping-Andersen, G. 1990. *The Three Worlds of Welfare Capitalism.* Princeton: Princeton University Press.

Gardawski, J. 2001. *Związki Zawodowe na Rozdrożu*. Warsaw: ISP.

———. 2009. 'Ewolucja polskich związków zawodowych' in J. Gardawski (ed.) *Polacy Pracujący a Kryzys Fordyzmu*. Warsaw: Scholar. 459–532.

Gardawski, J. and Meardi, G. 2010 'Keep trying? Polish failures and half-successes in social pacting' in P. Pochet, M. Keune and D. Natali (eds.) *After the Euro and the Enlargement: Social Pacts in the European Union*. Brussels: European Trade Union Institute. 371–394.

Ghellab, Y. and Vaughan-Whitehead, D. (eds.) 2003. *Sectoral Social Dialogue in Future EU Member States: The Weakest Link*. Geneva: ILO.

Gładoch, M. 2008. 'Meandry partycypacji pracowniczej w Polsce', *Dialog. Pismo Dialogu Społecznego*, 2. 59–64.

Grdešić, M. 2008. 'Mapping the paths of the Yugoslav model: Labour strength and weakness in Slovenia, Croatia and Serbia', *European Journal of Industrial Relations*, 14:2. 133–151.

Hassel, A. 2009. 'Policies and Politics in Social Pacts in Europe', *European Journal of Industrial Relations*, 15:1. 7–26.

Home Office 2009. *Accession Monitoring Report, May 2004—March 2009*. London: Home Office.

Kahanec, M., Zaiceva, A. and Zimmermann, K. 2009. 'Lessons from migration after EU enlargement' In M. Kahanec and K. Zimmermann (eds.) *EU Labor Markets After Post-Enlargement Migration*. Berlin: Springer. 3–46.

Kohl, H. and Platzer, H. 2007. 'The role of the state in Central and Eastern European industrial relations: The case of minimum wages' *Industrial Relations Journal*, 38:6. 614–635.

Kozek, W. 1999, 'Społeczne organizacje biznesu i jego związki w Polsce', in: W. Kozek (ed.)
Społeczne organizacje biznesu w Polsce a stosunki pracy. Warszawa: Wyd. B-P: 13–102.

Meardi, G. 2002. 'The Trojan horse for the Americanization of Europe? Polish industrial relations towards the EU', *European Journal of Industrial Relations*, 8:1. 77–99.

———. 2006. 'Social pacts on the road to EMU: A comparison of the Italian and Polish experiences', *Economic and Industrial Democracy*, 27:2. 197–222.

———. 2007. 'More voice after more exit?' *Industrial Relations Journal*, 38:6. 503–523.

———. 2012. *Social Failures of EU Enlargement : A Case of Workers Voting with Their Feet*. London: Routledge.

Meardi, G., Marginson, P., Fichter, M., Frybes, M., Tóth, A. and Stanojević, M. 2009. 'Varieties of multinationals', *Industrial Relations*, 48:3. 489–511.

Męcina, J. 2009. 'Prawo pracy w przebudowie—kierunki i cechy ewolucji zmian w prawie pracy' in J. Gardawski (ed.) *Polacy Pracujący a Kryzys Fordyzmu*. Warsaw: Scholar. 258–306.

Ost, D. 2000. 'Illusory corporatism in Eastern Europe: Neoliberal tripartism and postcommunist class identities", *Politics and Society*, 28:4. 503–530.

Parlevliet, J. and Xenogiani, T. 2008. *Report on Informal Employment in Romania*. Paris: OECD Development Centre, Working Paper 271.

Philips, K. and Eamets, R. (2009). Labour market flexibility and employment security in the Baltic States. In *Actas del VIII Congreso "Cultura Europea": VIII Congreso "Cultura Europea"; Pamplona, Spain; 26–29.10.2005*. (Eds.) Irantzu, P.; Maria, C.; Rosa, G.M.; Olejua, I.; Vazquez, J.; Villela, M. Universidad de Navarra, 2009, 385–394.

Schneider, F. and Buehn A. 2007. 'Shadow economies and corruption all over the world: Revised estimates for 120 countries', *Economics: The Open-Access, Open-Assessment E-Journal*. 1. 1–53.

Rugraff, E. 2006. 'Firmes multinationales et relations industrielles en Europe Centrale: Une approche institutionnaliste', *Relations Industrielles*, 61:3. 437–464.

Sommers, J. and Woolfson, C. 2008. 'Trajectories of entropy and "the Labor Question": The political economy of post-communist migration in the new Europe', *Debatte: Journal of Contemporary Central and Eastern Europe*, 16:1. 53–69.

Stanojević, M. 2010. 'Social pacts in Slovenia' In P. Pochet, M. Keune and D. Natali (eds.) *Social Pacts in the European Union*. Brussels: European Trade Union Institute. 317–344.

Surdykowska, B. 2008. 'Prześwietlanie rad pracowniczych', *Dialog. Pismo Dialogu Społecznego*, 2. 14–21.

Tóth, A. and Neumann, L. 2004. *National-level Tripartism and EMU in the New EU Member States and Candidate Countries*. Dublin: European Foundation for the Improvement of Living and Working Conditions.

Traxler, F. 2010. 'Corporatism(s) and pacts: Changing functions and structures under rising economic liberalism and declining liberal democracy' in P. Pochet, M. Keune and D. Natali (eds.) *Social Pacts in the European Union*. Brussels: European Trade Union Institute. 45–82.

Trif, A. 2008. 'Opportunities and challenges of EU accession: Industrial relations in Romania', *European Journal of Industrial Relations*, 14:2. 461–478.

Van Gyes, G., Vandenbrande, T., Lehndorff, S., Shilling, G., Schief, S. and Kohl, H. 2007. *Industrial Relations in EU Member States, 2000–2004*. Dublin: European Foundation for the Improvement of Living and Working Conditions.

Vanhuysse, P. 2006. *Divide and Pacify: Strategic Social Policies and Political Protests in Post-Communist Democracies*. Budapest: CEU Press.

Williams, C. 2009. 'Illegitimate wage practices in Central and Eastern Europe: A study of the prevalence and impacts of "envelope wages"', *Debatte: Journal of Contemporary Central and Eastern Europe*, 17:1. 65–83.

Woolfson, C. 2007. 'Pushing the envelope: The 'informalization' of labour in postcommunist new EU member states', *Work, Employment and Society*, 21:3. 551–564.

Woolfson, C., Calite, D. and Kalliste, E. 2008. 'Employee "voice" and working environment in post-communist new member states: An empirical analysis of Estonia, Latvia and Lithuania', *Industrial Relations Journal*, 39:4. 31.

6   Wage Regulation in the Private Sector
Moving Further away from a 'Solidaristic Wage Policy'?

Maarten Keune and Kurt Vandaele

INTRODUCTION

This chapter examines developments of the past decade or so with regard to the main features of national wage-setting institutions and wage policy in the private sector in the European Union (EU). In most of Western Europe, in the postwar decades, a so-called 'solidaristic wage policy' was adopted in pursuit of a fair distribution of income between capital and labor as well as within labor groups (Schulten 2002). This solidaristic wage policy translated into two main aims (ibid, p.74): (a) equal pay for work of equal value, implying that wages should not depend on individual company circumstances alone but should be standardized in multiemployer collective agreements, while pay raises should be in line with growth of the overall economy, enabling benefits to be shared between capital and labor in a manner ensuring that all workers participate in economic progress; and (b) a more egalitarian wage structure, reducing pay differences between higher and lower wage groups and counteracting market forces that result in increased wage differentiation. Since the 1980s, wage policy became increasingly market-driven and competition-oriented, including features such as wage moderation, a distribution of income between capital and labor that favors the former, and increased inequality within the labor force at large (Brandl and Traxler 2011). This development follows the displacement of Keynesianism with monetarist and neoliberal thought, in a context of expanded market relations (commodification) and increased global competition (Streeck and Thelen 2005).

Dramatic changes have taken place too in the Central and Eastern European (CEE) countries (see chapter 5, this volume). The postwar decades were defined by state-socialist systems in which wage differentiation was limited but wages were also, to a large extent, low and disconnected from productivity developments (Kornai 1992). Since the collapse of state socialism, radical changes have taken place in wage policy and wage-setting institutions in these countries (Kohl and Platzer 2004). Competitiveness became a major goal of wage policy, the market came to occupy a large role in wage setting and minimum wages were introduced. Again, the trend seems to be toward wage moderation, a distribution of income in favor of capital and increased wage inequality (Keune 2008).

Reinforcing these developments is the European Monetary Union (EMU), which fully emerged in 1999 and which strengthened calls for wage moderation and wage flexibility in the member countries of the Eurozone. One effect of EMU is that individual countries entering the Union lose a number of major instruments for adjusting to economic imbalances and shocks, including the possibility to change interest rates, exchange rates and money supply. Under EMU, monetary policy is the competence of the European Central Bank (ECB), which sets a common policy for all EMU members, with inflation as the one needle on the Frankfurt compass. This increases the importance of wage adjustments in the case of asymmetric shocks; indeed, under EMU wage moderation gains in importance also as a macro adjustment instrument. This is explicit under the present crisis: as governments miss macroeconomic adjustment instruments, the pressure on wages is mounting, especially in the public sector of countries most affected by the European sovereign debt crisis.

In this chapter we will discuss how far and with what implications the developments highlighted by Schulten have continued in the past decade or so. We will show that in the past twenty years pay has grown slower than productivity and with increased fragmentation in pay setting and outcomes. This is due to a series of factors: the pressures emerging from European integration and international competition, including a shift in power in favor of employers; pressures on public expenditure emerging in particular from EMU; social pacts geared to wage moderation; and the decentralization of collective bargaining and declining trade union power. We will pay due attention to differences between countries and continued divergence over time. In line with the neo-institutionalist literature on institutional change and the makeup of different types of capitalist systems (Crouch 2005; Hall and Soskice 2001; Hancké 2009), we should expect the specific shape to vary across (groups of) European countries, depending on different historical trajectories, institutional heritages, and the power constellations between labor, capital and the state. Hence, while a general trend is expected to be discernible, at the same time major variation between countries is predicted. Our key focus concerns the differences between countries with single-employer bargaining systems (SEBs) and those with multiemployer bargaining systems (MEBs) because it is expected that those wage-setting systems explain wage developments to a large extent.

A MAJOR INSTITUTIONAL DISTINCTION: SINGLE- AND MULTIEMPLOYER BARGAINING SYSTEMS

Wage outcomes are influenced by many factors. Paramount among them are the domestic institutional and legislative framework for wage bargaining as well as the relative bargaining power of (organized) labor and capital and their respective tactics and strategies. A crucial dimension of wage bargaining is the degree of coordination or interconnectedness between different collective bargaining units. Coordination influences the outcome of the bargaining process in multiple units by setting common standards or strategies, or because certain units (e.g., sectors) imitate the outcomes of other units. Wage-bargaining coordination can take different forms. The most straightforward form is wage-bargaining centralization above the level of the company, at the level of the sector or at the national level. The distinction between different levels of wage bargaining is sometimes vague in practice, however; in many countries bargaining occurs at various levels. Other major forms that wage coordination can take are state-imposed indexation, a statutory minimum wage, inter-associational coordination, intra-associational coordination and pattern bargaining.

A main division can be made between countries with SEB and MEB systems. In Western Europe, MEB (or functionally equivalent variants like pattern bargaining) were historically supported by employers because this practice 'effectively took the wage out of competition and guaranteed that key competitors would also be shut down in the event of a strike' (Flanagan 2008, p.410). Trade unions also favored coordinated wage setting because it imposes minimum wage standards on employers at the industry level or above, and it discourages a downward spiral over working conditions and wages. A high degree of coordination also makes it possible for unions to influence wage formation in small and medium-sized enterprises where they often have few members (Andersson and Thörnqvist 2007).

Of the EU members, Austria, Belgium, Denmark, Finland, France, Germany, Greece, Italy, Portugal, Slovakia, Slovenia, Spain and Sweden are generally considered MEB countries; whereas Bulgaria, Cyprus, the Czech Republic, Estonia, Hungary, Ireland, Latvia, Lithuania, Luxembourg, Malta, Poland, Romania and the UK are classified as SEB countries (Carley and Marginson 2011). Still, the two groups are not homogeneous and particularly in the MEB group one can find considerable diversity. Two main differences exist between the single- and multiemployer bargaining systems. One is that where collective bargaining takes place under MEB, sector-level collective bargaining is predominant and company-level bargaining takes place mainly within the parameters set by sector agreements; while under SEB, company-level bargaining predominates, even though in some sectors sector-level bargaining may take place (see also chapter 2, this volume). The other difference is that in countries with MEB the coverage of collective bargaining (i.e., the percentage of employees that are covered by collective agreements) is generally much higher than in countries characterized by SEB. High coverage is associated with a high membership rate of employers' organizations given the need for a mandate to negotiate collective agreements with trade unions for a large part of the economy. The lower bargaining coverage in the SEB countries implies, among others, that unilateral management decisions are of much stronger influence where wage

Table 6.1 Collective bargaining coverage and union density in SEB and MEB countries, 2010 (or last year available)

SEB	Coverage	Union density	MEB	Coverage	Union density
Bulgaria	30.0%	19.8%	Austria	99.0%	28.1%
Cyprus	52.0%	54.3%	Belgium	96.0%	52.0%
Czech	42.5%	17.3%	Denmark	80.0%	68.8%
Estonia	19.0%	6.7%	Finland	90.0%	70.0%
Hungary	33.5%	16.8%	France	90.0%	7.6%
Ireland	44.0%	33.7%	Germany	62.0%	18.6%
Latvia	25.0%	14.8%	Greece	65.0%	24.0%
Lithuania	15.0%	9.5%	Italy	80.0%	35.1%
Luxembourg	58.0%	37.3%	Netherlands	82.3%	19.0%
Malta	55.0%	51.0%	Portugal	45.0%	19.3%
Poland	38.0%	15.0%	Slovakia	40.0%	17.2%
Romania	70.0%	32.8%	Slovenia	92.0%	29.7%
UK	32.7%	27.5%	Spain	84.5%	15.9%
			Sweden	91.0%	68.9%
Average	39.6%	25.9%	Average	78.3%	33.9%
Deviation	16.1%	15.1%	Deviation	18.5%	21.8%

Source: Visser (2011).

setting is concerned. High coverage does not, however, necessarily require high trade union density. As Table 6.1 shows, the two can be quite disparate and in general coverage is substantially higher than union density. In this respect the French case is quintessential: whereas union density is at the very low level of 8 percent, bargaining coverage is universal. This is explained by the fact that public authorities can extend collective agreements to employers who are not members of the employers' associations that signed the agreement. The use of statutory extension schemes is very common in MEB countries, except for the Nordic countries where high union density does explain the high bargaining coverage.

PERSISTENT DIVERGENCE IN COLLECTIVE BARGAINING STRUCTURES AND COORDINATION

Looking at the dynamics in bargaining structures over time (Figure 6.1), decentralized wage bargaining has a long history in most SEB countries. Two countries demonstrate less historical continuity, however. The UK shifted

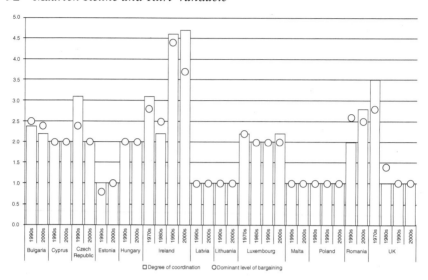

Figure 6.1   Dominant level of bargaining and collective bargaining coordination in SEB countries, 1970–2009 (ten yearly averages)

Source: Visser (2011).

Note: Level: 1 = local or company bargaining; 2 = sectoral or industry level, with additional local or company bargaining; 3 = sectoral or industry level; 4 = national or central level, with additional sectoral/local or company bargaining; 5 = national or central level; Coordination: 1 = fragmented bargaining, mostly at company level; 2 = mixed industry- and firm-level bargaining, with weak enforceability of industry agreements; 3 = industry bargaining with no or irregular pattern setting, limited involvement of central organizations and limited freedoms for company bargaining; 4 = mixed industry- and economy-wide bargaining; 5 = economy-wide bargaining.

away from multiemployer agreements toward decentralization in the 1980s due to state-led labor market reforms and the unions' inability to withstand the state's and employers' drive for decentralization. Ireland moved toward a centralized system of social pacts, including national wage agreements in the mid-1980s, but this system fell apart in 2009 when the government opted for a unilateral market and austerity-led adjustment rather than a negotiated package to confront its severe economic crisis (Regan forthcoming). Turning to the CEE countries, sectoral and national collective agreements in industry in Romania provide a framework for company negotiations, and agreements are automatically extended to cover all employees in the bargaining unit, but the dominant bargaining practice in the private services sector is exclusively SEB-based (Trif 2008). So, as in most CEE countries, the company level is the most important for setting the actual terms of employment and working conditions in Romania. Slovakia and Slovenia are the exceptions: they do not belong to the SEB cluster because their institutional framework for wage setting shows more similarities with the economies in the center-West of Europe.[1] Finally, with the exception of Ireland (until 2009) and Romania,

SEB countries are traditionally characterized by a low degree of wage coordination. Apart from their fragmented wage bargaining structure, this could be further explained by the absence or weak development of coordinating mechanisms and the weak coordination capacity of employers' organizations and trade unions, due to their fragmented organizational structure.

While the degree of wage coordination in most SEB countries has been relatively stable, bargaining has become more decentralized in the MEB countries after the 1970s (Figure 6.2), often accompanied by a decline in union density. The subgroup of Continental European countries has moved toward slightly less centralized bargaining structures. Even though the locus of collective bargaining in those countries is based more at lower levels today compared to the late 1970s, bargaining decentralization is not a universal trend. Moreover, if the 1990s form the reference period, changes for most countries since have been rather marginal (see also chapter 2, this volume). In Southern Europe, however, the countries point more toward decentralization (i.e., mixed sector and company bargaining). Finally, just like most countries within the Continental and Southern economies, several negotiation levels are in place in Northern Europe. In recent years, decentralization is a more marked trend in this part of Europe, with Finland moving its main negotiations from the central to the sector level in 2007 and with the other Nordic countries decentralizing more and more elements of wage bargaining to the company level, although still within sectoral frameworks (Keune 2011).

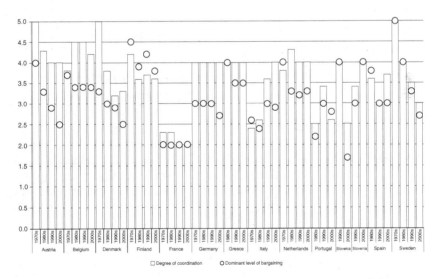

Figure 6.2 Dominant level of bargaining and collective bargaining coordination in MEB countries, 1970–2009 (ten yearly averages)

Source: Visser (2011).

Note: see Figure 1.

Dependent on the degree of multiemployer bargaining and pay synchronization, decentralization can occur in an organized or unorganized way (Traxler 1995). In the overall majority of the MEB countries decentralization happened in an organized way, meaning that unions and employers' organizations continue to set, in higher level agreements, the framework of rules and standards within which lower (company) level agreements are negotiated. For example, at sector level minimum increases of wages can be negotiated, while at company level actual increases are set. In this way, there is more flexibility at the company level to negotiate wages according to local circumstances, but at the same time sectoral unions and employers' organizations maintain a coordinating role. As a consequence, the degree of coordination has been less subject to change in the last decades. Despite the long-run decentralization trend, coordination remains relatively high in Continental and Southern Europe. A long-term exception is France with a significantly lower degree of coordination compared to its counterparts. Conversely, as will be explained in the next section, coordination has even been strengthened in Belgium, Italy and Spain in the 2000s. Equally, looking at Northern Europe, the degree of coordination is comparable with most MEB economies, despite standing at a lower level today than at the end of the 1970s. For the MEB countries, one can in fact replicate the conclusion that Schulten (2002, p.183) made, namely that 'there has . . . been no irreversible erosion of the institutional requirements for a solidaristic wage policy'. Nevertheless, the present crisis is taken as an opportunity by the European Commission and certain governments to put increased pressure on centralized wage-setting institutions and coordination processes, particularly in those countries hardest hit by recession (Aumayr et al. 2011).

Given that relative stability can be attributed to the MEB countries at the higher end of the coordination scale and given that stability is also the main characteristic for the SEB countries standing at the lower end, the two groups continue to diverge. There is one important exception within the MEB cluster, however. In Germany decentralization increasingly has a 'disorganized' dimension as the coverage of collective agreements declines, extensions are used less and less, and more and more employers leave the employers' organizations (Bispinck et al. 2010, pp.13–22; Keune 2008, pp.19–20; Streeck 2009). This decentralization is largely driven by the German employers with support from the major political parties and the government. Collective bargaining coverage has declined from 76 percent in 1998 to 65 percent in 2009 in West Germany and in the same period from 63 percent to 51 percent in East Germany (Bispinck et al. 2010, p.2). Also, opening clauses are increasingly included in sectoral collective agreements, allowing for more differentiation and decentralization of collective bargaining and in some cases for concession bargaining leading to deteriorating terms and conditions of employment for employees. Over time, the rationale behind opening clauses has shifted from allowing the adjustment and survival of companies experiencing severe but temporary economic difficulties, to sustaining competitiveness in general. In the metal industry, after the conclusion of the Pforzheim agreement in 2004, which established common rules and procedures for derogations, the number of companies effectively using opening clauses increased from seventy in September 2004 to 730 in April 2009 (Bispinck and Schulten 2011, p.7).

COORDINATION THROUGH NATIONAL SOCIAL PACTS

Macro-level social pacts have played an important part in wage setting and wage coordination. Social pacts can be defined as 'a set of formal or informal agreements between representatives of governments and organized interests who negotiate and implement policy change across a number of interconnected policy areas' (Natali and Pochet 2010, p.17). Such pacts were prominent in a number of Western European countries in the heydays of the central income policies of the 1960s and 1970s when Keynesian economic thinking was dominant. Pacts in those days focused on the redistribution of the fruits of economic growth through rising wages and greater wage equality. In later decades pacts have continued to be concluded, but their nature has changed. One major objective of the more recent social pacts is to strengthen the competitiveness of the national economy. Often under the auspices of governments, the 'social partners' have been trying to enhance international competitiveness on the supply side (Rhodes 1998). Apart from in general terms improving competitiveness in the globalizing economy, a series of pacts were also concluded in the 1990s to prepare for entry into EMU. These pacts had specific EMU-related objectives (i.e., to stabilize nominal exchange rates and to meet the convergence criteria set out in the Treaty of the EU concluded in Maastricht in 1992), including low inflation rates, falling public debt and low public deficits (Fajertag and Pochet 1997; 2001). These social pacts provide complex interlinkages between labor market reform, changing welfare state arrangements and wage restraint. A major element was the moderation of wage growth to reduce labor costs and inflation. This seems to point to the internalization of competitive pressures by unions and an orientation toward cross-class coalitions in the name of sustaining or improving national competitiveness (Streeck 1999).

Social pacts have mainly arisen in the MEB countries because these possess the necessary institutional prerequisites, and because this is where unions often have sufficient power to claim a place in reform processes. Pacts have been concluded in about half of the MEBs since 1990. Centered on inflationary targets, the reduction of public deficits and budgetary austerity, social pacts were concluded in Italy, Portugal and Spain in the wake of EMU accession (Pochet et al. 2010). Social pacts failed, however, in Greece due to the opposition of unions, particularly in the public sector, to neoliberal reforms, as a result of which the country could only enter the EMU in 2001 (Ioannou

2010). In Belgium attempts to conclude social pacts related directly to EMU entry failed as well; the federal government, however, imposed a statutory wage-setting system in 1996 that formally introduced wage moderation. In the Netherlands, a consensus on wage moderation within the 'shadow of the state' was already formalized in the 'Wassenaar agreement' in 1982, marking the start of competitive wage bargaining, often formalized in central agreements. This practice has continued in recent years (van der Meer and Visser 2010). In Germany, wage moderation has not been based on central agreements but on sectoral bargaining processes and exposed-sector pattern bargaining increasingly adopting a competitive supply-side bargaining strategy (Erne 2008, pp.99–103).

In Slovenia social pacts covering a range of policy areas have been signed at regular times since 1993, introducing and continuing a restrictive incomes policy (i.e., trying to achieve a consensus between the social partners on wage restraint) (Stanojevic 2010). The post–EMU entry pact of 2007 reasserts this policy with a strong emphasis on the country's competitiveness. In Slovakia, which entered the EMU in 2009, a social pact was signed in 2008, wherein the government committed itself to reducing the public deficit and the social partners, in turn, agreed on wage moderation. However, the major part of the socioeconomic measures for EMU entry had been previously introduced by the government in a unilateral way so that the social pact was very much an 'afterthought' (Bohle and Greskovits 2010, pp.348–351). In the Nordic countries the major case of social pacts is Finland, which has had a tradition of central incomes policy since 1968. This came to an end in 2007 when the Confederation of Finnish Industries decided not to participate further in central negotiations in order to increase the scope for flexibility and variable pay systems.

Some other countries continued to conclude social pacts after EMU entry, which might be explained by the continuing 'need to coordinate bargaining in the context of strong intermediate bargaining units and an asymmetrical interdependence of the exposed and the sheltered sector without clear leadership of the exposed sector in bargaining matters' (Traxler 2010, p.75). In other words, although the exposed sector might embark on effective wage moderation (mainly due to international competitiveness pressures) and thus exclude state 'intervention', it has been argued that social pacts might still be needed to dampen wage expectations in the sheltered sectors (largely consisting of the public sector). The concern here is that wage increases in these sectors might externalize the cost of those increases to the exposed sector, which would impair international competitiveness (Keune and Pochet 2010; Traxler and Brandl 2010). So far, the current economic crisis does not seem to have resulted in new social pacts, in spite of the very high 'problem load' faced by many countries. Instead governments most often pursue unilateral strategies around austerity packages.

As to wage moderation outcomes, the core element of most social pacts, by comparing the average productivity growth and wage growth (expressed as compensation—that is, wages plus employers' social contributions), Figure 6.3 shows that only in Belgium, Denmark, France and Italy has real compensation per employee been higher than the growth rate of labor productivity during the period 1999–2007 (i.e., before the start of the crisis). All other MEB countries, though obviously with cross-country differences, experienced wage moderation after EMU entry. Though wage moderation has often been recommended by the OECD and the European Commission as a way out of high and persistent unemployment, this has not necessarily resulted in a substantial improvement of employment performance (Stockhammer 2007). Furthermore, wage moderation was not evenly spread across all economic sectors and occupations, which significantly contributed to a growing income inequality and rising poverty rate across OECD member states since the mid-1980s (OECD 2011). Where wage development after 2007 is concerned, the data suggest that wages have outgrown productivity in recent years, but this largely reflects the impact of recession on lower-income jobs.

In the SEB countries social pacts have hardly been concluded, mainly because the unions and employers have only limited macrocoordination capacity and because wage moderation is often achieved through market forces. The major exception, as mentioned earlier, is Ireland, which concluded its first tripartite pact in 1987 (Regan forthcoming). Further, but less

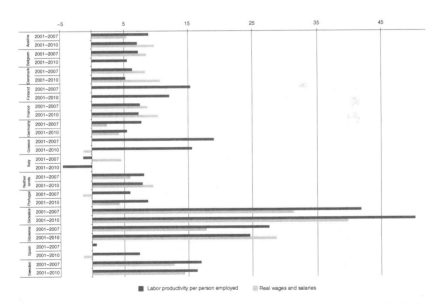

Figure 6.3 Labor productivity per person employed and real wages and salaries, compounded annual percentage changes for 2001–2007 and 2001–2010 in MEB countries

Source: EC (2011).

prominent, exceptions include Bulgaria, where one pact was signed in 2006, and Romania, where two pacts were signed in the early 2000s, but without the participation of the major unions. In addition, in Poland social pacts were *nearly* successfully concluded on several occasions in the 2000s. These exceptions show that, although in SEB countries pacts are clearly less likely to be concluded than in MEB countries, they are indeed possible.

Returning to economic outcomes, Figure 6.4 demonstrates that the gap between labor productivity and real compensation for almost all SEB countries is negative, allowing for real wage growth, in the period 2000–2007. There is, however, large country-to-country variation. To a certain extent, in most CEE countries there was a catching up of wages that had declined dramatically in the 1990s. Furthermore, although real wage growth was in general in most CEE economies in line with productivity improvements, real wage increases resulting from union wage bargaining were significantly below productivity trends, pointing to the low and decreasing coverage of collective wage agreements (Erne 2008, pp.98–99). Moreover, the increase in real wages was not enough to stem the decline in the wage share. Indeed, in both SEB and MEB countries it is possible to observe a clear decline in the wage share (i.e., the share of wages and employers' social contributions in GDP), with the decline since 1975 more pronounced in the SEB countries

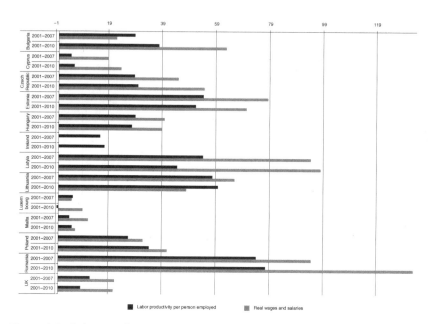

Figure 6.4   Labor productivity per person employed and real wages and salaries, compounded annual percentage changes for 2001–2007 and 2001–2010 in SEB countries

Source: EC (2011).

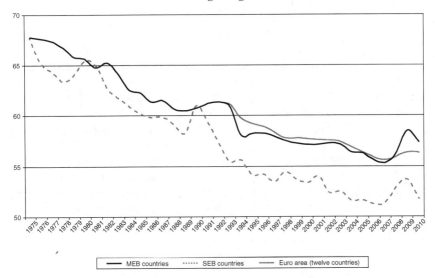

Figure 6.5 Wage share in MEB and SEB countries and the Eurozone (twelve countries), 1975–2010

Source: AMECO.

Note: Eurozone: Austria, Belgium, Finland, France, Germany, Greece, Ireland, Italy, Luxembourg, the Netherlands, Portugal and Spain. Data for West Germany only until 1990. No data for 1975–1989: Malta and Romania; 1975–1991: Hungary, Latvia and Poland; 1975–1992: Estonia and Lithuania; 1975–1994: Bulgaria, Cyprus and the Czech Republic.

(Figure 6.5). Hence, in the longer run it seems that wage moderation has been somewhat stronger in those countries where it results predominantly from market pressure than in those where it is an outcome of a bargaining process.

VPS: PROMOTING WAGE FLEXIBILITY

Whereas at the macro-level social pacts have often been an instrument aimed at improving national competitiveness through wage moderation, at the micro-level variable pay systems (VPS) have often been used in an attempt to strengthen company competitiveness. The three major types of VPS are individual and team-based performance-related pay (PRP), profit sharing (PS) and employee share ownership (ESO). Under variable pay systems, on top of a basic wage, workers receive performance-related variable pay elements that are dependent on the performance of the company as a whole, of the team to which a worker belongs or of the individual worker. VPS have a variety of aims (Arrowsmith, et al, 2010). Among them are improving firm performance and workers' productivity, skills, motivation and involvement; flexibilization in wage-setting through the adjustment of wage costs to firm performance; and/or the redistribution of wealth and the strengthening of economic democracy (in case of profit sharing and employee share owner-ship). However, it often remains unclear whether these additional aims are actually reached. The debates on variable pay are, to a significant extent, inconclusive: whereas many studies point to a positive relationship between VPS and productivity or firm performance, several others shed serious doubt on these results (see e.g., Robinson and Wilson 2006; Cox 2005; Lazear 2000).

For the present chapter, the particular significance of VPS is that they have an effect both on the distribution of income between capital and labor, and on wage differentiation among wage earners within the same company. In this section we will present comparative data on the use of the various types of VPS across the EU as well as differences between countries, sectors and enterprises of different sizes, and we will point to some elements explaining cross-country differences. Because of the lack of longitudinal data, a picture of the situation in 2009 will be presented. There seems, however, to be agree-ment in the literature that the use of VPS has been increasing in recent years (e.g., Welz and Fernándes-Macías 2008; van het Kaar and Grünell 2001). At the same time, there are very large differences between countries in the incidence of the different types of VPS, and the extent to which the use of VPS has been growing is dependent on country-specific factors as opposed to a general, cross-EU trend.

Of the three types of VPS distinguished here, performance-related pay, based on individual or team performance, is by far the most frequently used across Europe (Figure 6.6): 37.2 percent of companies with ten or more

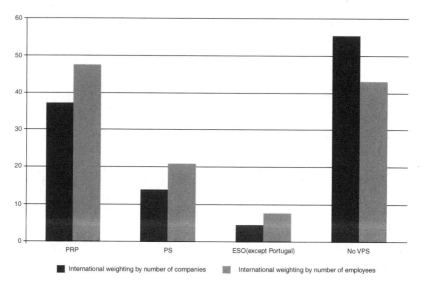

Figure 6.6   Types of VPS, EU27, 2009 (percent of companies with ten or more employees)

Source: European Company Survey (2009).

employees, employing 47.5 percent of employees in this group of companies, have some form of performance-related pay. There is a much lower incidence of both employee financial participation through profit-sharing schemes and employee-share-ownership schemes. What is more, over half of the enterprises with ten or more employees have no VPS whatsoever.

The incidence of VPS is closely related to three key factors: country, sector and company size. The largest differences are observed between countries, as shown in Table 6.2. For example, while in the Czech Republic no less than 71 percent of companies used PRP schemes, in Hungary only 19.8 percent of companies have such schemes. Profit sharing is meanwhile used in 35 percent of French companies but in no more than 2.9 percent of Italian companies. In addition, employee share ownership exists in 12.9 percent of Danish companies but in only 0.9 percent of Lithuanian ones. Meanwhile, no clear pattern related to the MEB-SEB distinction can be discerned. The

Table 6.2   Types of VPS per country (divided by SEB-MEB) in 2009 (percent of companies with ten or more employees)

Single-employer bargaining system				Multi-employer bargaining system		
	PRP	**PS**	**ESO**		**PRP**	**PS**	**ESO**
Hungary	19.8%	13.0%	3.4%	Italy	26.8%	2.9%	3.9%
Latvia	27.0%	10.4%	3.7%	France	28.3%	35.0%	4.7%
Ireland	28.2%	11.3%	6.4%	Belgium	30.2%	14.3%	11.4%
Cyprus	34.4%	5.7%	3.6%	Austria	31.3%	8.0%	2.1%
Malta	34.9%	4.3%	2.9%	Sweden	31.8%	23.5%	11.1%
Estonia	36.2%	17.7%	2.7%	Greece	34.3%	4.2%	1.6%
Bulgaria	37.1%	9.5%	7.3%	Netherlands	34.3%	26.8%	5.5%
UK	37.3%	8.2%	5.9%	Spain	40.3%	16.8%	3.4%
Luxembourg	37.6%	9.5%	3.6%	Germany	41.8%	14.1%	2.9%
Romania	40.5%	7.4%	10.8%	Denmark	43.3%	14.1%	12.9%
Lithuania	44.3%	7.1%	0.9%	Slovak Republic	56.3%	16.9%	2.5%
Poland	44.9%	7.2%	4.2%	Finland	63.6%	23.0%	5.0%
Czech Republic	71.0%	16.0%	1.0%	Slovenia	69.4%	13.3%	7.0%
Average	37.9%	9.8%	4.3%	Average	40.9%	16.4%	5.7%
Deviation	12.1%	3.9%	2.7%	Deviation	13.9%	9.0%	3.8%

Note: Sorted by PRP.

Source: European Company Survey (2009).

major difference between the two groups is a somewhat higher average for all three VPS types in the MEBs, but the differences are important only in the case of profit sharing. Also, the higher averages in MEBs are accompanied by higher standard deviations, indicating stronger internal differences.

The main explanatory factor of country differences relates to different national VPS-specific institutional contexts (i.e., different rules and regulations that govern the use of VPS in different countries). For example, the high level of PRP in the Czech Republic is linked to the fact that the Czech Labour Code—unique in this respect in the EU—strongly encourages performance pay. Similarly, the high level of profit sharing in French companies results from the fact that the country has a mandatory profit-sharing scheme for companies with a workforce of over fifty employees. In Denmark, multiple options and tax benefits exist in relation to employee share ownership and ESO schemes are increasingly a matter for collective bargaining. Indeed, through such statutory or collectively agreed regulations and promotional measures, the state and the social partners play a decisive role in promoting the use of VPS.

Clear differences in the use of variable pay schemes also exist between sectors (Figure 6.7). The three types of VPS are most prevalent in financial intermediation, followed by real estate and business services, and then by trade and repair. In health and social work, public administration and defense, and education, on the contrary, VPS is used to only a limited extent. The sectors with a high incidence of VPS often have a long tradition of individual and collective financial incentives. Another relevant factor is that

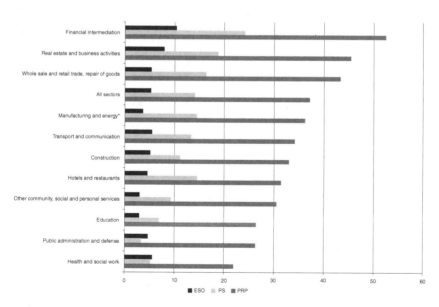

Figure 6.7 VPS by sector, EU27, 2009 (percent of companies with ten or more employees).

Source: European Company Survey (2009).

financial intermediation and business services have faced a tight labor market for highly educated labor in many countries in recent years, leading to the use of bonuses to attract employees and reward improvements in education and training (cf. van het Kaar and Grünell 2001).

Where size is concerned, the use of all three types of VPS increases steadily with the increase in the size of establishments (Figure 6.8). When companies with ten to nineteen employees are compared with those having 500 or more employees, PRP schemes are found to occur twice as often in the latter, PS schemes 2.3 times as often and ESO schemes 3.6 times as often. Of companies with 250 or more employees, over 60 percent make use of PRP schemes, while some 27 percent use PS schemes and some 13 percent have ESO schemes, all these percentages being well above the average. This is hardly surprising, in that the design and implementation of VPS schemes often requires substantial management involvement, administrative capacity and expertise in Human Resource Management (HRM) techniques (Cox 2005).

From this overview we can conclude that major differences exist between countries, sectors and company size in the use of VPS, with country-level institutional factors being of major importance. Performance-related pay is, meanwhile, by far the most important type of VPS, while employee share ownership is of minor significance. This suggests that VPS are employed much more often with the aim of increasing individual or group performance, competitiveness and wage flexibility, than for the purpose of redistributing wealth or strengthening economic democracy. Hence, the use of VPS seems to fit the trend from solidaristic to competitive wage policy; at the same

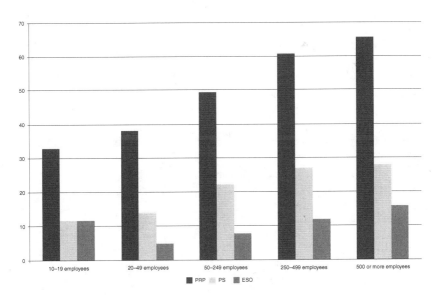

Figure 6.8 VPS by company size, EU27, 2009 (percent of companies with ten or more employees).

Source: European Company Survey (2009).

time, country-to-country variation is so great that it is hardly possible to speak of a general tendency.

LIMITING WAGE FLEXIBILITY VIA MINIMUM WAGES

A major factor in determining wage levels, wage flexibility and wage inequality is the minimum wage. A minimum wage places limits on wage flexibility by setting a wage floor in the labor market. Depending on the level at which the minimum wage is set, it can play an important role in containing wage inequality and low pay. The almost generalized decline of trade union density across Europe, combined in some countries with a falling coverage and/ or decentralization of collective wage bargaining, make the minimum wage all the more relevant in this respect. Other factors leading to increasing concerns about wage inequality and low pay are the rise of nonstandard flexible employment contracts and the growing use of opening clauses in collective agreements in certain countries, in particular Germany. Worries around low pay are further strengthened by the increased mobility of labor within the EU (Vaughan-Whitehead 2008; see also chapter 5, this volume).

Minimum wages can be set by law or by collective agreement. In Europe statutory minimum wages are the most common way of determining a minimum level below which wages cannot be set. Twenty out of the twenty-seven EU member states have a statutory minimum wage and Table 6.3 shows the levels of hourly minimum wages for these countries during the period 2002–2009. The most striking feature, initially, is the enormous difference in the level of the minimum wage, with the highest being more than ten times the lowest. When expressed in terms of purchasing power parity, the range between highest and lowest minimum wage levels shrinks, but, even so, the highest monthly minimum wage is still almost six times greater than the lowest (Keune 2011).

When observing the growth in the minimum wage over time, a difference emerges between the old and the new EU member states: in both nominal and real terms, minimum wage growth is higher in the new members than in the old. Over time, then, the gap between the old and new member states has been narrowing slowly, in line with the catching up of general wages (Keune 2008). Following the onset of the crisis, this trend would seem, however, to have come to a standstill, and even to have been reversed. In 2009 the hourly minimum wage saw its real value decline in nine countries, in some cases quite substantially (e.g., by 5.6 percent in Romania and 4.2 percent in Lithuania). Of these nine countries, eight are from the CEE new member states (i.e., this whole group except for Slovenia and Slovakia), while the ninth is the UK.

Figure 6.9 shows the relationship between the minimum wage and the average wage. In 2008, only in Luxembourg and Malta did the minimum wage represent over 50 percent of the average wage, while in ten countries it amounted to less than 40 percent of the average wage. This shows that in many countries the statutory minimum wage can play no more than a

Table 6.3   The statutory minimum wage in twenty EU countries, per hour, 2002 and 2009 (Euro)

Country	2002	2009	Growth	Real growth
Bulgaria	0.3	0.71	1.37	0.52
Romania	0.19	0.83	3.37	1.12
Lithuania	0.71	1.4	0.97	0.47
Hungary	1.03	1.47	0.43	−0.03
Latvia	0.49	1.47	2	0.86
Poland	1.02	1.7	0.67	0.43
Slovakia	0.88	1.7	0.93	0.47
Estonia	0.7	1.73	1.47	0.80
Czech Republic	1.28	1.82	0.42	0.19
Portugal	2.1	2.71	0.29	0.14
Slovenia	2.28	3.41	0.5	0.11
Malta	3	3.67	0.22	0.05
Spain	2.68	3.78	0.41	0.14
Greece	2.83	4.05	0.43	0.18
UK	4.6	6.43	0.40	0.20
Belgium	7.05	8.41	0.19	0.02
Netherlands	7.4	8.47	0.14	0.00
Ireland	5.97	8.65	0.45	0.19
France	6.67	8.71	0.31	0.15

Note: Sorted by level of minimum wage in 2009.

Source: Eurostat.

limited role in preventing low pay. What is more, between 2002 and 2008, in eleven countries the minimum wage lost ground to the average wage, most strongly in Ireland (minus 8 percentage points), Hungary (minus 5.4 percentage points) and the Netherlands (minus 5.1 percentage points). In most instances, the minimum wage seems unable to keep up with average wage developments in the labor market.

In Germany, Italy, Denmark, Austria, Sweden, Finland and Cyprus there exists no general statutory minimum wage. In these countries the setting of minimum wages is traditionally left to a large extent to unions and employers, which define minimum wages in collective agreements, mainly at the sectoral level (with the exception of Cyprus). In Cyprus, a statutory minimum wage exists but is applicable only to a limited number of occupations (sales staff, clerical workers, auxiliary healthcare staff and auxiliary

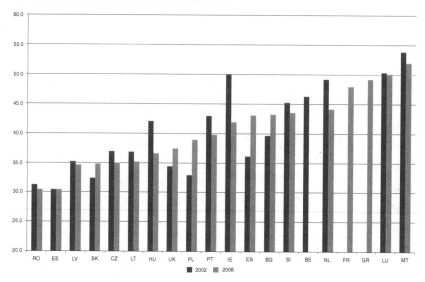

Figure 6.9 Monthly minimum wage as percent of average monthly earnings industry and services, 2002–2008

staff in nursery schools, crèches and schools). In Germany the minister of labor, under the *Arbeitnehmer-Entsendegesetz* (Posted Workers Law), can make a collectively agreed minimum wage binding on all employment in a sector, irrespective of whether or not the employer is directly bound by a sectoral collective agreement. Such minimum wages now exist for a limited number of sectors. One consequence of collectively agreed rather than statutory minimum wages is that minimum wages are not uniform but differ by sector and possibly also by type of job or region. What is more, in sectors where unions are weak, the agreed minimum wages may be low if compared to countries with a similar level of income. There is also a danger that certain sectors of the labor market, not covered by collective agreements, will lack any minimum standard. There is, as a result, in Germany in particular a vivid debate about whether or not a statutory minimum wage is desirable.

CONCLUSIONS

The major question discussed in this chapter has been whether we are witnessing a continued move away from a solidaristic toward a more competition-oriented wage policy. Various kinds of information have been provided in our effort to answer this question. First is the issue of wage-bargaining institutions, divided into multiemployer and single-employer bargaining systems. Although some decentralization has taken place in the MEB cluster, it has been organized in such a way that, broadly speaking, the systems have preserved high levels of bargaining coverage and a high coordination capacity. Moreover, governments have in a number of countries strengthened coordination through national social pacts. Coverage, coordination and social pacts have been much less important in the SEB countries. Within the MEB group an exception is Germany, where decentralization has become more disorganized in recent years. In the SEB group, the main exception was, for more than twenty years, Ireland with its tradition of concluding social pacts. However, since the breakdown of the centralized social partnership agreements in 2009, it remains to be seen whether the centralized agreements will be resurrected or whether local wage bargaining will prevail.

Hence, in the MEBs the institutional architecture for a solidaristic wage policy remains in place, whereas in the SEB it never—with a few exceptions—existed in the first place. At the same time, across Europe, the wage share has decreased, marking a gap between productivity improvements and wage growth and a shift in income from labor to capital, especially in the SEBs but also in the MEBs. This common trend has occurred, however, as a result of different mechanisms. Within the multiemployer bargaining systems it can be attributed, to a large extent, to wage moderation based on collective agreements and social pacts, whereas in the SEB systems wage moderation stems rather from market mechanisms and the unilateral imposition of wage levels. The organized nature of the MEB countries has then, in the longer term, a dampening effect on the shift of income from labor to capital, which is indeed stronger in SEB countries. The fact that MEB systems set more common standards can also be expected to limit the growth of wage inequality as compared to the SEB systems.

Two additional factors affecting wage setting have also been discussed in this chapter. The first is the increased use of variable pay systems and, in particular, performance-related pay, albeit with major cross-country differences. Most types of VPS are oriented more toward wage differentiation than toward the redistribution of wealth and hence correspond to a move away from a solidaristic wage policy. The second is the minimum wage, whether set by law or by collective agreement. Minimum wages, by establishing a floor for wage distribution, have a limiting effect on wage inequality though their impact is often weak.

To counter nationalist-inspired competition among states and to reorient wage policy toward more solidaristic objectives, workers and trade unions are trying to engage in transnational wage coordination to reduce wage competition and establish a more productivity-oriented wage policy (Glassner and Pochet 2011). Thus, despite the possibly contradictory interests of unions from high- and low-wage countries, the cultural and institutional variations between countries and the—supposedly—low interest shown by the rank-and-file membership, transnational cooperation and solidarity are on the union agenda (Gajewska 2009). Yet, given trade union weakness and the current neoliberal orientation of the majority of governments, together with developments at the European level ('Euro-Plus Pact') as well as in Germany, the largest economy in Europe, where disorganized decentralization is the trend, a more solidaristic wage policy seems, for the time being, unlikely.

NOTE

1. Luxembourg does not belong to the MEB countries, given that the focus of wage bargaining is on the company level.

REFERENCES

Andersson, M. and Thörnqvist, C. 2007. 'Determining wages in Europe's SMEs: How relevant are the trade unions? *Transfer*, 13:1. 55–73.

Arrowsmith, J., Nicolaisen, H., Bechter, B. and Nonell, R. 2010. 'The management of variable pay in European banking', International Journal of Human Resource Management, 21: 15. 2716–2740.

Aumayr, C., Cabrita, J. and Demetriades, S. 2011. *Pay developments—2010*. Dublin: European Foundation for the Improvement of Living and Working Conditions. Available at <http://www.eurofound.europa.eu/docs/eiro/tn1109060s/TN1109060S.pdf>

Bispinck, R., Dribbusch, H. and Schulten, T. 2010. 'German collective bargaining in a European perspective. Continuous erosion or re-stabilisation of multi-employer agreements?' WSI Discussion Paper No. 171. Düsseldorf: HBS.

Bispinck, R. and Schulten, T. 2011. *Sector-level bargaining and possibilities for deviations at company-level: Germany*. Dublin: European Foundation for the Improvement of Living and Working Conditions. Available at <http://www.eurofound.europa.eu/pubdocs/2010/874/en/1/EF10874EN.pdf>

Bohle, D. and Greskovits, B. 2010. 'Slovakia and Hungary: Successful and failed euro entry without social pacts', in P. Pochet, M. Keune and D. Natali (eds.) *After the Euro and Enlargement: Social Pacts in the EU*. Brussels: ETUI. 345–369.

Brandl, B. and Traxler, F. 2011. 'Labour relations, economic governance and the crisis: Turning the tide again? *Labor History*, 52:1. 1–22.

Carley, M. and Marginson, P. 2011. 'Negotiating the crisis: Social partner responses', in European Commission *Industrial Relations in Europe 2010*. Luxembourg: Publications Office of the European Union. 85–125.

Cox, A. 2005. 'The outcomes of variable pay systems: Tales of multiple costs and unforeseen consequences', *International Journal of Human Resource Management*, 16:8. 1475–1497.

Crouch, C. 2005. *Capitalist Divergence and Change: Recombinant Governance and Institutional Entrepreneurs*. Oxford: Oxford University Press.

Erne, R. 2008. *European Unions: Labor's Quest for a Transnational Democracy*. Ithaca, NY: Cornell University Press.

European Commission (EC) 2011. *Wages Trends in Europe in Perspective*. Luxembourg: Publications Office of the European Union.

Fajertag, G. and Pochet, P. 1997. *Social Pacts in Europe*. Brussels: ETUI.

———. 2001. *Social Pacts in Europe—New Dynamics*. Brussels: ETUI.

Flanagan, R. J. 2008. 'The changing structure of collective bargaining', in P. Blyton et al. (eds.) *The SAGE Handbook of Industrial Relations*. London: Sage. 406–419.

Gajewska, K. 2009. *Transnational Labour Solidarity: Mechanisms of Commitment to Cooperation within the European Trade Union Movement.* London: Routledge.

Glassner, V. and Pochet, P. 2011. 'Why trade unions seek to coordinate wages and collective bargaining in the Eurozone: Past developments and future prospects', ETUI Working Paper (forthcoming).

Hall, P. and Soskice, D. 2001. *Varieties of Capitalism: The Institutional Foundations of Comparative Advantage.* Oxford: Oxford University Press.

Hancké, B. (ed.) 2009. *Debating Varieties of Capitalism: A Reader.* Oxford: Oxford University Press.

Ioannou, C. A. 2010. 'Odysseus or Sisyphus' revisited: Failed attempts to conclude social-liberal pacts in Greece', in P. Pochet, M. Keune and D. Natali (eds.) *After the Euro and Enlargement: Social Pacts in the EU.* Brussels: ETUI. 83–108.

Keune, M. 2008. 'Introduction: Wage moderation, decentralisation of collective bargaining and low pay' in M. Keune and B. Galgóczi (eds.) *Wages and Wage Bargaining in Europe: Developments since the mid-1990s.* Brussels: ETUI-REHS. 7–27.

———. 2011. 'Wage flexibilisation and the minimum wage', in European Commission *Industrial Relations in Europe 2010.* Luxembourg: Publications Office of the European Union. 127–147.

Keune, M. and Pochet, P. 2010. 'Conclusions: Trade union structures, the virtual absence of social pacts in the new member states and the relationship between sheltered and exposed sectors', in P. Pochet, M. Keune and D. Natali (eds.) *After the Euro and Enlargement: Social Pacts in the EU.* Brussels: ETUI. 395–415.

Kohl, H. and Platzer, H. W. 2004. *Industrial Relations in Central and Eastern Europe: Transformation and Integration. A Comparison of the Eight New EU Member States.* Brussels: ETUI.

Kornai, J. 1992. *The Socialist System: The Political Economy of Communism.* Princeton, NJ: Princeton University Press.

Lazear, E. P. 2000. 'Performance pay and productivity', *American Economic Review,* 90. 1346–1361.

Natali, D. and Pochet, P. 2010. 'Introduction. The last wave of social pacts in Europe: Problems, actors and institutions', in P. Pochet, M. Keune and D. Natali (eds.) *After the Euro and Enlargement: Social Pacts in the EU.* Brussels: ETUI. 13–43.

OECD 2011. *Divided We Stand: Why Inequality Keeps Rising.* Paris: OECD.

Pochet P, Keune, M. and Natali, D. (eds.) 2010. *After the Euro and Enlargement: Social Pacts in the EU.* Brussels: ETUI.

Regan, A. forthcoming. 'The political economy of social pacts in the EMU: Irish liberal market corporatism in crisis', *New Political Economy.*

Rhodes, M. 1998. 'Globalisation, labour markets and welfare states: A future of competitive corporatism?' in M. Rhodes and Y. Mény (eds.) *The future of European welfare: A new social contract?* London: Macmillan. 178–203.

Robinson, A. and Wilson, N. 2006. 'Employee financial participation and productivity: An empirical reappraisal', *British Journal of Industrial Relations,* 44:1. 31–50.

Schulten, T. 2002. 'A European solidaristic wage policy?' *European Journal of Industrial Relations,* 8:2. 173–196.

Stanojević, M. 2010. 'Social pacts in Slovenia' in P. Pochet, M. Keune and D. Natali (eds.) *After the Euro and Enlargement: Social Pacts in the EU.* Brussels: ETUI. 317–344.

Stockhammer, E. 2007. 'Wage moderation does not work: Unemployment in Europe', *Review of Radical Political Economics,* 39:3. 391–397.

Streeck, W. 1999. *Competitive solidarity: Rethinking the "European Social Model".* MPIfG Working Paper 99/8, September 1999. Cologne: Max Planck Institute for the Study of Societies.

————. 2009. *Re-forming capitalism: Institutional Change in the German Political Economy*. Oxford: Oxford University Press.

Streeck, W. and Thelen, K. 2005. 'Introduction: Institutional change in advanced political economies', in W. Streeck and K. Thelen (eds.) *Beyond Continuity: Institutional Change in Advanced Political Economies*. Oxford and New York: Oxford University Press. 1–39.

Traxler, F. 1995. 'Farewell to labour market associations? Organised versus disorganised decentralisation as a map for industrial relations' in C. Crouch and F. Traxler (eds.) *Organised Industrial Relations in Europe: What Future?* Aldershot: Avebury. 3–19.

————. 2010. 'Corporatism(s) and pacts: Changing functions and structures under rising economic liberalism and declining liberal democracy', in P. Pochet, M. Keune and D. Natali (eds.) *After the Euro and Enlargement: Social Pacts in the EU*. Brussels: ETUI. 45–82.

Traxler, F. and Brandl, B. 2010. 'Preconditions for pacts on incomes policy: Bringing structures back in', *European Journal of Industrial Relations*, 16:1. 73–90.

Trif, A. 2008. 'Opportunities and challenges of EU accession: Industrial relations in Romania', *European Journal of Industrial Relations*, 14:4. 461–478.

van der Meer, M. and Visser, J. 2010. '"Doing together what is possible": Social pacts and negotiated welfare reform in the Netherlands', in P. Pochet, M. Keune and D. Natali (eds.) *After the Euro and Enlargement: Social Pacts in the EU*. Brussels: ETUI. 261–279.

van het Kaar, R. and Grünell, M. 2001. *Variable Pay in Europe*. EIRO Online. Available at <http://www.eurofound.europa.eu/eiro/2001/04/study/tn0104201s.htm>

Vaughan-Whitehead, D. 2008. 'Minimum wage revival in the enlarged EU: Explanatory factors and developments', in D. Vaughan-Whitehead (ed.) *The minimum Wage Revisited in the Enlarged EU*. Geneva: ILO.

Visser, J. 2011. *Data Base on Institutional Characteristics of Trade Unions, Wage Setting, State Intervention and Social Pacts, 1960–2010 (ICTWSS). Version 3.0.* Amsterdam: AIAS.

Welz, C. and Fernándes-Macías, E. 2008. 'Financial participation of employees in the European Union: Much ado about nothing?' *European Journal of Industrial Relations*, 14:4. 479–497.

7 Working Time in Europe

James Arrowsmith

INTRODUCTION

Working time is a vital feature of employment. It is an important determinant of efficiency, service and costs. It also impacts workers' earnings, workloads and rest and leisure. The determination of working time has therefore always been central to industrial relations. Working -time arrangements provide a strong indication of the balance of power between capital and labor.

The purpose of this chapter is to map and explain developments in EU working time in recent decades. The first part analyzes *trends* in working time, including patterns of long working hours, the uneven growth of part-time work, and forms of variable working time. It finds diversity but also a clustering of patterns that reflects different economic, institutional and social features of member states. It also confirms the continued transformation of working-time structures and forms, with more fragmented and flexible patterns, observed in the 1990s (Tregaskis et al. 1998).

The subsequent section briefly examines developments in the *regulation* of working time, focusing on the European working-time directive (WTD) and the changing collective-bargaining agenda at national level. Both sets of developments point to an increasing disorganization of working time in which the regulatory capacity of organized labor, as well as the state, is reduced. The overall argument of the chapter is that the historic forward march of labor over working time has largely halted. The determination of working time is now far more subservient to the so-called 'flexibility' agenda of employers than at any time since the European project began.

WORKING-TIME PATTERNS AND TRENDS

Working time should be one of the most consistent and straightforward of employment indicators to compare, yet mapping international trends is problematic. Official national surveys utilize different definitions, questions and terminology (Hoffmann and Greenwood 2001; Tijdens and

Dragstra 2007) and the European Labour Force Survey (ELFS) collects only limited information (Bell and Elias 2003). However a useful source of data, from which we draw heavily in this chapter, is provided by the European Foundation for the Improvement of Living and Working Conditions (Eurofound), and in particular its two large-scale surveys. The European Company Survey (ECS) was conducted in 2009 following its launch as the Establishment Survey on Working-Time and Work-Life Balance (ESWT) in 2004. It surveys management and, where possible, employee representatives at company level. The European Working Conditions Survey (EWCS), which draws on a random sample of workers, has a longer pedigree, having commenced in 1991 and repeated in 1995 and then on a quinquennial basis.

A snapshot of average working hours by sex, employment status and country is provided in Table 7.1. Two things are immediately apparent in terms of full-time hours. First, men tend to work longer hours than women. In only five countries is the male full-time average lower than forty per week; for women the figure is seventeen. Second, there are significant differences between countries, with men in the UK, for example, working 5.6 hours a week more on average than those in Denmark. Differences by sex tend to be less pronounced in terms of average duration of part-time work (though not in actual use, as discussed below). There is again a broad range between countries, with part-time work averaging just over twenty-four hours per week in Sweden and Hungary but only eighteen hours in Germany.

Full-Time and Long Hours

Hours of work are modest in historical terms. Early industrialization was based on what today would be seen as extreme hours, with a twelve-hour day and six-day week commonplace, but productivity growth helped drive a secular trend to reduced hours, especially for male workers (Ausubel and Grübler 1995). On aggregate measures this trend continued in Europe until recently, if at a slowing pace (Burchell et al. 2009). The national-level data reveals a more mixed picture, however. First, there is much diversity in the incidence of long working hours between countries. More than one in six of all workers in countries such as the UK and Austria regularly work forty-eight hours or more per week, compared to around one in twenty in Sweden and the Netherlands, for example; Greece is the outlier with a third of workers usually working forty-eight hours or more (Messenger 2010). Long working hours are also concentrated by gender and occupation, being more common for male plant and machine operatives, managers and professionals, as well as the self-employed.

Second, there are significant differences in terms of trends since the early 1990s. For example, between 1995 and 2006 there was little change in the incidence of long hours (i.e., 48-plus per week) in Spain (at around 15 percent),

Table 7.1   Average usual hours per week, EU and Norway, 2009

	Full time			Part time		
	All	Men	Women	All	Men	Women
EU27	40.4	41.2	39.3	20.1	19.2	20.4
AT	42.1	42.7	41.0	20.9	19.2	21.3
BE	39.1	39.7	38.1	23.9	24.5	23.8
BG	41.3	41.6	41.1	20.5	20.5	20.5
CZ	41.3	42.0	40.4	22.5	21.5	22.9
DK	37.7	38.0	37.2	19.2	16.7	18.5
DE	40.6	41.0	39.8	18.2	16.7	18.5
EE	40.6	41.1	40.0	21.5	21.8	21.4
IE	38.3	39.8	36.6	18.9	19.8	18.7
EL	40.7	41.6	39.4	20.4	21.8	19.9
ES	40.5	41.2	39.3	19.1	18.7	19.2
FR	39.4	40.1	38.4	23.2	22.5	23.3
IT	39.0	40.2	36.9	22.0	22.3	22.0
CY	40.8	41.6	39.9	21.7	21.7	21.7
LV	40.8	41.3	40.3	21.8	22.8	21.3
LT	39.7	40.1	39.3	21.5	21.9	21.2
LU	40.1	40.7	39.0	20.6	19.2	20.8
HU	40.5	40.8	40.1	24.1	24.5	23.9
MT	40.4	41.1	39.0	22.1	22.0	22.2
NL	38.9	39.1	38.2	19.8	19.2	20.1
PL	41.0	42.2	39.6	22.1	22.7	21.8
PT	40.2	40.9	39.3	19.7	20.2	19.5
RO	41.2	41.4	40.8	23.4	24.6	22.7
SI	41.1	41.5	40.7	20.9	20.6	21.2
SK	40.6	41.2	40.0	23.2	23.2	23.1
FI	39.0	39.9	38.1	19.8	18.3	20.5
SE	39.9	40.0	39.8	24.2	21.0	25.3
UK	42.2	43.6	40.1	19.1	18.0	19.3

Source: ELFS (Massarelli and Wozowczyk, 2010).

Germany, Denmark, Belgium and Finland (9–10 percent), and Sweden and the Netherlands (6 percent). In the UK, however, the overall incidence fell from nearly 23 percent to 17.7 percent, and dramatic falls were recorded in Portugal, from 21 percent to 12 percent, and Ireland, from 18 percent to 8 percent. These may be linked to transposition of the 1993 EU working-time directive (WTD), allied to sectoral and demographic change in the case of Portugal (Perista and Cabrita 2009), and with a clear role for national-level social partnership in Ireland (O'Connell et al. 2004). The UK is a more curious case in that the regulations implementing the WTD were severely undermined by an individual 'opt-out' provision (see below), though it is possible that it had a reflexive impact on behavior (Neathy and Arrowsmith 2001). However, it might also reflect the intensification of working time, with new technologies and forms of work organization 'facilitating the closing of the gaps in the working day' (Green and Whit-field 2009, p.206).

In contrast, many member states experienced an upward movement in average full-time hours, including Germany, Austria, Italy, Spain and France (European Commission 2007). In Austria, for example, the proportion of workers usually working forty-eight hours or more per week almost dou-bled from 9.7 percent in 1995 to nearly 18 percent in 2006, with almost all of the increase occurring since 2000 (Adam 2009). Much of this was due to the relaxing or reversing of collective agreements made in the 1990s, which reduced basic working time in return for greater flexibility. Downsizing and skills shortages may also have contributed to an increase in the incidence of excessive working time.

On the whole, the highest proportion of long-hours workers is found in the new member states (NMS), though several experienced significant reductions over the period 1995–2006 (Table 7.2). Six of the seven EU countries in which more than one in five male workers normally work over forty-eight hours a week are NMS—the Czech Republic, Hungary, Latvia, Poland, Romania and Slovakia (Burchell et al. 2009). In part, this is due to greater self-employment, though these countries also have higher figures for employees. Other factors include low pay, the relative importance of the primary sector, and underdeveloped institutions of collective bargaining (see chapter 5, this volume).

Explaining the patterns and dynamics of full-time and long working hours is complex because they are shaped by a number of demand, supply and insti-tutional factors. A first consideration is the level of economic development and productivity. From an employer's perspective, low productivity means longer hours are needed to produce goods and services; for employees, low pay (often a correlate of low productivity) makes additional hours attractive for earnings. Morley et al. (2009, p.5) observe a highly significant correlation of 0.693 between GDP per hour worked and average annual hours.

Related to this is the sectoral and occupational structure of a country, as long hours tend to be a feature of work in the primary sectors and heavy

Table 7.2 Percentage of all workers with usual weekly hours of forty-eight or more, EU NMS

	1995	2000	2006
BG	(–)	10	16
CY	(–)	18	14
CZ	21	20	17
EE	15	14	10
HU	12	11	7
LV	24	23	17
LT	17	7	3
MT	(–)	12	9
PL	(–)	23	23
RO	14	14	14
SK	15	13	15
SI	(–)	13	10

Source: EU LFS, in Messenger (2010, p.303).

Notes: Figures have been rounded; (–) = no data available; 1997 data used for CZ, EE, RO; 1996 for HU, SI; 1998 for LV, LT, SK; 2001 for PL.

industry, compared to service-sector and white-collar jobs. In manufacturing, long hours (and more variable hours) may be linked to the use of new 'just-in-time' and 'high-performance' work systems, together with performance management and variable pay arrangements, which increase pressures to meet targets (White et al. 2003). Long hours are also a feature of professional and management occupations and self-employment; half of those working more than forty-eight hours a week are in the top three income deciles (Morley et al. 2009). These workers ostensibly have greater autonomy over their hours of work, which suggests the importance of intrinsic factors promoting commitment to work (Burke and Cooper 2008). However, long hours might also reflect skills scarcity, professional norms and insecurity in a context of 'downsizing' and work externalization.

Further considerations are social, fiscal and regulatory structures. For example, a relatively high 'tax wedge' (the difference between labor costs and take-home pay due to social security contributions and taxes) tends to be associated with shorter annual hours worked per capita, as in Belgium, France, Italy and the Netherlands, and high marginal tax rates are particularly associated with shorter working hours (Leiner-Killinger et al. 2005). The growth of dual-earning families and a trend of having fewer children and at later ages also impacts on household decisions around working time (see below). Also important is the organization and regulation of labor markets. More highly regulated countries tend to have shorter hours (Bishop 2004), whether this is driven primarily by the state (e.g., France, Spain, Finland) or the social partners (e.g., Denmark, the Netherlands, Germany).

Part-Time Hours

Part-time work was largely unknown until the 1970s. Its driving force was rising female labor-force participation. This reflected a number of factors including increased employment opportunities due to the expansion of the service sectors and higher education; the impact of recession and inflation on household real incomes; equality legislation which made part-time work more attractive; and changing social norms, particularly in the traditionally conservative Catholic countries where women (especially married women and mothers) were largely absent from the workplace. The growth of female participation continued through the 1990s, when women formed 70 percent of the increase in the employed labor force in Europe (Visser 2004).

Part-time work is now a significant form of employment in the major economies, albeit concentrated in particular sectors and lower-skilled occupations (Sandor 2011). It is also heavily gendered; women are much more likely than men to work on a part-time basis, though it should be noted that only in the Netherlands are a majority of employed women part-time. Table 7.3 orders EU member states in terms of the incidence of female part-time work and also shows overall levels and changes over the ten years to 2008. Several points are immediately apparent. First is that the Netherlands has an exceptionally high rate of part-time work, with approaching half the workforce employed on this basis, including nearly a quarter of men. Elsewhere, male part-time work is unusual—only in Denmark (14.2 percent), Sweden (13.3 percent) and the UK (11.3 percent) do more than one in ten men work part-time, and in most other countries it is 5 percent or less—and mainly for those in labor market transitions, such as students, partial retirees and those seeking full-time work. Overall, part-time work is less common in the Mediterranean states (Italy, Spain, Portugal and France) and, especially, in the NMS.

There is also large variance in terms of the growth and scheduling of part-time work. First, part-time work in the EU27 increased by 14.5 percent between 1998 and 2008, from 15.9 percent of employment (6.3 percent male and 28.7 percent female) to 18.2 percent (7.9 percent male and 31.1 percent female). However it almost doubled in Italy and Luxembourg in this period, grew by half in Spain, and increased between 20–40 percent in Germany, Austria, Belgium, Sweden and the Netherlands. Significant growth was also observed in several of the NMS, albeit from a low base, whereas others recorded relative declines. Second, part-time work is also heterogeneous in terms of its duration and scheduling. It typically comprises between twenty and thirty hours a week, but the incidence of short part-time

Table 7.3 Part-time work as percentage of employment, 2008

Country	Female workforce	Total workforce	Change (total) 1998–2008
NL	75.3	47.3	21.6
NO	45.7	29.4	–
DE	45.4	25.9	40.8
UK	41.8	25.3	3.3
AT	41.5	23.3	48.4
SE	41.4	26.6	34.3
BE	40.9	22.6	40.0
LU	38.3	18.0	97.8
DK	36.5	24.6	10.3
IE****	31.5	16.8	1.8
FR	29.4	16.9	−2.3
IT	27.9	14.3	95.9
MT	25.5	11.5	69.1**
ES	22.7	12.0	53.8
FI	18.2	13.3	16.7
PT	17.2	11.9	8.2
PL	11.7	8.5	−18.3
SI	11.4	9.0	47.5*
CY	11.4	7.8	20.9*
RO	10.8	9.9	−37.3
EE	10.4	7.2	−16.3
EL	9.9	5.6	0.0
LT	8.6	6.7	−34.3**
CZ	8.5	4.9	−14.0
LV	8.1	6.3	−50.8
HU	6.2	4.6	21.1
SK	4.2	2.7	17.4
BG	2.7	2.3	−20.7***

Source: Employment in Europe 2009.

Notes: *1999–2008, **2000–2008, ***2001–2008 ****1998–2004. Norway data = 2004, from Parent-Thirion, et al. (2007).

work (i.e., less than twenty hours) is highly dispersed, from around one in six female part-timers in Sweden, to one in four in Austria, Denmark and France, two in five in Finland and Germany, and around half in the UK and the Netherlands (Bielenski et al. 2002). Scheduling patterns also vary within and between countries. A part-time worker might work fewer but full days each week, or work for part of every day; she or he might even work alternate 'full-time' weeks or fortnights or for longer periods (for example, around school holidays). In fact, heterogeneity is a common trend; the Euro-found data indicates that 'part-time work organisation has diversified, with more companies using multiple forms' (Riedmann 2010, p.17).

Again, patterns of usage and growth are shaped by a dynamic interre-lationship between institutions (working-time laws, welfare and childcare arrangements, tax and benefits systems, collective bargaining); the economy (levels of unemployment and tertiarization); and culture (gender and family roles). Many countries removed restrictions on part-time work in the 1990s and equality legislation (including the 1997 part-time work directive [97/81/EC], which prohibited lower pay and benefits) might also have stimulated labor supply (Hegewisch 2005). Social-partner initiatives are also relevant in a number of cases, notably in the Netherlands, where a series of agree-ments in the 1980s and 1990s sought to reduce working hours as a means to redistribute work, as well as increase labor flexibility.

Significantly, the extent and form of female participation remains strongly influenced by the provision and cost of childcare (Corral and Isusi 2007). In France, there is a low incidence of part-time work that, furthermore, involves longer hours (one common 'part-time' contract is a nonworking Wednesday, when schools are normally closed). This is attributed to relatively generous childcare subsidies, together with family-based taxation arrangements and a system of social security contributions linked to headcount (Daune-Richard 1998; Boulin et al. 2004). Support for working parents is generally greatest in the postcommunist states-although provisions 'are declining in the transition to the market economy' (Lewis and den Dulk 2010, p.247)—and still more so in Northern Europe. This helps explain why fewer than one in ten Danish and Swedish mothers with dependent children are not in employment, and only one in seven in Finland, whereas in Portugal it is more than one in three, Spain and Ireland nearly two in five, and Greece approaching half (Lewis 2009). In the UK, a high level of female part-time work is usually explained by the restrictive effect of expensive private childcare (Gash 2008).

Household decisions around the distribution of paid and unpaid work are also heavily influenced by the gender pay gap (the relatively higher earn-ing capacity of men), and tax and benefit arrangements (Anxo 2004). The historically slow growth of part-time work in Germany, for example, has been linked to a tax system that favors the 'male breadwinner' model; this is reinforced by relatively high wages in the West and the legacy of universal childcare in the East (O'Reilly and Bothfeld 2004; Bosch 2009). In Ireland, in contrast, strong economic growth within a 'liberal' fiscal and welfare configuration (including highly 'privatized' childcare) saw part-time work double between 1991 and 2000 (O'Connell et al. 2004).

A key factor driving part-time work on the demand side is the expansion of the service sector in many countries. Employers in public services such as education and health, with large numbers of professional workers, often accommodate part-time preferences due to labor market pressures. Employers in sectors such as retail and 'horeca' (hotels, restaurants and catering) are also willing and able to offer part-time work because of their demand, cost and productivity configurations (Arrowsmith 2010). First, demand is usually variable in a largely predictable pattern, which facilitates the scheduling of part-time hours to cover peaks and extended opening. Second, a large number of jobs are lower-skilled, which reduces the duplication costs of training. Third, part-time work better maintains productivity in what can be routine yet pressured jobs. It also offers a larger labor pool for absence cover, which is important in sectors with high labor turnover. However, this concentration of part-time work in service-sector occupations means that much of it—outside the professions—is low-paid (Bettio and Verashchagina 2009). Low pay in the service sectors is a condition of labor intensity and competitive pressures on margins; the substitutability of workers in lower-skilled work; and lower trade union density reflecting the transaction costs of organizing dispersed workplaces. It also often amounts to a charge on workers for employers meeting their preferences or needs for part-time work (Walsh 1990). In many countries, one effect of this low pay concentration is to reinforce preferences for full-time work (Ruivo et al. 1998).

Annual Leave

Much of the postwar decline in overall working time in Europe was due to the growth of paid leave, whether introduced by legislation or collective bargaining (Blyton 1985). This trend slowed in the early 1980s, after four weeks became the annual full-time norm, but picked up again in the 1990s. In a context of wage restraint (especially in the Eurozone countries), holiday entitlement became a means for unions to deliver productivity-related gains at a time when employers were less willing to accommodate further reductions to basic weekly hours. Its growth also reflected changes in the law, notably the 1993 WTD which established a twenty-day basic entitlement, granted in addition to public holidays (except in the UK until 2009), and extended on a pro-rata basis to part-time and temporary employees.

Again, though, there is enormous national variation in practice. Employers provide an average fifteen days off in Latvia but twenty-nine in Germany and thirty-one in France, according to Eurostat's Structure of Earnings Survey (2006). Total entitlement (i.e., with public holidays) ranges from an average twenty-eight days in Hungary to 40.5 days in Germany—a 45 percent difference which equates to 2.5 working weeks (Carley 2010). Significantly, the relationship between paid leave and working-time duration is negative, so that full-time workers in countries with lower average weekly hours also tend to enjoy a greater number of paid days off. 'Time poor' countries include Ireland, the UK, Greece, Estonia, and Poland, whereas workers in France, Spain, Slovakia and Slovenia tend to enjoy both more extensive paid leave and a shorter working week. Paid leave is thus less compensation for long hours but instead reflects national differences in productivity and labor market institutions.

WORKING-TIME FLEXIBILITY

Flexibility of working time is increasingly important for employers and employees. The main forms for organizations include overtime, shift work and, increasingly, hours-banking arrangements. Employee flexibility involves discretion around the scheduling of working time, as well as other measures to accommodate 'work-life balance' (WLB).

Overtime

Overtime involves the fluctuation of workers' hours above the contracted basic, and is usually voluntarily induced by wage premia. Paid overtime is used by more than two-thirds (68 percent) of EU establishments, extending on average to half the workforce (Riedmann 2010). There are significant country differences, with high users including Germany, the Netherlands, Finland and Denmark (all with over 80 percent of establishments); relatively low use is reported in most Southern European countries and the NMS. Paid overtime is common for 'blue-collar' employees, especially in manufacturing with its often variable and unpredictable demand. Its principal benefit is that it is simple to administer and does not incur the direct or administrative costs (including training) associated with permanent or temporary hiring (Calmfors et al. 2005). It is also easy to reverse, accommodating downturns without losing skilled staff. Both rationales become more compelling in an increasingly competitive and volatile environment. For salaried staff, particularly at more senior levels, overtime is less likely to be financially compensated, though 'time off in lieu' arrangements might apply. However, competitive pressures have increased 'unpaid overtime' in different countries (Nicolaisen 2011). In the UK, around 5 million employees regularly work unpaid overtime, with one in five of these contributing more than ten hours per week (Sweeney et al. 2011).

Decisions regarding overtime usually fall outside the scope of collective bargaining, though the overall framework might be subject to joint arrangements (Kummerling et al. 2009). Here, an interesting development concerns the reduction of overtime. In principal, there is a common interest in reducing high levels of overtime given union concerns about overwork and the fact that it introduces perverse incentives to 'spin out' work. Such discussions are reported by 56 percent of employee representatives in the EU, though again there are strong country differences, from 75 percent in Belgium and over

60 percent in Italy, Germany and the Netherlands, down to around one in five in Ireland and less than one in ten in the UK (Kummerling et al. 2009). This reflects national differences in workplace industrial relations and the capacity of the actors to accommodate alternative arrangements to overtime such as shift work and, especially, annualization and working-time accounts.

Shift Work

Shift working has long been a feature of continuous-process and capital-intensive industries, as well as service sectors with long operating times. Around 16 percent of the EU workforce is engaged in shift work, rising to a quarter of horeca workers and a third of those in healthcare (Parent-Thirion et al. 2007). Shift work can also be used on a periodic basis to meet upswings of demand. Though it often involves atypical or 'unsocial' hours, shift workers tend to have more standardized schedules than others. The proportion with very long (or very short) hours is also half that of non–shift workers (Parent-Thirion et al. 2007).

Shift work is one area of working time that demonstrates diminishing country differences. In 1979, the proportion of the (non–service sector) workforce involved in shift work ranged from one in ten in the Netherlands, one in seven in Denmark, around one in five in Ireland, (West) Germany and Italy, a quarter in Belgium and approaching a third in the UK and France (Blyton 1985). Today, it is universally widespread; nearly a third of European establishments use shift work, with no strong country differences observed (Riedman 2010).

Working-Time Accounts and Annualized Hours

Working-time accounts (WTAs) allow for variation around an average standard work week, within agreed parameters, and are often introduced to reduce overtime. Hours can be averaged over any period but usually pertain to a month or a quarter; annualized hours (AH) systems apply a similar principle over the working year. Essentially, overtime is made compulsory and distributed across the workforce, with higher consolidated salaries and/or fewer overall working hours often granted by way of compensation. Overall, two in five (39 percent) EU establishments utilized some form of WTA in 2009, an increase from the third (32 percent) recorded in 2004–2005 (Riedmann 2010).

These types of schemes are more common in the Nordic countries and Austria and Germany, where AH operates in 28 percent of companies and time banks cover 37 percent of workers (Messenger 2004). In contrast, they are rarely found in Southern Europe, the NMS, Ireland, or the UK, where they face the entrenched obstacles of low pay and institutionalized overtime. Introducing and managing such schemes has to address horizontal problems of different interests and tradeoffs within the workforce as well as between management and labor; hence they are normally widely disseminated in countries well-served by effective institutions of collective bargaining or (as in France) those with a strong legislative stimulus (Arrowsmith 2007).

The Chimera of Employee-Centered Flexibility

The issue of WLB basically involves addressing long working hours and increasing employee discretion over working time. It has become an increasingly important policy and trade union concern across Europe under the twin pressures of long and increasingly destandardized (unsocial, irregular and unpredictable) hours. For example, whereas two thirds of French employees worked the same hours each day in 1978, by 1991 it was just over half (Spurgeon 2003). In the Nordic countries and the Netherlands, 55 percent of workers now work variable hours and 47 percent have variable start and finish times; the comparable figures for the Mediterranean countries are lower but still considerable at 33 percent and 38 percent (Riedmann 2010). Approaching half (45 percent) of employees in Europe work evenings in a typical month, and one in five work some nights (Morley et al. 2009).

Rather than better balancing paid work with other obligations, the trend is the other way. As Gornick (2010, p.239) observes, in the last two decades or so 'legions of European workers may have gained shorter hours at the cost of more nonstandard work scheduling and, in many cases, reduced control and predictability'. A 2004 ad hoc LFS survey of twenty states found that less than a quarter of primary-aged workers (ages twenty-five to forty-nine) had 'any real flexibility' in the hours that they worked, and these were mainly in the public sector and professions (Morley et al. 2009). Eurofound data indicates that overall, two thirds of employees in the EU have no influence over their working time; this rises to three quarters in the Mediterranean and NMS countries. Only in the Nordic countries and the Netherlands do a majority of workers have at least some input into their hours of work (Morley et al. 2009; Hurley and Wolf 2008).

At the same time, there has been a widespread intensification of working time (Green and McIntosh 2001). In Ireland, for example, a survey conducted in 2003 and again in 2009 found that the number of private-sector employers using flexible working time almost doubled in the period, and the proportion of employees reporting increased pressure at work rose by nearly two-thirds (Russell and McGinnity 2011). This conjunction of long, variable and highly utilized hours has implications for the overall quality of life, not just quality of working life (Scherer and Steiber 2007). There are externalized costs at the personal, household and ultimately societal levels.

THE REGULATION OF WORKING TIME

The 1993 WTD is one of the most significant and contested labor laws at the European level. Collective bargaining is also an important form of working-time regulation in many countries, often mandated under national law.

Recent developments in both areas have not on the whole been favorable to labor, however.

Legal Regulation: The WTD Saga

The 1993 WTD (Council Directive 93/104/EC on aspects of the organization of working time) was introduced as a measure to improve the safety and health of workers. The main provisions are a maximum average working week of forty-eight hours, calculated over a seventeen-week reference period; a limit for night workers of eight hours, on average, per twenty-four, and a requirement for regular health screening; a rest break of at least twenty minutes after six consecutive hours of work; daily and weekly rest periods of at least eleven hours and thirty-five hours respectively; and a minimum of four weeks annual paid leave, pro rata for part-time and temporary employees.

The terms of the directive were uncontroversial in most of the then-dozen member states as existing provisions ensured broadly equal or higher standards. However, strong opposition was expressed by the British government, not least because the UK had nearly half of the 7 million male workers in the EU working forty-eight hours or more a week at the time. This prompted a concession unique in health and safety law by which member states could make provisions for individuals to 'opt out' of the maximum work week provision. The opt-out was granted, subject to review after ten years, in order to provide the UK the opportunity to bring its working-time practices into line with other member states. In reality it removed any real pressure to do so (Neathy and Arrowsmith 2001).

The Commission's review of the directive began in 2003, by which time the British government found it was no longer isolated. First, an amendment of the WTD in 2000 extended it to previously excluded sectors such as transport, sea fishing, and doctors in training.[1] The latter was especially significant, following rulings by the European Court of Justice in the SIMAP (2000) and Jaeger (2003) cases.[2] These established that time spent on call at the workplace constituted working time for the purposes of the WTD even if no recourse was made of these hours and workers were permitted to rest, or indeed sleep. This had major implications for sectors such as health and residential care and a number of countries including France, Germany, the Netherlands and Spain introduced legislation to enable the opt-out for health-sector work. The second factor which shifted the political agenda was EU enlargement because many of the NMS also had relatively long working hours. The number of member states making some use of the opt-out rose from one in 2000 to four in 2003 and fifteen in 2009—five universally and ten for specific sectors.

The Commission presented its first recommendations concerning revision of the WTD in September 2004. It contained three main proposals: that the individual opt-out be retained, but with tighter restrictions; that the 'inactive' part of on-call time not be considered as working time; and that member states could extend reference periods up to twelve months. The European Trade Union Confederation (ETUC 2005) called the proposals 'a flagrant disregard of all the social paragraphs in EU Treaties and Charters' and claimed that they 'would lead to the first-ever social policy directive that would introduce a regression compared to the previous situation, and would in fact herald the burial of Social Europe'. The proposals were rejected by the European Parliament and in response, the Commission's revised proposals of May 2005 accepted the phased end of the opt-out while maintaining that inactive on-call time not be counted as working time (nor rest time). The revised proposals also included a new provision, Article 2b ('Compatibility between working and family life'), whereby member states must 'encourage the social partners to conclude agreements at the appropriate level establishing rules for improving compatibility between working life and family life'. Furthermore, employers would be required to inform workers in good time of any changes in their pattern of working time, and workers would be able to request changes to their working hours and patterns, which employers would be obliged to consider.

It then took the European Council more than three years to arrive at a common position. This basically endorsed the Commission's original proposals, with the provision that opted-out workers would not normally work more than an average of sixty hours per week. It also accepted the new Article 2b. Parliament and the Council then entered months of negotiation through the Conciliation Committee process but without success—the first time that it had failed to arrive at a resolution. In March 2010 the Commission therefore launched a consultation with the EU-level social partners on a comprehensive review of the WTD given what the Commission termed 'fundamental changes' to working patterns since it was originally introduced. The social partners began a nine-month period of negotiations in November 2011 from divergent positions, which made an overall agreement seem highly unlikely.

What does this saga tell us about the regulation of working time in Europe? First, that regulation is an intensely political process with enlargement compounding the difficulties of reaching consensus. Second, that there are competing conceptions of working time in which the coalition of employer representatives and member states committed to a liberal interpretation of labor market flexibility are in the ascendancy over those prioritising workers' safety, health and well-being. A similar contestation is observed at national level, where France serves as the exemplar case. The 'Robien law' (1996) and 'Aubry laws' (1998 and 2000) went far beyond the WTD by introducing a series of incentives and obligations for employers to reduce full-time working hours to thirty-five per week or 1,607 per year. The objective was to combat unemployment, not simply by work-share but by improving productivity and competitiveness through local bargaining around work reorganization and working-time flexibility. By 2001, 62 percent of the workforce worked a thirty-five-hour week, with various forms of WTAs commonplace (Fagnani and Letablier 2006).

In recent years, however, the thirty-five-hour week came under mounting pressure from employers, even if it remained popular with the public. The turning point was the 2004 agreement of workers at the Bosch plant in Lyon to extend their week by one hour without pay, under threat of work relocation to the Czech Republic. The company utilized a new legal provision permitting company-level agreements to undercut those at higher levels, and other employers soon followed suit. Collectively agreed average weekly hours rose by a whole thirty-six minutes in the year to 2009 alone (Carley 2010). The government also introduced a series of measures reducing the taxes and restrictions on overtime.

The case of France, along with the tortured progress of the WTD, demonstrates how states face demands to loosen the legal regulation of working time under the pressure of internationalization. A similar process operates through collective bargaining channels, often facilitated by decentralization. Here, employers have become increasingly assertive not just for flexibility per se, but *cost-effective flexibility* by means of a higher basic working week as well as various hours-banking schemes to reduce overtime costs and introduce a greater degree of compulsion.

Collective Bargaining over Working Time

Working time has been described as 'a tug-of-war between employer and worker . . . won by the side with greater bargaining power at the time' (Golden 2006, p.47). Certainly, collective bargaining was the most important mechanism driving the postwar trend to reduced working hours in Western Europe, and it is no coincidence that hours of work tend to be shorter in countries with the most robust and 'highly articulated' systems of industrial relations (Lehndorff 2000). However, as the tide began to turn against labor, two distinct trends emerged. First, in the 1990s, bargained reductions in working time became increasingly conditional on increased flexibility, especially in countries with 'insider' or 'social market' systems such as Germany, the Netherlands and Scandinavia (Berg et al. 2004). This trend rapidly faded at the turn of the century, since when reductions in working hours have 'scarcely featured on the collective bargaining agenda in most countries' (Carley 2010, p.5). Union priorities shifted to wages and jobs with the 'dot-com' recession and, while employers remained intensely concerned with flexible scheduling to improve customer responsiveness, reduce unit costs and fully exploit the digital revolution, they were less willing in an increasingly internationalized competitive environment to countenance further reductions in basic hours (Keune 2006).

Instead, company-level agreements began to *extend* working hours often without, or with only partial, pay compensation (Calmfors et al. 2005). In Germany, a landmark agreement at Siemens in 2004 raised standard weekly hours from thirty-five to forty without increasing pay (an effective hourly pay cut of 12.5 percent), and workers at one of Daimler Chrysler's plants agreed to a gradual increase from thirty-five to thirty-nine hours with only partial compensation (Bispink 2006). This followed IG Metall losing its first strike in fifty years when it failed to achieve a cut from thirty-eight to thirty-five hours in the eastern Länder after all but nine employers held out against a four-week strike. Other companies concluding similar agreements included MAN, Thomas Cook, Lufthansa and hundreds of small and medium-sized firms (Arrowsmith 2004). More than three quarters of a million public sector workers also saw their hours increased by a 2006 sector agreement. Employers in neighboring countries such as Belgium, the Netherlands and France adopted similar negotiating positions. In countries such as Finland, where trade unions were especially weakened by high unemployment, employers pursued radical approaches to flexibilization (Lähteenmäki 2002).

These developments were facilitated by the decentralization of collective bargaining in the 1990s, when countries such as Germany, Austria, Denmark, Italy, Spain, Sweden and Belgium introduced various opening clauses and derogations to sector-level agreements (Marginson and Sisson 2006). This process, if anything, accelerated at the turn of the decade. In Germany, for example, the watershed 'Pforzheim Agreement' of 2004 delivered a wage deal acceptable to IG Metall but at the price of a revised framework for overtime and, crucially, shifting much working-time bargaining to company level. As noted above, and in contrast to earlier periods, local trade unions and works councils were less able to regulate this flexibility resulting in hundreds of 'supplementary agreements' to increase hours (Haipeter and Lehndorff 2005).

The decentralization of collective bargaining resulted from the internationalization of markets, which reduced the encompassing governance capacity of sector agreements (see chapter 2, this volume). Internationalization also increased competitive pressures, so that firms wanted greater scope to customize work organization and working time to their own needs. Hence, across Europe, collective agreements became more and more 'instruments of flexibilisation' (Keune 2006, p.25), but now with longer rather than shorter hours attached.

Another factor behind the lengthening of basic working time was, perversely, sustained high levels of unemployment. The EU15 average unemployment rate was 10 percent throughout the 1990s, and around 9 percent for the EU27 until a fall in 2005–2008. This weakened the bargaining power of labor. As noted above, too, larger firms were able to leverage bargaining power through increasingly credible threats to relocate or invest elsewhere. In multinational companies (MNCs), which grew rapidly in the 1990s, working-time flexibility was facilitated not just by 'coercive comparisons' between countries and plants but by a process of attitude structuring through internal benchmarking (Arrowsmith and Marginson 2006). Practices such as time accounts and 'compressed working weeks' were disseminated across MNC subsidiaries on the basis of matching arrangements elsewhere; these then influenced national practices in a second round of benchmarking by other companies within national systems. MNCs were thus at the forefront of agreements around more flexible and extended working time arrangements (Marginson and Meardi 2009).

This extension of working time came to an abrupt halt with the global financial crisis (GFC) that began in 2008. Evidence from the European Restructuring Monitor shows that many companies tried to reduce hours rather than numbers employed, even in heavily hit sectors such as automotives (Hurley and Finn 2009). Short-time working was more common in those countries that provided state support, which usually required agreements on working-time flexibility as a condition for eligibility (Bosch 2009). There was thus a strong role for collective bargaining in governing the use of short-time work, with intersector agreements in France and Poland, sector-level agreements in Sweden and Germany, and extensive company-level agreements in Belgium, the Czech Republic, Denmark, Germany, Italy and Sweden (Carley 2010). Large firms, especially in sectors with higher-skilled employees such as metalwork, led the way (Glassner et al. 2010). In contrast, the adjustment process in the UK and many of the NMS was much more likely to involve layoffs and large-scale redundancies (Glassner and Galgóczi 2009).

At the same time, the fallout from the GFC basically weakened the position of organized labor still further. Though demonstrating the utility of collective bargaining, specifically in response to crisis, it reinforced trends to decentralization and concessions around the flexibilization of working time already well-established even in the most 'organized' industrial relations systems (Glassner and Keune 2010; Carley and Marginson 2010). Collective agreements became more and more oriented to employers' demands for working-time flexibility on the premise of saving jobs (Sweeney et al. 2011).

CONCLUSIONS

This chapter began with a review and analysis of developments in working-time patterns in Europe. The duration of working time, especially long hours and part-time hours, is heavily gendered but also strongly mediated by country-level factors such as tax and benefits systems, economic development and productivity, social norms and regulation by law and collective bargaining. There has been a widespread growth in flexible working time arrangements, notably overtime, shift work and WTAs, with the latter accelerating in recent years in many countries. However, employee-centered flexibility is limited to certain occupations and country clusters in the face of a general deregularization and intensification of working time.

The second part of the chapter examined significant developments in the regulation of working time. The story of the WTD demonstrates the increasing importance of the liberal (i.e., weak) interpretation of the role of employment law amongst political élites at the EU and national levels, in the name of 'subsidiarity' and flexibility. But it is perhaps developments within collective-bargaining systems that should pose the greatest concern. The internationalization and intensification of competition, the growth of MNCs with the potential to relocate investment and jobs, persistent unemployment and the decentralization of collective bargaining have all served to weaken organized labor. The bargaining agenda shifted from reduced-for-more-flexible hours in the 1990s, to a more recent situation in which negotiations served to increase basic hours at the same time as granting employers still greater control over scheduling. The impact of the GFC, which introduced a pause in the drive for longer hours, also furthered concession bargaining over working time in the cause of saving jobs.

According to the ILO, 'decent work' involves decent pay, stimulating tasks, mechanisms for employee voice and a degree of control over the duration, scheduling and intensity of the hours spent at work. In a similar vein, the Lisbon strategy made 'more and better jobs' the employment mission of the EU. But it is currently failing in this. Record numbers are excluded from working time altogether, with youth unemployment historically high at 20.9 percent. Millions more have marginal control over their hours of work, are over- or underemployed or confined to temporary work which has massively increased in recent decades. Tellingly perhaps, the Commission's lynchpin *Europe 2020 Strategy for Smart, Inclusive and Sustainable Growth* makes little mention of working time, except to note that the WTD is under review and that 'Europeans work short hours—10 percent less than their US or Japanese counterparts'. In the US, of course, the phenomenon of 'the overworked American' has long been noted (Schor 1993), and Japan is the only country in the world that legally recognizes death by overwork. Not the kind of benchmarks to be used lightly.

NOTES

1. Specific directives governing working time also apply in the transport sectors: 1999/63/EC (sea); 2000/79/EC (air); 2002/15/EC (road); and 2005/47/EC (rail).
2. *Sindicato de Médicos de Asistencia Pública (SIMAP) v. Conselleria de Sanidad y Consumo de la Generalidad Valenciana*, Case C-303/98; Landeshauptstadt Kiel v. Norbert Jaeger, Case C-151/02.

REFERENCES

Adam, G. 2009. *Working Time in the European Union: Austria*. Dublin: Eurofound.
Anxo, D. 2004. 'Working time patterns among industrialized countries: A household perspective', in J. C. Messenger (ed.) *Working Time and Workers' Preferences in Industrialized Countries*. Abingdon: Routledge. 60–107.
Arrowsmith, J. 2004. 'Counting the hours', *People Management*, 10:18. 36–41.
———. 2007. 'Why is there not more "annualised hours" working in Britain?' *Industrial Relations Journal*, 38:5. 423–438.

————. 2010, 'Industrial relations in the private sector', in T. Colling and M. Terry (eds.) *Industrial Relations in Britain, 3rd edition.* Oxford: Blackwell. 178–206.

Arrowsmith, J. and Marginson, P. 2006. 'The European cross-border dimension to collective bargaining in multi-national companies', *European Journal of Industrial Relations*, 12:3. 245–266.

Ausubel, J. H. and Grübler, A. 1995. 'Working less and living longer: Long-term trends in working time and time budgets', *Technological Forecasting and Social Change*, 50. 113–131.

Bell, D. and Elias, P. 2003. 'The definition, classification and measurement of working time arrangements: A survey of issues with examples from the practices in four countries', *Conditions of Work and Employment Series, No. 4.* Geneva: International Labour Office.

Berg, P., Appelbaum, E., Bailey, T. and Kalleberg, A. L. 2004. 'Contesting time: International comparisons of employee control of working time', Industrial & Labor Relations Review, 57. 3.

Bettio, F. and Verashchagina, A. 2009. *Gender Segregation in the Labour Market: Root Causes, Implications and Policy Responses in the EU.* Luxembourg: Publications Office of the European Union.

Bielenski, H., Bosch, G. and Wagner, A. 2002. *Working time preferences in sixteen European countries.* Dublin: Eurofound.

Bishop, K. 2004. 'Working time patterns in the UK, France, Denmark and Sweden', *Labour Market Trends*, March. 113–122.

Bispinck, R. 2006. 'Germany: Working time and its negotiation', in M. Keune (ed.) *Collective Bargaining and Working Time in Europe: An Overview.* Brussels: ETUI-REHS. 111–129.

Blyton, P. 1985. *Changes in Working Time: An International Review.* Beckenham: Croom Helm.

Bosch, G. 2009. 'Working time and working time policy in Germany', JILPT Report No. 7, Tokyo.

Boulin, J.-Y., Lallement, M., and Silvera, R. 2004. 'Working times in France: Institutional methods of regulating and new practices', in J. O'Reilly (ed.) *Regulating Working Time Transitions in Europe.* Cheltenham: Edward Elgar. 17–200.

Burchell, B., Cartron, D., Csizmadia, P., Delcampe, S., Gollac, M., Illéssy, M., Lorenz, E., Makó, C., O'Brien, C. and Valeyre, A. 2009. *Working Conditions in the European Union: Working Time and Work Intensity.* Dublin: Eurofound.

Burke, R. J. and Cooper, C. L. 2008. *The Long Hours Culture: Causes, Consequences and Choices.* Bingley: Emerald Publishing.

Calmfors, L., Corsetti, G., Honkapohja, S., Kay, J., Leibfritz, W., Saint-Paul, G., Sinn, H.-W. and Vives, X. 2005. *EEAG Report on the European Economy*, Issue 3.

Carley, M. 2010. *Working time developments—2009.* Dublin: European Foundation

Carley, M. and P. Marginson 2010. 'Negotiating the crisis: Social partner responses', in P. Marginson (ed.) *Industrial Relations in Europe 2010.* Luxembourg: Publications Office of the EU.

Corral, A. and Isusi, I. 2007. *Part-time Work in Europe.* Dublin: Eurofound.

Daune-Richard, A.-M. 1998. 'How does the "societal effect" shape the use of part-time work in France, the UK and Sweden?' in J. O'Reilly and C. Fagan (eds.) *Part-Time Prospects: An International Comparison of Part-Time Work in Europe, North America and the Pacific Rim.* New York: Routledge. 214–231.

European Commission 2007. *Employment in Europe 2007.* Luxembourg: Publications Office of the EU.

European Trade Union Confederation, 2005. *ETUC Statement: Revision of the Working Time Directive.* http://www.etuc.org/a/1839.

Fagnani, J. and Letablier, M. T. 2006. 'The French 35-hour working law and the work-life balance of parents: Friend or foe?' in D. Perrons, C. Fagan, L. McDowell, K. Ray and K. Ward (eds.) *Gender Divisions and Working Time in the New Economy*. Cheltenham: Edward Elgar. 79–90.

Gash, V. 2008. 'Preference or constraint? Part-time workers' transitions in Denmark, France and the United Kingdom', *Work, Employment and Society*, 22:4. 655–674.

Glassner, V. and Galgóczi, B. 2009. 'Plant-level responses to the crisis: Can jobs be saved by working less?', *ETUI Policy Brief*, Issue 1/2009.

Glassner, V., Jagodzinski, R. and Kluge, N. 2010. 'Collective bargaining and the economic crisis' in *Benchmarking Working Europe 2010*. Brussels: ETUI/ ETUC. 59–74.

Glassner, V. and Keune, M. 2010. 'Collective bargaining responses to the economic crisis in Europe', *ETUI Policy Brief*, Issue 1/2010.

Golden, L. 2006. 'How long? The historical, economic and cultural factors behind working hours and overwork', in R. J. Burke (ed.) *Research Companion to Working Time and Work Addiction*. Cheltenham: Edward Elger. 36–57.

Gornick, J. C. 2010. 'Limiting working time and supporting flexibility for employees: Public policy lessons from Europe', in K. Christensen and B. Schneider (eds.) *Workplace Flexibility: Realigning 20th-Century Jobs for a 21st-Century Workforce*. Ithaca: Cornell University Press. 223–244.

Green, F., and McIntosh, S. 2001. 'The intensification of work in Europe', *Labor Economics*, 8. 291–308.

Haipeter, T. and Lehndorff, S. 2005. 'Decentralized bargaining of working time in the German automobile industry', *Industrial Relations Journal*, 36:2. 140–156.

Hegewisch, A. 2005. 'Individual working time rights in Germany and the UK: How a little law can go a long way' in A. Hegewisch (ed.) Working Time for Working Families: Europe and the United States. Washington, DC: Friedrich Ebert Stiftung.

Hoffmann, E. and Greenwood, A.M. 2001. 'Statistics on working-time arrangements: An overview of issues and some experiences', *Statistical Journal of the United Nations*, 18:1. 51–63.

Hurley, J. and Finn, M. 2009. *Europe in Recession: Employment Initiatives at Company and Member State Level*. Dublin: Eurofound.

Hurley, J. and Wolf, F. 2008. *Revisions to the European Working Time Directive: Recent Eurofound Research*. Dublin: Eurofound.

Keune, M. 2006. 'Collective bargaining and working time in Europe: An overview', in M. Keune and B. Galgóczi (eds.) *Collective Bargaining on Working Time: Recent European Experiences*. Brussels: ETUI-REHS. 9–29.

Kummerling, A., Lehndorff, S., Coppin, L. and Ramioul, M. 2009. *Social Dialogue, Working-Time Arrangements and Work-Life Balance in European Companies*. Dublin: Eurofound.

Lähteenmäki, S. 2002. 'Flexible working in Finland—Sign of a new industrial relations or just the opposite?' in I. U. Zeytinoğlu (ed.) *Flexible Work Arrangements: Conceptualizations and International Experiences*. London: Kluwer Law International.

Lehndorff, S. 2000. 'Working time reduction in the European Union: A diversity of trends and approaches', in L. Golden and D. M. Figart (eds.) *Working Time: International Trends, Theory and Policy Perspectives*. London and New York: Routledge. 38–56.

Leiner-Killinger, N., Madaschi, C. and Ward-Warmedinger, M. 2005. 'Trends and patterns in working time across Euro area countries', *ECB Occasional Paper Series* No. 41.

Lewis, J. 2009. *Work-Family Balance, Gender and Policy*. Cheltenham: Edward Elgar.

Lewis, S. and den Dulk, L. 2010. 'Parents expectations of flexible work arrangements in changing European workplaces' in K. Christensen and B. Schneider (eds.) *Workplace Flexibility: Realigning 20th-Century Jobs for a 21st-Century Workforce*. Ithaca: Cornell University Press. 245–261.

Marginson, P. and Meardi, G. 2009. *Multinational Companies and Collective Bargaining*. Dublin: Eurofound.

Marginson, P. and Sisson, K., with Arrowsmith, J. 2006. *European Integration and Industrial Relations: Multi-Level Governance in the Making*. Houndmills: Palgrave Macmillan.

Massarelli, N. and Wozowczyk, M. 2010. 'European Union Labour Force Survey—Annual Results 2009', *Data in Focus, 35/2010*. Eurostat.

Messenger, J. C. 2004. 'Working time at the enterprise level: Business objectives, firms' practices and workers' preferences' in J. C. Messenger (ed.) *Working Time and Workers' Preferences in Industrialized Countries: Finding the Balance*. Abingdon: Routledge. 147–192.

———. 2010. 'Working time trends and developments in Europe', *Cambridge Journal of Economics*, 35. 295–316.

Morley, J., Sanoussi, F., Biletta, I. and Wolf, F. 2009. *Comparative Analysis of Working Time in the European Union*. Dublin: European Foundation.

Neathy, F. and Arrowsmith, J. 2001. 'Implementation of the working time regulations', *Employment Relations Research Series Report No. 11*. London: Department of Trade and Industry.

Nicolaisen, H. 2011. 'Changes in the regulation of overtime under different collective bargaining regimes: A comparison of Irish, Norwegian and Swedish banking', *European Journal of Industrial Relations*, 17:1. 7–23.

O'Connell, P. J., McGinnity, F. M. and Russell, H. 2004. 'Working-time flexibility in Ireland' in J. O'Reilly (ed.) *Regulating Working Time Transitions in Europe*. Cheltenham: Edward Elgar. 240–279.

O'Reilly, J. and Bothfeld, S. 2004. 'Regulating working time transitions in Germany' in J. O'Reilly (ed.). *Regulating Working Time Transitions in Europe*. Cheltenham: Edward Elgar. 86–122.

Parent-Thirion, A., Fernández Macías, E., Hurley, J., and Vermeylen, G. 2007. *Fourth European Working Conditions Survey*. Dublin: Eurofound.

Perista, H. and Cabrita, J. 2009. *Working Time in the European Union: Portugal*. Dublin: Eurofound.

Riedmann, A. 2010. 'Working time flexibility' in *European Company Survey 2009: Overview*. Dublin: Eurofound. 5–22.

Ruivo, M., de Pilar González, M., and Varejão, J. M. 1998. 'Why is part-time work so low in Portugal and Spain?' in J. O'Reilly and C. Fagan (eds.) *Part-Time Prospects: An International Comparison of Part-Time Work in Europe, North America and the Pacific Rim*. New York: Routledge. 199–213.

Russell, H. and McGinnity, F. 2011. *Workplace Equality in the Recession? The Incidence and Impact of Equality Policies and Flexible Working*. Dublin: The Equality Authority.

Sandor, E. 2011. *European Company Survey 2009: Part-time Work in Europe*. Dublin: Eurofound.

Scherer, S. and Steiber, N. 2007. 'Work and family in conflict? The impact of work demands on family life in six European countries', in D. Gallie (ed.), *Employment Regimes and the Quality of Work*. Oxford: Oxford University Press, 137–178.

Schor, J. B. 1992. *The Overworked American*. New York: Basic Books.

Spurgeon, A. 2003. *Working Time: Its Impact on Safety and Health*. Geneva: ILO.

Sweeney, B., Curterelli, M., Aurnayr, C., Vargas, O., Cabrita, J. and Broughton, A. 2011. *Industrial Relations and Working Conditions Developments in Europe 2010*. Dublin: Eurofound.

Tregaskis, O., Brewster, C., Mayne, L., and Hegewisch, A. 1998. 'Flexible working in Europe: The evidence and the implications', *European Journal of Work and Organizational Psychology*, 7:1. 61–78.

Tijdens, K. and Dragstra, A. 2007. 'Research Note: "How many hours do you usually work?"', *Time and Society*, 16:1. 119–130.

Visser, J. 2004. 'Negotiated flexibility, working time and transitions in the Netherlands' in J. O'Reilly (ed.). *Regulating Working Time Transitions in Europe*. Cheltenham: Edward Elgar. 123–169.

Walsh, T. J. 1990. 'Flexible labour utilisation in the private service sector', *Work, Employment and Society*, 4:4. 17–30.

White, M., Hill, S., McGovern, S. and Mills, C. 2003. 'High-performance management practices, working hours and work–life balance', *British Journal of Industrial Relations*, 41: 2. 175–195.

8 Transformations in Work Organization and Labor Regulation

Ludger Pries

INTRODUCTION

The topic of work organization has been of increasing importance to practitioners and scholars since the 1980s. The worldwide success of Japanese manufacturing companies at that time could not be explained simply by technological innovation nor by exploitation of cheap labor, but by the specific Japanese (lean and flexible) production system. During the 1990s the economic dynamic was thought to shift to service industries and the knowledge work of high-qualified employees. New forms of work organization like 'high performance systems', project work and virtual cross-border cooperation attracted scientific and practical attention in both the productive and service sectors.

The aim of this chapter is twofold: first to describe crucial tendencies of change of working organization in a comparative perspective, and then to explain whether and how such changes are related to joint labor regulation. Are these shifts based on management prerogative and control, or do they presuppose a certain degree of workers' individual and/or collective participation and involvement? Therefore, in the first section the relation between work organization and labor regulation will be discussed. Then the most important shifts in work organization since the 1980s will be indicated, followed by an analysis of the interrelations between work organization and labor regulation. A discussion of future tendencies and options concludes the chapter.

WORK ORGANIZATION AND THE ROLE OF LABOR REGULATION

Work organization can be understood broadly as the structures and processes (configuration) of distributing and coordinating the tasks and elements necessary to produce certain goods or services in and between work units, whether this concerns persons, groups, departments, plants and/or companies. Work organization has been an important scientific topic since the seminal studies of Adam Smith on the division of labor, Karl Marx on the labor process, Frederick W. Taylor on 'scientific management' and Max Weber on the ideal-type of bureaucratic administration. Based on these classical studies, at least four approaches can be distinguished. In a *techno-functionalist* view work organization is conceptualized as the organizational part of the production process of goods or services, mainly understood as (a) the 'neutral' separation and distribution of work tasks to organizational positions; and (b) the mechanisms of coordination and integration of these work tasks into one entire work process or workflow. This line of thinking can be summarized as follows: 'things have to get done; how is work distributed and combined?' Accordingly, the main aspects of work organization studied in this perspective were the degree of specialization of activities, of standardization of procedures, formalization of documentation and centralization of authority. The configuration of work positions and the flexibility of adapting to changing environments were also included. The specific configurations of these elements were explained by the situational or 'environmental' factors relevant to the work organization (Brown 1992; Child 1972).

A second perspective is the *utilitarian* approach. Here work organization is conceptualized in terms of individual 'rent seeking' based on rational choice, principal-agent and contract theory. In accordance, work organization is seen as combining corporate organizational needs with individual qualifications and interests. It consists mainly of the system of job descriptions and selective incentives. Principal-agent and contract theory focus on the dilemma and possible strategies of a principal (in this case, the employer) and his/her agents (in this case, employees) to optimize their corresponding duties and opportunities. As the agent by definition disposes of exclusive knowledge and relations, work organization mainly consists of mechanisms to invite, convince and oblige agents to do what the principal expects them to do (Williamson 1994).

A third line of thinking is the *culture-interactionism* approach. Work organization is understood as derived from the implicit and explicit norms and values of leaders and members of the corresponding organization. The specific distribution of tasks is less an outcome of functional needs than of social values (e.g., of pyramidal leadership or horizontal coordination, of material incentives or immaterial recognition and esteem) and symbolic interaction (e.g., remembering and citing certain 'heroes' or special historical events of the work organization). Work organization is thus a 'negotiated order' based on settled social institutions, discourses and struggles around how things should be done (Strauss 1978). This reflects 'societal effects' as the division of jobs, 'leadership span' between workers and supervisors, and mechanisms of work coordination vary significantly between countries, even when controlling for size, ownership and sector. Societal institutions like the labor market, labor regulation regime and education system help explain these variations (Maurice et al. 1980;

Kelliher and Anderson 2003). Neo-institutionalism argues that organizations adapt their structure and strategy to the expectations of their 'organizational field'—even sometimes against the specific organizational imperatives of rationality and efficiency (Meyer and Rowan 1977; Powell and DiMaggio 1991).

A fourth tradition of conceptualizing work organization may be termed the *power and politics* approach. In a capitalist market economy and society the organization of work can be seen as a battlefield of diverging individual and collective interests, and this perspective strongly informs the industrial relations tradition (e.g., Pulignano and Stewart 2006). In particular, the so-called Labour Process Debate looked at the organization of work as the main mechanism to resolve the 'transformation problem' of realizing the potentiality of labor power into work action. Simple, technical and bureaucratic systems of labor control were distinguished (Edwards 1979). 'Responsible autonomy' and self-control vied with direct forms of control as means to secure loyalty and flexibility from the workforce (Friedman 1977). At the same time, Crozier and Friedberg (1979) analyzed work organization as an arena for the strategic and tactical plays of actor groups, defined by common status or position (e.g., research and development groups, project groups, sales versus production groups) or by joint beliefs, norms and commitments (see Poole 1986). This resembles the concept of 'work politics' elaborated by the German scholars Jürgens and Naschold (1984).

To summarize, work organization relates to much more than its techno-functionalist and utilitarian aspects. It includes themes such as culture, power relations, negotiations and the strategies of collective actors, and is embedded in societal institutions. For this reason it is necessary to relate work organization to labor regulation. Labor regulation can be defined as the individual and collective negotiation, determination and monitoring of the conditions and relations of work, employment and participation. Employment relations refer to the norms, expectations and practices of the work contract itself; work relations refer to the norms, expectations and practices of enacting and controlling work (Poole 1986). The aspects of participation relations deal with the norms, expectations and practices of the participation of workers and employees in strategic and operative decisions.

In any given organization of work, participants do not simply execute standardized tasks or follow narrowly defined worksheets; they are participating in a process of interpreting rules and norms, adapting standards to new situations, and exploring creative solutions to the problems inevitably involved in the complex process of productive cooperation. Besides, and based on this 'primary participation', workers also often participate in a formal way in operative and sometimes strategic decisions. For example, shop stewards or works councils participate in the regulation of working time or job assignation, and union or other worker representatives participate in company committees or boards of administration such as in France, Germany and Spain (European Commission 2008).

As elaborated elsewhere (Pries 2010), there are eight crucial dimensions of labor regulation to be distinguished.

- issues and topics of regulation (salaries, work time, contract duration, training, internal horizontal and vertical mobility, job description and assignment, achievement, autonomy, improvements, proposal, participation);
- arenas of regulation (individual contract, collective bargaining, agreements at plant level, by law, public discourse);
- spatial reach of the regulation (local, regional, national, supranational, transnational, global);
- mode of regulation (informal-formal, substantial-procedural);
- type of conflict regulation (norm generation, norm interpretation, direct versus bypassed conflict);
- dominant actor groups (individuals, unions, employer associations, companies, shop stewards, works councils, professional groups, NGOs, social issue networks, public authorities);
- prevailing sources of power (social, cultural, economic, organizational, political capital); and
- specific actors' constellation (liberal-individual, political bargaining, collective bargaining, institutionalized concentration, unilateral discretion) and shared ideology and political discourse (antagonistic class struggle, utilitarian business negotiations, populism, corporatism, social partnership).

All of these dimensions of labor regulation are intertwined with work organization (Eurofound 2009b, p.49). In sum, therefore, work organization needs to be analyzed in relation to its intersections with the corresponding labor-regulation regimes and in a multidimensional way, not least if we are to understand crucial trends in the transformation of work organization.

THE TRANSFORMATION OF WORK ORGANIZATION SINCE THE 1980s

The era of the 1980s introduced revolutionary change in the internationalization of firm activities, the use of new information and communication technology (ICT), the movement from industrial-manual to knowledge-based and virtual work, and in the growing significance of intelligent work organization—mainly in the trends of marketization, decentralization and internalization of control. There are four fundamental shifts of work organization in this regard.

From Stable Material to Fluid Social Transformation

From industrialization until recent times, work processes were largely characterized by the manual productive combination of material elements into new physical products and outcomes. Stamped iron parts, wheels, seats, screws, etc., were assembled into cars; bricks, cement, tubes, windows, etc., were integrated into a house; meals were cooked and served for clients in a restaurant. Historically, hours were largely fixed and earnings calculated based on time cards and paid in cash. Since the 1980s, though these activities remain important, the nature and meaning of work organization has shifted from simple material transformation to the social transformation of information, knowledge and expectations involving innovative software and hardware programs of control, new immaterial goods and promises such as the symbols, stories, icons, etc., in media and cultural business (Pries 1991). The car is built as a promise of freedom; the meal is served as a promise of well-being; gratifications are organized as promises of making money and of recognition. Even the traditional employee working in the supermarket checkout is not only collecting money but also has to live the promise of treating the customer as the king (Rifkin 2001). Furthermore, new digitalized media (e-journals, computer games, online trailers and movies) and new cultural and service business (in tourism, financial services and online-healthcare) restructure the traditional patterns of work organization. In Microsoft Windows Beta-version software programming, in online computer games or individualized T-shirt production based on customers' own online design, the distinction between production and consumption or producer and consumer are blurred (Toffler 1980; Voß and Rieder 2005; Kalkowski 2007; Blättel-Mink and Hellmann 2010).

Of course, stating a shift in centrality from simple material transformation to social transformation does not mean that material production is irrelevant—cars, after all, are primarily a means of transport. But it does strongly signal profound changes in the nature (volume and quality) of work. The static-structural aspects of work organization lose relative weight as compared to the dynamic-procedural aspects. For instance, classic Taylorist work organization (in contrast to craft or workshop forms) was based on the separation, standardization and specialization of roles, activities and procedures. In many ways, the constraints that this paradigm offers in terms of inflexibility and structured conflict means that work organization is increasingly shifting from stable material to fluid social transformation, for example utilizing teams as basic units of work organization.

From the Workplace toward Project Teams and Direct Participation

In its influential Green Paper 'Partnership for a New Organization of Work', the European Commission identified 'a shift from fixed systems of production to a flexible, open-ended process of organizational development'

(European Commission 1997, p.5). This concept of continuous change has been variously described as 'the flexible firm' or 'high-performance' workplace, which utilizes functional flexibility based on teams. There is no one model, and in many respects this is nothing new; Schulten (1997) observed that during the 1920s there were experiments with group work at Daimler Benz, and in the 1970s there was a broader debate around the so-called 'humanization of work' program. As indicated above, a major reason for focusing on work organization in the 1980s was the worldwide success of Japanese companies utilizing high-involvement methods (Abo 1994; 1998).

In terms of the quantity and quality of group/team work scholars concur that there is a plurality of very different types, frequency and coverage. In a European-wide survey, Benders et al. (2001) found that 'the degree of self-management is low. . . . The application of group work is modest. In the investigated European organizations, group work is in its infancy. However, there are distinct cross-national differences in the use of group work within Europe' (Benders et al. 2001, p.215). Similar conclusions are reached elsewhere (Murray et al 2002; Greenwood and Randle 2007), with the observation that group work is also most thoroughly developed in certain sectors and occupations as well as countries. Here, a major development is the move toward a 'knowledge society' involving work in knowledge-intensive areas of the secondary and tertiary sector (research, development, culture and media, science, laboratories, etc.). Work in these sectors and occupations more commonly involves project work, and the shorter the project duration and the more overlapping the projects or work groups for each employee implies a more fluent, fragmented and individualized organization of work (Abel and Pries 2007). More generally, however, another European survey (Eurofound 2007, p.35f) found that: 'In the EU15, teamwork is chiefly found among white-collar workers in the top three ISCO job categories. At the same time, however, a high incidence of teamwork prevails in the craft and related trade workers category. . . . The same tendency emerges in the ACC12'. The report also pointed to the challenging aspects of teamwork: 'Working in a team generally means a higher pace of work and working to tight deadlines both in the new and old EU Member States'. A similar conclusion emerged from a more recent study, which observed a growing trend toward teamwork but also that this 'is not necessarily accompanied by a higher degree of autonomy and control over work among employees or a reduction in hierarchical and control structures within enterprises' (Eurofound 2011, p.31).

Virtualization of Work Cooperation and Teleworking

In the traditional work process the workforce is normally concentrated in time (a work shift) and space (a factory, shop or office). Remarkable in relatively recent times is the increasing virtualization and fluidity of cooperation. Virtualization means the spatial and temporal decoupling of a work process. What once might have been referred to as an 'onion model' of small and spatially concentrated working units located within broader work departments or factories and even bigger national conglomerates, now could be organized as a transnational work group distributed over different workplaces even around the world (Aneesh 2006; Kratzer 2005). These ICT-based forms of work organization change the workflows in time and space and have deep impacts on cooperation and control.

For example, in a review of existing studies on the 'deboundaring' of work, Eichmann and Hermann (2004) describe a general flexibilization of the work organization. Seven basic aspects of change are identified: (1) a stronger focus on processes instead of structures; (2) more flexible assignments from persons to work places; (3) more cooperative and interactive work; (4) increasing involvement of employees in work organization; (5) task integration; (6) the outsourcing of functions and tasks; and (7) delegation of responsibilities (see also Eurofound 2007; 2009a). Thus, the increasing importance of teleworking, which more clearly impacts higher-qualified employees, is due to two new tendencies of work processes and work organization. On the one hand, productive processes, which in former times were organized in one establishment, now span different locales (eWork, eOutsourcing, cloud-working); on the other hand, pluri-local work organizations emerge from newly established productive networks, by joint ventures or partnerships that lead to telecooperation and virtual joint-work organization.

A crucial challenge to such virtualized and pluralistic forms of cooperation relates to the modes of coordination/control of tasks and processes. Ideally, typically four patterns of coordination may be differentiated, each with different effects. A first could be termed *norm-based cultural coordination*. In this case, shared values and a common cultural language is the basis for (intrinsic) coordination. When cooperation in different countries is concerned, intercultural competences and sensitivity as well as strong normative commitment to the pluri-locally operating organization is needed. The tension between organizational culture and country cultures explains much of the failures of cross-border assignments (Dülfer and Jöstingmeier 2008). A second pattern is *authority-based hierarchical coordination*. Even in a highly decentralized form of work organization, some activities might follow a top-down process of coordination, and this pattern is easier to handle in mono-local than in pluri-local or pluri-cultural settings. A third type is efficiency- and competition-based *simulated market coordination*. This is focused on measures of coordination that imitate competitive features of the market. The coordination process between different work units (teams, projects, departments or plants) implies to share, compare and evaluate online and offline production indicators and other kinds of information concerning output and cost indicators. This could be useful for quantifiable work processes but is difficult to operationalize for complex knowledge work. A fourth pattern can be characterized as coordination and networking in *distributed power structures*. The main 'bonding cement' of the work organization in this case consists of social coalitions based on mutual trust and reciprocity (Cooke 2004; Ibarra-Colado 2006).

From 'Work Organization' toward 'Management of Work'

As argued above, the notion of work organization as a relatively fixed matrix of work positions and cooperative relations within and between workplaces is increasingly changing to a more fluid model of work procedures, workflows and assignations of persons to positions (Abel and Pries 2007; Liebowitz 2005; Eurofound 2007). As formal and 'external' control of work becomes more and more difficult (i.e., rigid, expensive, inefficient), so in the past two decades has management increasingly paid attention to mechanisms of intrinsic motivation and commitment (Meyer et al. 1989). At the same time, new ICT-based strategies of control were pursued (leading in many cases to conflict with individual rights of data privacy protection). This tension between intrinsic and ICT-based mechanisms of work control has been in the main discussed for high-qualified personnel, and again relates to modes of labor regulation (Menezes and Wood 2006; Doellgast 2008; Kluge et al. 2007; Boxall and Macky 2009).

High-performance forms of work organization can be characterized by the following elements: competences and responsibility are decentralized to the level of those who actually do the work (workplaces, work groups, projects), with few levels of hierarchy in general; and high qualifications and commitment are found, as well as trust and a 'discursive coordination' of work (Minssen 2006). As an example, Kirchner and Oppen (2007) analyzed data of the representative German factory panel (Betriebspanel/IAB) from 1995 to 2004 to distinguish four trends of new forms of work organization: group work, internal business centers, delegation of responsibility, and reorganization of department and functional areas. They found that almost 80 percent of all establishments between 1993 and 2004 introduced at least one of the innovative patterns of work organization. The authors argue, however, that only the different elements in combination are innovative and sustainable, with the delegation of responsibilities constituting the most important trend. Some see 'high-commitment' systems as an increasingly strategic approach in human resource management (Gollan et al. 2006). They offer scope to motivate staff through intrinsic job quality considerations, by reward-based remuneration and by greater discretion over working time through flex-time and remote working arrangements.

RELATIONS BETWEEN WORK ORGANIZATION AND LABOR REGULATION

Hence, since the 1980s, work organization has been a crucial and important area for transformation and new developments in the field of employment. New forms of work organization had different aims: from the 'humanization of work' and higher involvement of employees through to a flexibilization of work processes and cost reduction, which might lead to increasing control and work intensity as much as employee commitment and motivation. Power relations and labor regulation account for much of the variation observed across (and within) different countries and sectors (other parts of variation have to be explained by recurring to the four approaches mentioned at the beginning).

Shifts in Work Organization Lead to Changes in Labor Regulation

Shifts in work organization normally have significant impacts on power relations and labor regulation, if often as unintended consequences. The decentralization and marketization of work organization contributed to new forms of human resource management and to the direct participation of workers in for example group work and quality circles (Müller-Jentsch 1998). Works councils also play an important and increasing role in the implementation process of new forms of work organization including through more flexible collective agreements (Müller-Jentsch 1998; see also chapter 3, this volume). The results are not necessarily determined. To take one example, Boxall and Macky (2009) revisited the international state of research concerning high performance work systems or organizations (HPWOs) and their impact on labor relations in traditional production environments. They found that at 'the heart of high-involvement work reforms are practices that attempt to reverse the Taylorist process of centralising decision making and problem solving in the hands of management. . . . In these contexts, movement towards a high-involvement goal implies making better use of employee capacities for self-management, personal development and problem solving' (Boxall and Macky 2009, p.9). The authors identified—mainly positive—impacts of these new strategies of (high-performance) work organization on working conditions in general and also on some aspects of labor regulation—for example, in the field of increasing autonomy from direct control and in higher quality of workplace communication. Conversely, Osterman (2000, p.193) argues that 'there is very little evidence that HPWOs have delivered on the promise of "mutual gains"' (see also Ramsay et al. 2000).

Similarly, research involving highly qualified workers in the digital economy revealed five tendencies of change in labor regulation arrangements for these types of workers (Abel and Pries 2007; Gollan et al., 2006; Pulignano 2009). First, group work and project work tends to promote a mixture of collective and self-representation; high-qualified persons make use of their 'primary power' (knowledge, scarcity value, employment alternatives) and, at the same time, accept collective workers' representation (e.g., via works councils) (Hauser-Ditz et al. 2008; Hoose et al. 2010). A second tendency is the decentralization of collective labor regulation from the regional and sector level toward the company and workplace level. The most cited example is the so-called opening clauses in many recent collective agreements in Germany, which allow works councils at the local level to adapt and specify the distribution of working hours. The third trend is a shift from material-substantial toward procedural regulation. The case of negotiating working-time collective agreements at regional and/or plant level is also a good example here. A fourth tendency is the increasing significance of the virtualization of collective action and protest. Pulignano (2009, p.191), for example, holds that ICT could help 'to establish a new form of regulation where workers, activists and trade union officials organize through networks and influence the agenda of capital through innovative strategies and policy making'. The fifth aspect refers to the shifting roles and power of collective actors like unions, works councils and other plant-level committees, work groups and project teams. For example, if work groups and project teams come to develop more and more responsibilities, then many of the issues formerly regulated and controlled by works councils or shop stewards become decided directly by team members themselves. In this way, the decentralization process of work organization has a direct impact on the main agents and levels of labor regulation.

Labor Regulation and Work Organization Intertwined

Notable early examples of innovative work organization as an outcome of labor regulation initiatives include the working groups introduced in the Volvo automobile assembly in Sweden and the 'humanization of work' program in Germany, referred to above (Ulich 1994). In the first case, a policy of job enrichment, job enlargement and of higher qualifications for workers led to the replacing of the conveyor belt by a system of workstations (Berggren 1998). The latter was a political initiative pushed by the unions and the Social Democratic Party. It ran from 1974 until 1989 and offered resources to companies and research institutes for specific projects aimed at improving the work situation in similar fashion to Volvo but applied across a range of companies and sectors. Interestingly, although unions supported the general program, many union officers and also works councils were suspicious about aspects of decentralization involved, such as work groups, as they feared losing influence over the work process and workers themselves (Kern and Schumann 1984).

One crucial lesson from these initiatives is that there is no 'zero-sum game' involving work organization and labor regulation. Not only in Germany, unions and workers' representation bodies at local levels feared that giving more responsibilities and power to work groups would lead to less power and influence for the official collective representative organizations. In many cases too, management representatives feared losing control and influence by this decentralizing of work organization. Although labor regulation mechanisms and bodies do not necessarily need to lose control when work organization is decentralized, it is also true that the interplay between both is quite complex (Sisson 1999; Frick 2002). When work organization is decentralized and the plant or higher-level interest representations and regulations weaken, the labor regulation regime as a whole may become decomposed and atomized. With the pressures of everyday production needs, and introduced pressures such as individualized or group incentives for high performance, work groups might reduce internal job rotation and intensify work. In this sense, based on the degree of delegation of responsibility, conservative and progressive strategies of high-performance work practices may be differentiated, and work organization strategies will vary according to sector, competitive factors and company size (Kirchner and Oppen 2007).

There could be another typical relation between labor regulation and work organization. When work organization becomes decentralized, but labor regulation remains centralized and strong, the responsible bodies of labor regulation could try to bureaucratically control and delimitate work groups and workers' participation at decentralized levels. For example, cases of a control effort by works councils and unions toward work groups were reported in the early stages of work group introduction in Germany and elsewhere (Kissler 1996). More generally, however, a Europe-wide study found that 'direct and indirect participation existed side-by-side in more than 70 percent of establishments. Overall, the presence of employee representatives was neutral so far as the diffusion of direct participation was concerned. The same was true of collective bargaining and union membership' (Sisson 1999). Similarly, a more optimistic view (in the techno-functionalist tradition) is presented by Coupar (2007). Using case studies from the UK health sector, the author reveals tendencies of an interrelation between shifting work organization, higher innovation and employee involvement, which indicates a mutually strengthening relationship between new work organization initiatives and a more proactive role of workers in labor regulation. However, he also noted that much of this depended on having 'an inclusive management style' (Coupar 2007, p.37).

CONCLUSION: BETWEEN MARKETIZATION AND INSTITUTIONALIZATION

Some general conclusions can be drawn. First, the relation between work organization and labor regulation has to be approached in a multidimensional frame and a bidirectional way. Work organization influences labor regulation and vice versa. Second, there is no 'one best way' of designing work organization and of approaching this field by labor regulation. The specific national-social institutions structuring work and employment, the economic and political situation of a national economy and of companies in an increasingly transnational environment define the specific restrictions and opportunities in each situation. Third, empirical evidence indicates that a productive, fair and sustainable work organization is highly compatible with—and perhaps even requires—a transparent and strong labor regulation regime at different levels. Organizations have to find their specific 'fit' according to trajectory, environment, contingency and actor groups (Hauser-Ditz et al. 2010). Hence, the fundamental shifts in work organization observed since the 1980s involve a wide set of influencing factors and have a more or less direct impact on labor regulation patterns at company, regional, national and international level. In particular, the shift from fixed (Tayloristic) forms of work organization to more flexible work processes—as part of an overall tendency toward accelerated value chains and more fluid economies and societies in general—has pushed labor relations to became more flexible and more decentralized too. This does not necessarily mean less regulated but more disposed to speedier adaptation at the local level when and if required.

Notwithstanding general common tendencies, however, empirical findings also suggest that the cultural-institutional settings of national societies and the corresponding actors' strategies do influence the specific outcomes and patterns of change. In the twenty-first century it is possible that the contours of a cooperative and sustainable model of work organization and labor regulation are emerging, which are able to reconcile productivity, innovation, high standards of labor and employee participation. A high-efficiency, flexibility and innovation model of work organization seems to be associated with high qualification, commitment and individual as well as collective participation. Thus, to end on a positive note, it could be that the dynamics and innovative forces of capitalism themselves hollow out the traditional Tayloristic, techno-functionalist and utilitarian approaches of work organization and open the way for employees' participation and labor politics in particular at local levels. Much depends on how policy makers, workers and their representatives, as well as employers, approach and regulate issues of power and control under the new forms of work organization that potentially offer greater worker inclusion in decision making.

REFERENCES

Abel, J. and Pries, L. 2007. 'Shifting patterns of labor regulation: Highly qualified knowledge workers in German new media companies', *Critical Sociology*, 33. 101–125.

Abo, T. (ed.). 1994. *Hybrid Factory: The Japanese Production System in the United States*. Oxford: Oxford University Press.

Abo, T. 1998. 'Hybridization of the Japanese production system in North America, newly industrializing economies, South-East Asia, and Europe: Contrasted configurations' in R. Boyer, E. Charron, U. Jürgens and S. Tolliday (eds.) *Between Imitation and Innovation: The Transfer and Hybridization of Productive Models in the International Automobile Industry*. New York: Oxford University Press. 216–230.

Aneesh, A. 2006. *Virtual Migration: The Programming of Globalization*. Durham: London.

Benders, J., Huijgen, F. and Pekruhl, U. 2001. 'Measuring group work; findings and lessons from a European survey', *New Technology, Work and Employment*, 16:3. 204–217.

Berggren, C. 1998. 'A Second comeback or a final farewell? The Volvo trajectory, 1973–1994' in by M. Freyssenet, A. Mair, K. Shimizu and G. Volpato (eds.) *One Best Way? Trajectories and Industrial Models of the World's Automobile Producers*. Oxford and New York: Oxford University Press.418–439.

Blättel-Mink, B. and Hellmann, K.-U. (eds.) 2010. *Prosumer Revisited: Zur Aktualität einer Debatte*. Wiesbaden: VS-Verlag.

Boxall, P. and Macky, K. 2009. 'Research and theory on high-performance work systems: Progressing the high involvement stream', *Human Resource Management Journal*, 19:1. 3–23.

Brown, R. K. 1992. *Understanding Industrial Organisations: Theoretical Perspectives in Industrial Sociology*. London and New York: Routledge.

Child, J. 1972. 'Organizational structure, environment and performance: The role of strategic choice', *Sociology*, 6:1. 1–22.

Cooke, B. 2004. 'The managing of the (third) world', *Organisation*, 11:5. 12–25.

Coupar, W. 2007. 'Employee participation, corporate cultures and innovation: Review and case study from the Health Care Sector—Country Report from the United Kingdom' in N. Kluge, K. Kollewe and P. Wilke (eds.) *Innovation, Participation and Corporate Culture: A European Perspective*. Working Papers from Project TiM, No. 9, University of Rostock. 13–38.

Crozier, M. and Friedberg, E. 1979. *Macht und Organisation: Die Zwänge kollektiven Handelns*. Königstein: Athenäum-Verlag.

Doellgast, V. 2008. 'Collective bargaining and high-involvement management in comparative perspective: Evidence from U.S. and German call centers', *Industrial Relations*, 47:2. 284–319.

Dülfer, E. and Jöstingmeier, B. 2008. *Internationales Management in Unterschiedlichen Kulturbereichen*. München: Oldenbourg Verlag.

Edwards, R. 1979. *Contested Terrain: The Transformation of the Workplace in the Twentieth Century*. London: Heinemann.

Eichmann, H. and Hermann, C. 2004. *Umbruch der Erwerbsarbeit—Dimensionen von Entgrenzung der Arbeit. Auszug aus dem EAP-Zwischenbericht*. Wien: Forschungs- und Beratungsstelle Arbeitswelt.

European Commission 1997. *Partnership for a new organization of work—Green Paper. Supplement 4/97 to the Bulletin of the European Union*. Luxembourg: Office for Official Publications of the European Communities.

——— 2008. *Employee Representatives in an Enlarged Europe Volume 2 (Directorate-General for Employment, Social Affairs and Equal Opportunities, Unit F.2)* Luxembourg: Office for Official Publications of the European Communities.

Eurofound (European Foundation for the Improvement of Living and Working Conditions) 2007. 'Teamwork and high performance work organization'. [online] Available at <www.eurofound.europa.eu/ewco/reports/TN0507TR01/TN0507TR01.htm>

——— 2009a. *Working Conditions in the European Union: Work organization*. Luxembourg: Office for Official Publications of the European Communities.

——— 2009b. *European Company Survey 2009: Overview*. Luxembourg: Office for Official Publications of the European Communities.

——— 2011. 'Recent developments in work organisation in the EU27 member states and Norway'. [online] Available at <www.eurofound.europa.eu/ewco/studies/tn1102013s/tn1102013s.htm>

Frick, B. 2002. 'High performance work practices und betriebliche Mitbestimmung: komplementär oder substitutiv?' *Industrielle Beziehungen*, 9. 79–102.

Friedman, A. 1977. *Industry & Labour: Class Struggle at Work and Monopoly Capitalism*. London: Macmillan.

Gollan, P. J., Poutsma, E. and Veersma, U. 2006. 'New roads in organizational participation?' *Industrial Relations: A Journal of Economy and Society*, 45:4. 499–512.

Greenwood, I. and Randle, H. 2007. 'Team-working, restructuring and skills in UK and Sweden', *European Journal of Industrial Relations*, 13. 361–377.

Hauser-Ditz, A., Hertwig, M. and Pries, L. 2008. *Betriebliche Interessenregulierung in Deutschland. Arbeitnehmervertretung zwischen demokratischer Teilhabe und ökonomischer Effizien*. Frankfurt and New York: Campus Verlag.

Hauser-Ditz, A., Hertwig, M., Pries, L. and Rampeltshammer, L. 2010. *Transnationale Mitbestimmung? Zur Praxis Europäischer Betriebsräte in der Automobilindustrie* Frankfurt and New York: Campus Verlag.

Hoose, F., Jeworutzki, S. and Pries, L. 2010. *Führungskräfte und betriebliche Mitbestimmung. Zur Praxis der Partizipation am Beispiel der chemischen Industrie*. Frankfurt and New York: Campus Verlag.

Ibarra-Colado, E. 2006. 'Organisation studies and epistemic coloniality in Latin America: Thinking otherness from the margins', *Organisation*, 13. 463–488.

Jürgens, U. and Naschold, F. (eds.). 1984. 'Arbeitspolitik. Materialien zum Zusammenhang von politischer Macht, Kontrolle und betrieblicher Organisation der Arbeit', *Leviathan Sonderheft 5*. Opladen: Westdeutscher Verlag.

Kalkowski, P. 2007. 'Work-requirements and commitment in knowledge-intensive projects'. Paper prepared for SASE (Society for the Advancement of Socio-Economics) Conference 30.06.2007/Copenhagen. Available at <www.sofi-goettingen. de/index.php?id=184>

Kelliher, C. and Anderson, D. 2003. 'For better or for worse? An analysis of how flexible working practices influence employees' perceptions of job quality', *The International Journal of Human Resource Management*, 19:3. 419–431.

Kern, H. and Schumann, M. 1984. *Das Ende der Arbeitsteilung?* München: C.H. Beck.

Kirchner, S. and Oppen, M. 2007. *Das Ende der Reorganisationsdynamik? High Performance Work Practices als Muster der Reorganisation in Deutschland*. Discussion paper SP III 2007–103. Berlin: WZB.

Kissler, L. (ed.). 1996. *Toyotismus in Europa. Schlanke Produktion und Gruppenarbeit in der deutschen und französischen Automobilindustrie* Frankfurt: Campus Verlag.

Kluge, N., Kollewe, K. and Wilke, P. (eds.). 2007. *Innovation, Participation and Corporate Culture: A European Perspective* (Working Paper No. 9, Chair of Organizational and Business Psychologie). Rostock: University of Rostock.

Kratzer, N. 2005. 'Employment organization and innovation—Flexibility and Security in "Virtualized" Companies', *Technology Analysis & Strategic Management*, 17:1. 35–53.

Liebowitz, S. J. 2005. *Industrial Organization and the Digital Economy*. Cambridge MA: MIT Press.

Maurice, M., Sorge, A. and Warner, M. 1980. 'Societal differences in organizing manufacturing units: A comparison of France, West Germany and Great Britain', *Organisation Studies*, 1. 59–86.

Menezes, L. M. and S. Wood. 2006. 'The reality of flexible work systems in Britain', *International Journal of Human Resource Management*, 17:1. 106–138.

Meyer, J. P., Paunonen, S. V., Gellatly, I. R., Goffin, R. D. and Jackson, D. N. 1989. 'Organizational commitment and job performance: It's the nature of the commitment that counts', *Journal of Applied Psychology*, 74:1. 152–156.

Meyer, J. W. and Rowan, B. 1977. 'Institutionalized organizations: Formal structure as myth and ceremony', *American Journal of Sociology*, 83:2. 340–363.

Minssen, H. 2006. 'Challenges of teamwork in production—Demands of communication', *Organization Studies*, 27:1. 103–124.

Müller-Jentsch, W. 1998. 'Der Wandel der Unternehmens- und Arbeitsorganisation und seine Auswirkungen auf die Interessenbeziehungen zwischen Arbeitgebern und Arbeitnehmern', *Mitteilungen aus der Arbeitsmarkt- und Berufsforschung (MittAB)*, 3. 575–584.

Murray, G., Bélanger, J., Giles, A. and Lapointe, P.-A. (eds.) 2002. *Work and Employment Relations in the High Performance Workplace* London and New York: Routledge.

Osterman, P. 2000. 'Work reorganization in an era of restructuring: Trends in diffusion and effects on employee welfare', *Industrial and Labour Relations Review*, 53:2. 179–196.

Poole, M. 1986. *Industrial Relations: Origins and Patterns of National Diversity*. New York: Routledge and Kegan Paul plc.

Powell, W. W. and DiMaggio, P. J. (eds.) 1991. *The New Institutionalism in Organizational Analysis*. Chicago: University of Chicago Press.

Pries, L. 1991. *Betrieblicher Wandel in der Risikogesellschaft. Empirische Befunde und konzeptionelle Überlegungen*. Opladen: Westdeutscher Verlag.

Pries, L. 2010. *Erwerbsregulierung in einer globalisierten Welt*. Wiesbaden: VS-Verlag.

Pulignano, V. 2009. 'International cooperation, transnational restructuring and virtual networking in Europe', *European Journal of Industrial Relations*, 15:2. 187–205.

Pulignano, V. and Stewart, P. 2006. 'Bureaucracy transcended? New patterns of employment regulation and labour control in the international automotive industry', *New Technology, Work and Employment*, 21:2. 90–106.

Ramsay, H., Scholarios, D., and Harley, B. 2000. 'Employees and high-performance work systems: Testing inside the black box', *British Journal of Industrial Relations*, 38:4. 501–531.

Rifkin, J. 2001. *The Age of Access: The New Culture of Hypercapitalism, Where All of Life Is a Paid-For Experience*. New York: Putnam.

Schulten, T. 1997. 'New forms of work organisation in Germany: Reactions to the European Commission's Green Paper "Partnership for a New Organisation of Work"'. [online] Available at <www.eurofound.europa.eu/eiro/1999/03/feature/de9903288f.htm>

Sisson, K. 1999. 'A new organisation of work: The EU Green Paper and national developments'. Paper prepared for Eurofound/EIRO. [online] Available at <www.eurofound.europa.eu/eiro/1999/03/study/tn9903201s.htm>

Strauss, A. 1978. *Negotiations: Varieties, Contexts, Processes, and Social Order*. San Francisco: Jossey-Bass.

Toffler, A. 1980. *The Third Wave*. New York: Bantam.

Ulich, E. 1994. 'Gruppenarbeit damals—Lehren aus dem HdA-Programm' in K. Krahn, G. Peter and R. Skrotzki (eds.) *Immer auf den Punkt*. Dortmund: Montania. 45–57.

Voß, G. and Rieder, K. 2005. *Der arbeitende Kunde—Wenn Konsumenten zu unbezahlten Mitarbeitern werden*. Frankfurt: Campus Verlag.

Williamson, O. E. 1994. 'Transaction cost economics and organization theory' in N. J. Smelser and R. Swedberg (eds.) *The Handbook of Economic Sociology*. Princeton, NJ: Princeton University Press. 77–107.

9 Governing Complexity, Diversity and Uncertainty in the Changing European Space

Valeria Pulignano

INTRODUCTION

The employment regimes of Western industrialized societies have been in the grip of a far-reaching structural transformation since the end of 1970s, which considerably accelerated during the 1990s and in the new millennium. A wide range of literature highlights the growing complexity of governance deriving from the widening and deepening of the European Union (EU), and its implications for employment and social policy more specifically. In particular, increased competition among (and within) socio-economically and politically diverse member states, allied to the neoliberal macroeconomic vision steering the process of European integration, have contributed to make the European approach to social and employment policy appear difficult and often tentative in its scope. The eastern enlargement of ten new member states (the Czech Republic, Estonia, Hungary, Latvia, Lithuania, Poland, Slovakia, Slovenia, Bulgaria and Romania) from Central and Eastern Europe since 2004 has far-reaching implications, exacerbating regime competition in Europe's integrated market and threatening to stall the further Europeanization of the institutions and processes of labor market regulation (Marginson 2006).

A longstanding tenet of the European social model is the case for ad hoc social policy intervention in order to create a 'level playing field', which facilitates economic growth by promoting social integration and avoiding the 'dumping' of labor standards across EU countries. Yet, more recently, it can be also argued that social and employment policy has become subordinated to macroeconomic governance, which is in turn dictated by restrictive monetary policy and a broader neoliberal agenda (Goetschy 2003). Thus, the main concern is whether we can reconcile rapidly advancing market integration (post-Maastricht in the monetary, finance and credit sphere) and political and social integration. This is increasingly challenged by developments such as the increasing internationalization of businesses, the rise of labor market 'flexibility', the enhancement of free movement of labor and migration, collective bargaining decentralization, and the deregulation of employment protection governing the individual and collective relationship.

Moreover, by eliciting new political orientations at the EU level, the 2008 financial and economic crisis has exacerbated this scenario because of the continuing push for wage flexibility and restructured working conditions under austerity. In particular, because of the transfer of monetary sovereignty to the European Central Bank and the recent fiscal limitations imposed to national government policy, industrial relations, labor market and welfare policy in Europe have been declared to be the fields for major structural reforms as a major precondition for economic recovery and competitiveness in Europe (Allard and Everaet 2010). As the European Commission (2011, p.20) has put it 'reforms on labour markets and in particular in relation to wage-setting mechanisms need to ensure efficient adjustment of labour costs in order to facilitate absorption of macroeconomic imbalances and to reduce unemployment'.

There has thus been a growing debate in the social policy and industrial relations literatures around the nature (intent and effect) of the governance mechanisms used by the EU in its social and employment policy. On the one side, 'soft' approaches have been strongly criticized on the basis that they displace more effective legal instruments underpinning the community method of European social integration (Trubek and Trubek 2005). We do not reject this argument, but we also acknowledge that 'hard' law in itself is a necessary but not a sufficient condition for the creation of a context where the social dimension of Europe is effectively promoted; as Schmid (2008, p.64) observes, 'hard law is not necessarily more effective than soft law'. Accordingly, 'soft' measures can complement (not substitute for) legal instruments in order to better cope with the increasing complexity and uncertainty of the wider and deeper European Union. This is because 'soft' governance measures may be better positioned to engage and influence the behaviors of the social actors at European and national levels.

If we look at developments in social and employment regulation at the European level, particularly since the early 1990s, we can argue that a more inclusive form of regulation appeared involving a combination of 'hard' and 'soft' methods. Social dialogue probably represents the most important example of the way 'hard' (i.e., European directives) and 'soft' (i.e., framework agreements) elements came together. At the macro-level, the open method of coordination (OMC) emerged to attempt an active coordination of national labor markets and employment policies but by introducing fairly loose and, to some, ritualistic forms of governance. The question as to what extent the appearance of 'soft' forms of regulation lead to a correspondent shift from 'hard' law is perhaps deceptive, per se. This is because it is the combination of 'soft' and 'hard' mechanisms that makes regulation truly effective in realizing the European space.

The next sections briefly examine the nature of the political and economic transformations that have occurred in Europe over the last four decades, highlighting the increasing complexity, diversity and uncertainty that these have generated for inter- and intracountry governance in Europe. Section three offers an analysis and assessment of the measures of social governance adopted in Europe to cope with these transformations. In section four the aim is to present an account of the complementary role that 'soft' governance measures can have in structuring Europe's (social) market economies. The final section draws a concluding argument.

WHICH TRANSFORMATIONS IN THE EUROPEAN ZONE?

Change in employment systems and social policy is propelled by two related developments, each of a genuinely epoch-making character. First, the societies of the industrialized West have been in the grip of a far-reaching, complex and accelerating structural *economic* change since the late 1970s. Among the main features of this transformation are: the conjunction of a number of technological revolutions, in particular in the field of communication and information; rapid regional and global economic integration; changes in corporate structures and scale; and the restructuring and reorganization of work. Secondly, the *political* process of 'European opening' has enforced rapid change within (and across) member states. This principally has a twofold character: the development of a Single European Market (SEM) in 1992, and the ending of the economic and political isolation of Central and Eastern Europe (CEE) with enlargement since 2004. Following the Single Market Program, 1991 saw the agreement on the Maastricht Treaty, which indicated the establishment of the European Union and its project of the creation of a single European currency by 1999. The inclusion into the treaty, which came into force in the autumn of 1993, of competencies for justice and home affairs, foreign and security policy, the introduction of an EU citizenship, and other substantive and institutional changes were intended to add a political dimension to the previously essentially economic process of European integration. Further elements in the fundamental economic and political transformation of Europe are the agreement between the European Community (EC) and the European Free Trade Association (EFTA) on the creation of an European Economic Area (EEA), with structures similar to that of the Single Market, and the accession of a number of other Western and CEE countries to the European Union from the beginning of 1995.

Economic integration and EU enlargement have had profound implications for the regulatory arena of employment relations. First, as Lecher and Platzer (1998) argue, industrial relations rules and processes have acquired an unprecedented importance in competition between sites to attract economic activity. Not only are factors set by collective bargaining, such as pay, working time and flexibility in work organization crossing national borders and entering into mutual competition, but this competition also encompasses the broader social climate within which the regulation of employment relations takes place. Growing market internalization and the increasing international mobility of capital and labor have increasingly promoted 'regime competition' at both local and cross-national level (Marginson 2006). Second, the process of EU eastern enlargement has reinforced these tendencies. Reviewing the implications of industrial and employment relations in Poland for arrangements in 'old' member states, for example, Meardi (2002) suggested that enlargement might turn out to be the 'Trojan horse of the Americanization of Europe'. This argument indirectly sheds light on the efficiency-seeking motives behind the growing number of multinationals investing in CEE countries (Marginson and Meardi 2006). It also underlines the need for EU-level intervention to establish and entrench the core sectoral and cross-sectoral institutional architecture of industrial relations in the new member states, as relying on internal dynamics within these societies will not suffice.

Hence, a multidimensional process of regime competition has emerged. It ranges across different elements, including not only labor regulation and labor costs but also labor quality, skills and productivity and different forms of labor flexibility—qualitative as well as quantitative. The comparison of labor costs, labor flexibility and labor performance underpins business decisions to relocate activities abroad. In other words, the threat to relocate is bound up with the 'coercive comparisons' of labor costs and performance across sites and countries that are central to the management systems of multinational producers (Coller 1996). In this context, management places pressure on the local workforce, and local negotiations leverage concessions over costs and labor flexibility. The economic and financial crisis of 2008–2009 only served to reinforce concession bargaining as it further shifted the balance of power between management and labor at the company level (Glassner et al. 2011).

In this context of increasing competition, capital concentration and mobility, European structures for the governance of employment became both more urgent and yet weaker. The original objective of the 'social dimension' in Europe was to counter the risk of a 'race to the bottom' in terms of wages and working conditions as a result of European economic integration. Yet the social regulatory capacity at the European level remained limited. This can be explained in terms of three broad features (Marginson and Sisson 1998): the primacy of the economic focus of the political project of Europe; the narrow scope of international competence in the field of industrial relations and opportunities for political obstructionism (e.g., the requirement to secure unanimity in the Council of Ministers for matters others than health and safety and the working environment); and the weakness of the European social partners in relation to their constituent national affiliates. At the same time, the traditional instruments of European ('hard') law became increasingly ill-adapted to the widening institutional and economic diversity of national systems, especially within a period of sometimes turbulent economic and social change. Though new 'soft' forms of governance emerged in response, there have been doubts concerning their effectiveness at national and local levels. In the following sections we review both these approaches and assess their potential and limitations.

FORMS OF GOVERNANCE

Three phases of EU-level social and employment policy may be identified. In the 1970s, policy coordination was still largely regarded as a means to help promote the 'harmonization' of employment systems between member states. Accordingly, the aim was to adopt supranational regulatory instruments, mostly European Directives, to facilitate the general improvement ('upwards harmonization') of working conditions. The end of the 1980s and the beginning of 1990s coincided with a second phase characterized by the development of social dialogue between the EU social partners, with scope for collective agreements to be implemented by their national affiliates. Since the mid-1990s a new set of European rules emerged aimed less at harmonizing institutions via legislation than at achieving a form of convergence based on the force of opinion. These so-called 'soft' governance measures were developed in order to address the problems of vertical and horizontal coordination in the increasingly complex European space. These are now considered in turn.

Community Law

The Treaty of Rome, which was originally signed in 1957 by Belgium, France, Italy, Luxembourg, the Netherlands and West Germany in order to establish the European Economic Community, represented the base of the development of European social regulation. In particular, Article 117 of the treaty referred to the need to facilitate the improvement and harmonization of working conditions across the different member states. Accordingly, for example, equal pay for women and the free movement of workers were included in the treaty (Article 119 and Article 48–51, respectively) in order to facilitate this. In addition, other articles have been included in the treaty, requiring the Commission to promote close cooperation between member states in the social field, particularly in matters which relate to employment, labor law and working conditions, vocational training, social security, the right of association, and collective bargaining between employers and employees.

The peak years of EU legislation were the 1970s, when it was feared that countries with inferior employment conditions would gain an unfair advantage in the common market. European legislation (i.e., European Directives) were introduced aimed at the eradication of social discrimination based on sex, as well as to avoid social dumping in working conditions across the different member states. As Hyman (2010) argues, the presence of a center-left government in most European countries also pushed for more ambitious efforts to ensure upward harmonization at this time. This halted with a shift to the right in European politics (notably Margaret Thatcher's election in the UK in 1979) and the abandonment of the postwar Keynesian consensus. However a number of directives (equality between men and women, health and safety in the workplace) as well as certain aspects of labor law (collective redundancy, transfer of undertakings and insolvency of the employer) were adopted in a context of economic downturn and growing labor militancy.

Much of the early academic discussion on the formation of the European economic space assumed that the political authority and competence of the European level would expand as the result of the European Union (see, for example, Lecher and Platzer 1998). In reality, there was never a move to a federal harmonized Europe, simply because national governments were effective protectors of their autonomy and legislation required unanimous vote in the Council of Ministers. Accordingly, Europe is now generally considered not as a super-state in the making but as an arena governed by the diplomatic maneuvers of the member states, hence the emphasis on 'subsidiarity' (Hyman 2010). The principle of 'subsidiarity' (regulation at the national or local level where appropriate) imposes constraints on the capacity of the EU to adopt supranational regulatory instruments while attributing to the EU the legal competence to regulate only insofar as such capacity is formally assigned in the treaties. Jacques Delors's vision as Commission President in the late 1980s of a strong 'social dimension'—which materialized with the creation of a European 'social chapter' (formally the Community Charter of Fundamental Social Rights for Workers)—effectively stalled with the neoliberal turn in the UK and then successive waves of enlargement. This compounded the political problems of establishing consensus, even with the extension of qualified majority voting (QMV) to employment and industrial relations matters.

Yet the period after Maastricht—which also introduced the agreement on Economic and Monetary Union (EMU)—was characterized by a revitalization of employment legislation by the EU. A series of directives, which are binding instruments but which leave the form of implementation to be decided at national level, were introduced in the early 1990s and 2000s. These include directives on working time (1993, 2003), the European Works Council (1994), the European company (2001), information and consultation at national level (2002), the statute of the European cooperative (2003), antidiscrimination (2000), equality between men and women (2004), and free movement of workers (2004). It is argued that this was linked to the prospective accession of CEE states, which would introduce a large block lacking the traditions of social Europe and with a competitive interest in preventing new employment regulation (Hyman 2008). Certainly, there have been few 'hard' measures since the EU enlargement of 2004.

The question remains, however, as to how far the directives had a significant and structural impact, or whether they were essentially minimalist legislation that created a very low level of protection and little change. On the matter of potential impact, by looking at some key examples (e.g., the free movement of labor, information and consultation and antidiscrimination), we can note that the process of national implementation has been quite diverse. In some cases (e.g., the directive stipulating equal treatment of national and community workers; see Pochet 2008) national adoption is still pending, and so the regulation cannot yet be enforced. Provisions to combat age (and some aspects of sex) discrimination continue to represent a particular challenge, as most member states had no prior legislation in this area. In others, directives have been implemented in most member states, but the quality of the transposition process is quite ambivalent and dubious. A useful example is the transposition of the information and consultation directive in the UK via the 2004 Information and Consultation of Employees (ICE) Regulations. Although the ICE Regulations are unquestionably a major development in British employment law, observers suggest that they have proved to be something of a 'damp squib' as far as impact in practice is concerned (see Hall et al. 2009).

Social Dialogue

A) *Inter-Professional and Sector-Level*
The social dialogue emerged following the election of Jacques Delors as Commission President in 1985, linked to the introduction of Article 118a of the treaty to encourage improvements in the working environment, especially as regards the health and safety of workers. The Commission was also mandated to develop the dialogue between management and labor at the European level, which could, if the two sides considered it desirable, lead to relations based on agreements. This institutionalized the role of European social dialogue, which began with the groundbreaking Val Duchesse process in 1985. Delors also pressed for a European social charter, which was adopted in 1989 by eleven member countries, with the UK dissenting. This was followed by the Social Chapter agreed at Maastricht in December 1991. The Social Chapter enlarged EU competences in the employment field and extended the range of social issues on which European legislation could be adopted by QMV. However, it is important to note that this provision did not apply to pay, the right of association, the right to strike or the right to impose lockouts.

The Social Chapter also created the social partners' route to European legislation. Social partners at the European community level could, if they wished, choose to negotiate agreements on the matter in question in place of the traditional legal instruments, such as a directive or a regulation. Such agreements could—if requested by the trade unions and employers and agreed to by the EU's Council of Ministers—subsequently be given the binding force of a directive. In accordance, trade unions and employers' organizations are considered 'partners' of the state in formulating and administering social policy. Hence, these procedures are consistent with the classic formula for corporatist concertation as 'a mode of policy formation in which formally designed interest associations are incorporated within the process of authoritative decision-making and implementation' (Schmitter 1981, p.295). The EU-level regulatory procedure of social dialogue is characterized by dense contact and interdependence between the Council, the social partners, the Commission, and, to some extent, the European Parliament. In addition, the Council of Social Affairs and Employment Ministers have an important role to play both informally and formally. As at the national level, effective negotiations at the European level need some backing from the state, in this case the institutions of the EU, in particular the European Commission.

Under the post-Maastricht arrangements a number of framework agreements were reached which contributed to important legislation. First was the 1995 social partner agreement on parental leave, subsequently implemented as a directive, followed by agreements on aspects of atypical employment, such as part-time work and temporary work, which were also later accorded the binding force of a directive. Despite the relative decline in legislative activity in the 2000s the social partners declared their continuous commitment to European intersector social dialogue. In particular, in November 2002 they adopted a joint three-year program committed to continuing dialogue on a broad agenda encompassing employment, enlargement and workers' mobility. Two 'frameworks of actions' were agreed during the same timeframe: one concerning the lifelong development of competencies and qualifications (2002) and the other on gender equality (2005). This was followed by an agreement in 2007 on a set of guidelines on flexicurity and a new framework covering harassment and violence at work, and in 2009 a revised framework on parental leave was agreed.

It has been argued that the intensity and the quality of the consultation and negotiation around relevant social policy issues continued to inform new regulation in the area of employment (Pochet 2008). For example, in 2007 the social partners were consulted by the Commission on six different subjects: active inclusion; seafaring jobs in the EU; cross-border transfers of undertakings; reconciliation of professional and family life; and musculoskeletal disorders. The Commission also referred to the social partners when revising or proposing relevant directives, such as European Works Councils (EWCs) and working time. In July 2008 the Commission introduced a new draft directive to combat discrimination outside the workplace as the result of intense consultation and negotiation activity with the social partners, adding to the existing package of antidiscrimination that the Commission presented in November 1999. All of this indicates a continuing flow of regulatory outcomes that represent the medium-long-term effect of the ongoing consultation activity between the social partners.

In contrast, social dialogue at the *sectoral* level took place within heterogeneous and more or less established structures, such as joint committees and informal working parties until 1998 when the Commission introduced a new unified framework to increase the incidence and quality of employment-related social dialogue at the European sector level. The establishment of the education sector social dialogue committee (SSDC) in June 2010, incorporating the newly created European Federation of Education Employers and the European Trade Union Committee for Education, was the thirty-ninth SSDC established since 1998. The SSDCs have adopted more than 500 texts in the form of autonomous agreements, codes of conduct, guidelines and frameworks of action, many of which commit the parties to monitor implementation in the member states and to take follow-up action as required.

If we assess the impact of sectoral social dialogue, we can at first note that some of the texts adopted have been effective in stimulating further social regulation in Europe. Since 1995, four out of the seven collective agreements from the sectoral level social dialogue were turned into social directives. Two of the latter are an adaptation of the working time directive to the transport sectors (seafarers in 1998 and civil aviation in 2000), and the other two are agreements concluded in the railways sector in 2004 (one fully transposed into a directive in 2005 and the other partly so in 2007). On average one text coming from the social partners has been extended *erga omnes* by a directive almost every two years. Moreover, whereas in the past, sectoral social dialogue was primarily geared to the 'joint lobbying' of the European institutions, since 2003 it appears to be generating more documents that reflect 'reciprocal commitments' (Degryse and Pochet 2011). This has led some commentators (e.g., Pochet 2008) to argue that, although within the limits set by member state politics (as in the case of temporary agency work), the development of sectoral social dialogue as a soft governance process has fostered the creation of important sector-based 'hard' directives. As indicated above, this can be explained by the Commission having undertaken more consultation (under Treaty Article 154), which opened a window of opportunity for the social partners.

B) Euro-Company Level

At the European company level, the key development for social dialogue was the adoption in 1994 of the European Works Council (EWC) directive 94/45/EC (revised in 2009). The aim of the EWC directive was to coordinate national provisions in order to create a European legal framework for transnational information and consultation within community-scale enterprises (those with at least 1,000 employees in the EEA countries, including 150 in at least two of these). The existence of rights of worker representation at the European level within multinational companies, along with information and consultation rights, amounted to significant progress toward the establishment of a regulatory setting for employment in Europe. This is because EWC initiatives can be coordinated with trade union strategies at both national and European level in order to provide an impetus to transnational collective bargaining. Multinational companies too have become more amenable to signing agreements with EWCs. Telljohann et al. (2009, p.512) identified seventy-three European agreements concluded between 1996 and mid-2008; more were reached following the economic crisis, especially in the metal sector, with currently at least eighty-five agreements in place. By mid-2011, the European Commission listed 102 agreements that have a European scope, of which fifteen include non-EEA member states. The vast majority of these framework agreements concluded at the European company level were signed by EWCs, the majority in cooperation with the European Industry Federations (EIFs) and most also cosigned by national unions; in addition, in the minority of cases where the EIF alone signed the agreement, EWCs were involved either in the negotiation and/or the monitoring process.

However, agreements concluded at the European company level vary in form and content. Only in a minority of cases do they involve genuine negotiation on key aspects of employment, such as pay and working conditions. Conversely, many appear to be driven by management's interest to transfer 'soft' policies (such as concerning equal opportunities, health and safety, skills and competences) to their subsidiaries. Yet, in some sectors the negotiation of European Framework Agreements (EFAs) is a way through which trade unions have attempted to widen the scope of the cross-border coordination of collective bargaining in the absence of a legal framework for transnational collective bargaining (Pulignano 2010). This is typical, for example, of some industries that are exposed to international product-market competition such as the metal sector, and the European Metalworking Federation (EMF) has been active in defining the conditions and rules under which it receives mandates from the different national unions to negotiate EFAs at the European company level.

It is argued that understanding the social actors' strategies at the European, national and local levels and, more importantly, their degree of coordination, is crucial in order to assess the extent to which cross-national negotiation at the company level has been pursued and with what effect (da Costa et al. 2012). For example, in the auto industry, an intense process of bargaining activity developed at the beginning of the 2000s at the cross-country company level directed at achieving common socially responsible approaches by management and unions with regard to company restructuring with a view to avoiding major job losses. The EFAs concluded that Ford and GM are of particular significance because they contributed to reducing the number of collective redundancies under company restructuring. Also important was an agreement in ArcelorMittal in 2009 on the anticipation of change at the company level. These remain exceptions, however; as noted above, in other multinationals personnel matters were at the core of the negotiation of EFAs, such as equal opportunities and professional development (as in the case of Areva in 2006, 2010 and 2011 and in Thales in 2009 and 2010), or a profit-sharing plan negotiated at EADS in 2011.

Overall, the conclusion of various European-level agreements for the transnational regulation of employment in Europe reflects a process which Marginson and Sisson (2004) label as 'virtual collective bargaining'. The growing character that these agreements have assumed and the scope they have offered to both the trade unions and management in Europe to coordinate their strategies, policies and actions across borders, suggests an increasing contribution to forms of bargaining with relevant social outcomes for the workers involved.

C) The Open Method of Coordination

The European Union's open method of coordination (OMC) was primarily intended to orient member states' policies toward common strategic priorities, such as employment, poverty and social exclusion through the adoption of shared action frameworks. From a political-institutional perspective, the OMC—or better, the various applications of the OMC—is amongst the most 'soft' of the measures of governance undertaken at the European level since the 2000s in order to cope with increased complexity. Notwithstanding this, the OMC has been seen as an important and original experiment in the promotion of policy change on a continental basis, geared toward modifying not only objectives and policy measures in the areas involved, but also the interaction dynamics among the many actors operating in such areas (Ferrera and Sacchi 2004). As Zeitlin and Pochet (2005) argue, the OMC process has fortified the logic of mutual learning, benchmarking, best practice and peer pressure to achieve objectives.

How, then, does this work? First, it involves the definition of common objectives to guide national policy. The conceptualization of the lines along which national policies are formulated takes place at the supranational level. The Lisbon European Council (2000) also proposed combining those guidelines with specific timetables for achieving the goals over the short, medium and long term. It also established quantitative and qualitative indicators and benchmarks, tailored to the needs of different member states and sectors. In so doing the aim was to strengthen the aspect of coordination as one of the main leading principles of the European Employment Strategy. The second step therefore consists of translating EU guidelines into national action plans. Here the multilevel dialogue that characterizes the Employment Strategy is naturally at the heart of the OMC. Arguably, however, the dialogue is refined and pushed further in order to make the EU objective efficient, by leaving to each member state the definition of the most appropriate implementing measures. Therefore, as Arrowsmith et al. (2004) argue, the birth of the OMC is found in the elevation of benchmarking as the tool to resolve the horizontal and vertical collective action problems that often bedevil the development and implementation of decision-making processes at the EU level.

Nevertheless, it is this complexity that makes assessment of the OMC difficult and controversial, not least given the proliferation and increased variety of OMC processes. The most robust critiques concern its intrinsically 'soft' (even voluntary) approach, which must necessarily weaken its efficacy as a tool of coordination and which may be used displace 'hard' regulatory instruments even in domains where the EU already possesses legislative powers (Goetschy 2003). The OMC is also held to have lacked substantive impact in the member states; rather, the process constitutes an exercise in symbolic politics where national governments repackage existing policies to demonstrate their apparent compliance with EU objectives (Scharpf 2002). At best, then, the OMC is a defensive adjustment to the constraints imposed on European social policy by the single market, the EMU, and globalization; at worst it represents a mechanism for unlearning the lessons of the postwar European model of socially embedded capitalism (Offe 2003).

And yet, there is no evidence of the OMC undermining the production of substantive pieces of legislation in the social field, or of it contributing to the reduction of social legislation (Pochet 2009). On the contrary, some commentators claim that this new EU mode of governance is particularly suitable for addressing a range of common European concerns while respecting legitimate national diversity. It commits member states to work together in reaching shared goals and performance targets, without seeking to homogenize their policy regimes and institutional arrangements (Hemerijck and Berghman 2004). In this respect, it may amount to a more flexible, efficient and integrated policy tool than the traditional legislative approach (Borras and Jacobsson 2003), suited to efforts to coordinate in the highly heterogeneous and unpredictable European space (Arrowsmith et al. 2004). In some ways too, the OMC offers a partial answer to the 'democratic deficit', defining and building consensus around common objectives and values, and enhancing participation and accountability at national and local levels (Ferrera 2001). Recent studies have also argued that the OMC has contributed to changes in national policy thinking by incorporating EU concepts and categories (such as activation, prevention, gender mainstreaming, lifelong learning, etc.) into domestic debates and exposing policy makers to new approaches (Zeitlin 2011). Problems of clarity, consistency and weak integration into national policy making remain (Frazer and Marlier 2011), but these processes seem to have a value when horizontal coordination and cross-sectoral integration of interdependent policy areas need to be guaranteed, as well as vertical coordination between levels of governance enhanced.

COMPLEMENTARY EMPLOYMENT GOVERNANCE MEASURES IN EUROPE

The continuous socioeconomic and political transformations that have occurred in the European space since the 1970s means that the situation at the EU level is characterized by increasing uncertainty as the result of growing heterogeneity and complexity. Global (and regional) market integration, free movement of capital and labor, and increasingly flexible rules to ensure the new market-based order have made coordination across (and within)

European member states increasingly difficult. Moreover, by reinforcing uncertainty the 2008–2009 financial crisis contributed to an increased risk of social disintegration (Degryse and Pochet 2011; Erne 2011).

European complexity is a product not just of growing diversity across (and within) the member states; it also relates to the nature of the problems and issues that need to be socially and democratically addressed. As Crouch (2010) emphasizes, the fundamental issue is workers' certainty in their lives as broadly conceived, which more concretely means the provision to them of secure and decent employment. Increasingly, the very process of regional economic integration implies the need for national, sector or firm-level governance to be set in a broader (multinational or international) context in order to address the social consequences of ever-growing complexity and uncertainty.

In principle, the management of complexity in the current European space requires new dynamic measures of governance able to respond more flexibly and rapidly to the fundamental changes occurring in the way market economies, as well as the organizations within them, are managed. This implies that the traditional top-down community method, which aims at maintaining control from above, mainly through the use of legislation, is essential but nevertheless no longer sufficient to manage the levels of complexity generated by the process of Europeanization. In this chapter we argue that inter- and intranational diversity makes common rules increasingly problematic. The impact of legislation can generate disparate and different effects. Therefore, we consider governance measures that stimulate coordination, interaction and networking among multiple actors at different levels for the continuous consultation and negotiation as equally important. Ideally, 'soft' governance measures are designed to be iterative and adaptable, and commonly agreed as a result of a process of mutual learning and communication among the social actors (Arrowsmith et al. 2004). Thus, they should be able to coordinate horizontally and vertically by increasing the involvement and the participation of the agents, in particular national governments and social partners, to influence their behaviors and approaches to cohere to European common interests more generally. This has strong parallels with what Barnard and Deakin (2000, p.341) call 'inducing second-order effects on the part of the social actors', involving the elaboration of customized local solutions within a guiding framework of principles and a process of monitoring and review that the actors can support.

This leads to another important implication, that there is not necessarily a 'tradeoff' between prescriptive 'hard' law and 'soft' governance measures. First, as Pochet (2008) notes, since the launch of the EU employment strategy in 1997, the number and the scope of social directives did not fall. This can be explained, as discussed above, by the ongoing engagement of the national and European social partners through consultation and the joint exchange of ideas and mutual learning, as well as bargaining activity at the transnational level of multinationals. Therefore it may be argued that the social partners' interests in coordinating policy outcomes with regard to socioeconomic issues has stimulated and sustained the development of social regulation. Second, the link between 'soft' and 'hard' measures is in certain circumstances explicit. As Léonard (2008) states, the European social partners are more crucial today because they are now formally entrusted to produce texts that can potentially be transposed into Community legislation by a Council decision. The most advanced example of this is the employment equality directive, which as indicated above was accompanied by different steps taken at the EU level.

Furthermore, from a different perspective, it can also be argued that community law does not necessarily imply *erga omnes* a broader space for social regulation. This is for two main reasons. First, as Hyman (2010) shows, the Commission monitors whether directives are transposed into national law, but not whether these laws are then enforced. National courts may (and indeed should) take EU law as their point of reference. However, whereas in some countries, such as the UK, there is evidence of the impact this has had for the progression of a social agenda, in other countries this is less evident and very difficult to evaluate. Second, European legislation has contributed to the process of marketization which increasingly defines contemporary Europeanization. The 'deregulatory' effects of this legislation on aspects of employment are very clear. We refer here, most notably, to the Services Directive (2006/123/EC), which contributed to the creation of a single market for services in Europe without enhancing (rather, potentially undermining) the social aims and objectives of the treaty. In accordance, providers located in one country have open access to all other countries' markets, and as such, they have a wider scope for subordinating workers' rights and standards to the right of free movement and competition.

If, as we claim in this chapter, 'soft' governance measures can offer a strong complementary basis to facilitate and reinforce 'hard' legislation, it is also acknowledged that the process of reaching such outcomes is politically highly contested. We refer here to a lack of, even a declining, appetite for EU social regulation on the part of many member states, let alone employers—which is why the agency work directive took so long to be endorsed, and why the EWC and working-time directives took so long to be revised. Also relevant is the recent formulation of Europe 2020, as proposed by the Commission in March 2010 and approved in amended form by the June 2010 European Council. The European 2020 governance strategy seems to challenge the foundation of a combined and integrated mechanism of 'hard' and 'soft' governance. First, it is unclear how the headline targets of Europe 2020, which are focused on poverty, social exclusion, pensions and health care, will be monitored, renewed, evaluated and acted upon within the governance architecture; the relationship between the new and preexisting governance measures (in particular the OMC) is not clear. Second, the 2008–2009 financial crisis reinforced the primacy of EU economic concerns, perversely 'strengthening the power of financial markets instead of breaking or at least curbing it' (Dräger 2011, p.23). No substantial regulation of financial markets has taken place, despite all the official rhetoric about the need to correct and prevent irresponsible behavior. As a result, it is plausible to expect the interests of finance capital under the Europe 2020 strategy to gain a much stronger influence on economic policy making, including using 'soft' governance mechanisms to pursue the 'neoliberal trajectory' further (Baccaro and Howell 2011). Already, a common feature of the crisis is an undermining of the collective dimension of labor regulation and a weakening of labor and social rights in Europe.

CONCLUSION

The lack of institutional capacity at the EU level, which is in stark contrast to existing national social systems, has long been noted as one of the weakest features of the process of Europeanization and a major obstacle to building a social Europe (Teague 2001). Twenty years from the Maastricht Treaty, there remains only very limited competencies at the EU level to contribute to the development of a European social model 'from above', but in any case this is an unrealistic and inappropriate benchmark and, in various ways, the EU has contributed to the creation of a new dimension of European integration, which involves emergent forms of European employment relations. This process is fragmented and highly contested, but nonetheless it cannot be completely discounted. Indeed, as this chapter has pointed out, the emergence of new forms of employment policy and regulation has been at least conceived and developed in response to the very socioeconomic transformations associated with market integration.

The measures adopted to create the conditions for the enhancement of a space for the regulation of employment at the EU level have been various and in most cases hotly debated. A particular theme is whether flexible (so-called 'soft') measures of governance may be better able than traditional law to manage the problems of complexity and diversity as well as periods of economic and social uncertainty. It is clear, on the one hand, that 'soft' measures per se cannot constitute the sole governance mechanism for the EU employment strategy given the very fragmentation involved in this multilayered dynamic of transformation. Rather, we have argued in this chapter that such approaches can complement, rather than substitute for, more robust or 'hard' forms of regulation. Indeed, 'soft' and 'hard' (top-down) forms of regulation should be understood not as a simple dichotomous shift but as representing a continuum of approaches to the contemporary European space. For any alternative to the macroeconomic neoliberal vision of marketization in the EU, it is not enough to enact 'hard' law measures alone. It is important to consider the capacity of community measures overall, irrespective of their 'soft' or 'hard' nature, to function as complementary and purposive means of learning. Yet this is why we are concerned with regard to the new economic governance architecture of Europe 2020. By overlooking how to enhance the relationships between 'soft' and 'hard' mechanisms, the new approach seems to reinforce the dominance of the financial markets rather than giving more specific substance to social policy strategies. Hence, there is some foundation to the belief that a stalling of 'social Europeanization' is likely to become an enduring feature of the EU landscape for some time to come.

REFERENCES

Allard, C. and Everaet, L. 2010. *Lifting Euro Area Growth: Priorities for Structural Reforms and Governance, International Monetary Fund.* IMF Staff Position Note SPN/10/19.

Arrowsmith, J., Sisson, K. and Marginson, P. 2004. 'What can "benchmarking" offer the open method of coordination?' *Journal of European Public Policy*, 11:2. 311–328.

Baccaro, L. and Howell, C. 2011. 'A common neoliberal trajectory: The transformation of industrial relations in advanced capitalism', *Politics & Society*, 39. 521–563.

Barnard, C. and Deakin, S. 2000. 'In search of coherence: Social policy, the single market and fundamental rights', *Industrial Relations Journal*, 32:2. 136–153.

Borras, S. and Jacobsson, K. 2003. 'The open coordination method and the new governance patterns in EU'. Paper presented at the workshop 'OMC and Economic Governance in Europe, Center for European Studies, Harvard University, 28 April.

Coller, X. 1996. 'Managing flexibility in the food industry: A cross-national comparative case study in European multinational companies', *European Journal of Industrial Relations*, 2:2. 153–172.

Crouch, C. 2010. 'British industrial relations: Between security and flexibility' in M. Terry and T. Colling (eds.) *Industrial Relations: Theory and Practice.* Blackwell, London.

da Costa, I., Pulignano, V., Rehfeldt, U. and Telljohann, V. 2012. 'Transnational negotiations and the Europeanisation of industrial relations: Potentials and obstacles', *European Journal of Industrial Relations*, 18:2. 1–15.

Degryse, C. and Pochet, P. 2011. *Monetary Union, Economic Coordination and Democratic legitimacy.* ETUI Policy Brief, 5.

Dräger, K. 2011. *Sado-Monetarism Rules OK? EU Economic Governance and Its Consequences.* Paper presented at the 17th Euro Memo Group workshop on alternative economic policy in Europe, 16–18 September, Vienna.

Erne, R. 2012. 'European industrial relations after the crisis: A postscript' in S. Smismans (ed.) *The European Union and Industrial Relations—New Procedures, New Contexts.* London: Taylor & Francis.

European Commission 2011. *Macro Economic Report to the Communication from the Commission to the European Parliament, the Council, The European and Social Committee and the Committee of Regions.* Annual Growth Survey 2012, Brussels: CEC.

Ferrera, M. 2001. 'The European Social Model between "Hard" Constraints and "Soft" Coordination', unpublished paper presented to the *Social Models and EM: Convergence, Co-existence? The Role of Economic and Social Actors*, Economic and Social Committee, Brussels, 19 November.

Ferrera, M. and Sacchi, S. 2004. *The Open Method of Coordination and National Institutional Capabilities.* Paper presented at the 16th annual meeting of the Society for the Advancement of Socio-Economics, Washington, 8–11 July.

Frazer, H. and Marlier, E. 2011. 'Strengthening social inclusion in the Europe 2020 strategy by learning from the past', in F. Marlier, D. Natali and R. Van Dam (eds.) *Europe 2020: Towards a More Social Europe?* Work & Society Series, 69, Brussels.

Glassner, V., Keune, M., and Marginson, P. 2011. 'Collective bargaining in a time of crisis: Developments in the private sector in Europe', *Transfer: European Review of Labour and Research,* 17. 303–322.

Goetschy, J. 2003. 'The European employment strategy, multi-level governance and policy coordination' in J. Zeitlin and Turbek D. M. (eds.) *Governing Work and Welfare in a New Economy: European and American Experiments.* Oxford University Press, Oxford. 59–87.

Hall, M., Hutchinson, S., Purcell, J., Terry, M. and Parker, J. 2009. 'Implementing information and consultation: Evidence from longitudinal case studies in organisations with 150 or more employees', *Employment Relations Research Series* no. 105. 1–78.

Hemerijck, A. and Berghman, J. 2004. 'The European social patrimony: Deepening social Europe through legitimate diversity', in T. Sakellaropoulos and J. Berghman (eds.) *Connecting Welfare Diversity within the European Social Model.* Intersentia, Antwerp.9–54.

Hyman, R. 2008. Britain and the European social model: capitalism against capitalism? *IES Working Paper, 19.* Brighton: Institute for Employment Studies.

———. 2010. 'British industrial relations: The European dimension' in M. Terry and T. Colling (eds.) *Industrial Relations: Theory and Practice.* Blackwell, London.

Lecher, W. and Platzer, H.-W. (eds.) 1998. 'Introduction: Global trends and the European context' in W. Lecher and H.-W. Platzer (eds.) *European Union—European Industrial Relations?* London: Routledge. 1–20.

Léonard, E. 2008. 'European sectoral social dialogue: An analytical framework', *European Journal of Industrial Relations,* 14. 401–419.

Marginson, P. 2006. *Between Europeanisation and Regime Competition: Labour Market Regulation Following EU Enlargement.* Warwick papers in Industrial Relations, 79, February.

Marginson, P. and Sisson, K. 1998. 'European collective bargaining: A virtual prospect?' *Journal of Common Market Studies,* 36:4. 505–528.

———. 2004. *European Integration and Industrial Relations: Multi-Level Governance in the Making.* London: Palgrave.

Marginson, P. and Meardi, G. 2006. 'EU enlargement & the FDI Channel of industrial relations transfer', *Industrial Relations Journal,* 37:2. 92–110.

Meardi, G. 2002. 'The Trojan horse for the Americanization of Europe? Polish industrial relations towards the EU', European Journal of Industrial Relations, 8:1. 77–99.

Offe, C. 2003. 'The European model of 'social' capitalism: Can it survive European integration?' *Journal of Political Philosophy,* 11:4. 437–469.

Pochet, P. 2008. *Social Europe: Does Hard Law Still Have a Role to Play?* Working Papers Series no. 2. Brussels: European Trade Union Institute.

———. 2009. *The Community Method: Obstinate or Obsolete?* London: Basingstoke, Palgrave.

Pulignano, V. 2010. 'European integration and transnational employment regulations: The company-level experience of EFAs in the metal sector in Europe", *European Labour Law Journal,* 1. 81–88.

Scharpf, F. 2002. 'The European social model: Copying with the challenge of diversity, *Journal of Common Market Studies,* 40:4.

Schmid, G. 2008. *Full Employment in Europe: Managing Labour Market Transitions and Risks.* London: Edward Elgar.

Schmitter, P. 1981. 'Interest intermediation and regime governability in advanced industrial/capitalist polities' in S. Berger (ed.) *Organizing Interests in Western Europe*. New York: Cambridge University Press. 285–327.

Teague, P. 2001. 'Deliberative governance and EU social policy', *European Journal of Industrial Relations*, 7:7. 7–26.

Telljohann V., da Costa, I., Muller, T., Rehfeldt, U. and Zimmer, R. 2009. 'European and international framework agreements: New tools of transnational industrial relations', *Transfer*, 3–4. 505–525.

Trubek, D. and Trubek, L. 2005. 'Hard and soft law in the construction of social Europe: The role of the open method of coordination', *European Law Journal*, 11:3. 343–364.

Zeitlin, J. 2011. 'Towards a stronger OMC in a more social Europe 2020: A new governance architecture for EU policy coordination' in F. Marlier, D. Natali and R. Van Dam (eds.) *Europe 2020: Towards a More Social Europe?* Work & Society Series, 69, Brussels.

Zeitlin, J. and Pochet, P. 2005. *The Open Method of Coordination*. Brussels: PIE-Peter Lang.

10 Employability

Jonathan Winterton and Nigel Haworth

INTRODUCTION

The principal purpose of this chapter is to explore the question of employment flexibility for employees, captured by the term 'employability'. In a period when employers have sought more and more contractual flexibility in employment, through outsourcing, contingent work and new forms of pay and working time, and with high rates of structural unemployment in many countries, employability has become an increasingly important concern for workers and trade unions, as well as policy makers. The chapter is organized into five sections. The first addresses theoretical debates surrounding the changing nature and multifaceted character of employability. This is done through a literature review of state intervention to promote training and employability, contextualized within a historical perspective tracing supply-side interventions since the mid-1980s. Inputs that contribute to the enhancement of employability are also considered through engaging with the literature around lifelong learning and commenting on the changing nature of jobs and skills within an expanding Europe. Assumed outcomes of employability are also explored, with a focus on external flexibility (and concepts of 'flexicurity'), mobility and portfolio careers.

The second section involves a review of EU policy relating to responses to unemployment and more specifically EU policy in the field of employability. The development of the European Employment Strategy (EES) is analyzed with respect to the changing role of employability in the Employment Guidelines and the Joint Employment Report. The third section then focuses on an analysis of eight countries identified for empirical research: Belgium, France, Germany and the UK among the 'old EU15', and Lithuania, Malta, Romania and Slovenia among the 'new EU' member states. The choice of countries is driven by a need to capture variation in labor market, employment relations and training regimes in exploring the relationship between labor market regulation, social dialogue and employability. Evidence is derived from the employment chapters of national reform program (NRP) reports, the Joint Employment Report of the Commission and commentary in the academic literature.

Finally, some conclusions are offered concerning how employability has been interpreted over recent years, including country diversity in approaches. *Theoretical* confusion is inherent in the concept of employability, which neatly supported the switch from a focus on unemployment to an emphasis on employment rates. In *policy* terms, employability evolved from the most important pillar at the outset of the EES to an implicit objective in the plethora of initiatives underpinning Europe 2020. *Practice*, in the implementation of active labor market measures, training and inclusion initiatives, exhibits considerable diversity at the level of member states and reflects both the theoretical ambiguity and increasing opacity of employability in NRP reports.

THEORETICAL DEBATES SURROUNDING EMPLOYABILITY

In tracing the antecedents of employability, Gazier (1998; 2001) identified no less than seven different ways in which the term had been used, each associated with a particular historical and geographical context, but here the concern is with its use in the policy context in Europe since the 1980s. It is no coincidence that a resurgence of interest in employability emerged at the same time as neoliberal economic ideas were becoming hegemonic. The election of the first Thatcher Government in May 1979 marked the appearance of these policies in Europe, with labor market restructuring viewed as a route to competitive advantage as well as a mechanism for reducing unemployment, especially among young people (Ashton et al. 1990). In this political transformation from Keynesian welfare state to 'Schumpeterian workfare state' (Jessop 1992, p.9), the goal of full employment was replaced by 'employability' in a 'work and opportunity-focussed welfare state' (Finn 2000; Evans 2001, p.260). For Jessop (1992, p.18) the defining feature of the Schumpeterian workfare state is 'a concern to promote innovation and structural competitiveness in the field of economic policy; and a concern to promote flexibility and competitiveness in the field of social policy.' These twin concerns reflect increasingly global competition and a focus on supply-side interventions, in contrast with the Keynesian emphasis on managing the demand-side of the economy to maintain 'full employment' (ibid, pp.9–15). Hence, the origins of employability in European employment policy can be traced to such supply-side concerns at national level in the 1980s, particularly in countries that were adopting active labor market policies, evidently in the UK (Lindsay 2002), but also Denmark (Hespanha and Møller 2001) and the Netherlands (Hemerijck and Kuin 1999). The OECD *Jobs Study* (OECD 1994) endorsed such polices and had an influence on the subsequent development of European policy (see the next section).

The issue of employability rapidly became pervasive in policy literature but with various meanings and no consensus definition (Philpott 1999). To take the UK as an example, HM Treasury (1997, p.1) in connection with the first UK Employment Action Plan, defined employability in terms of a goal that 'all those capable of work are encouraged to develop the skills, knowledge, technology [sic] and adaptability to enable them to enter and remain in employment throughout their working lives'. A policy document from the UK Department for Education and Employment in the following year offered as a definition 'the capacity to move self-sufficiently within the labor market to realise potential through sustained employment' (Hillage and Pollard 1998, p.11). The Confederation of British Industry (CBI 1999, p.1) used employability in the sense of 'the possession by an individual of the qualities and competencies required to meet the changing needs of employers and customers and thereby help to realise his or her aspirations and potential in work'. These definitions around individual competences that are held to enhance an individual's chances of obtaining, maintaining and moving more easily to different employment, have been widely adopted, yet they remain problematic. For example, McQuaid and Lindsay (2005, p.202) warn that the emphasis on individual employability in labor market policy raises a risk 'that the "interactive" elements of the concept of employability have been lost amongst a welter of discussions centering on how best to activate and "up-skill" the unemployed and other disadvantaged groups.' Similarly Philpott (1999) describes a two-part approach to employability: providing access to employment via labor market activation strategies and up-skilling through lifelong learning initiatives, but this is still essentially a supply-side solution devoid of its interactive element with demand (Peck and Theodore 2000).

Overall, the vocabulary of employability has been associated with a series of paradigm shifts: in intervention terms from unemployment to 'unemployability'; in production terms from Fordism to a knowledge-based economy; in ideological terms from providing security to providing competence (Serrano Pascual 2004; Lindsay and Serrano Pascual 2009). Employability thus defined plays a pivotal role in balancing flexibility and security, as captured by the term 'flexicurity' (see chapter 11, this volume). In this new construct, security is attained through personal employability rather than through state-sponsored or employers' welfare. As Serrano Pascual (2009, p.56) remarks, 'This semantic displacement of the notion of security is emblematic of the contemporary tendency to make of the fight against dependency, the emphasis on autonomy, and the promotion of individual responsibility, the fundamental pillars of the new culture of work'. In other words, employability has been 'hollowed out' in supply-side labor market policy: 'the interactivity supposedly at the centre of the concept appears to have been replaced by a singular focus on the individual and what might be termed their "employability skills"'. (McQuaid and Lindsay 2005, p.205). In similar fashion Brown et al. (2003, p.110, p.111q) argue that policy invariably 'fail(s) to grasp the *duality of employability*, a duality that reflects the interaction of individual characteristics and labor market demand given that employability can be defined as *the relative chances of acquiring and maintaining different kinds of employment*' [emphasis in original].

Neglecting the demand side of employability effectively shifts responsibility for unemployment to the unemployed (Evans et al. 1999; Kleinman et al. 1998), yet supply-side measures are insufficient without demand-side measures to create employment opportunities. The importance of demand factors has been recognized in local labor market policies designed to reduce long-term unemployment (Campbell 2000), including in relation to rural unemployed who have barriers to employment as a result of geographical isolation (Lindsay et al. 2003). Even in urban environments with available work, the 'employability gap' of the long-term unemployed, reinforced by multiple deprivations that maintain social exclusion (Hollywood et al. 2000), could only be addressed by providing mechanisms of support to build basic work habits and develop relevant skills with the active involvement of employers themselves (Lindsay 2002; McQuaid and Lindsay 2002). However, the assumption that engagement with employers will promote employability neglects the difficulty of operating in a market context with no means of influencing employers' demand for, and use of, skills (Streeck 1989). The problem is not simply one of matching supply and demand, or aligning learners' interests with employers' needs, but also of how these needs are generated and articulated, the extent to which skills apparently desired will actually be deployed, and how such 'needs' are communicated to providers and learners. Another consequence of the emphasis on individual employability is a renegotiation of the psychological contract or 'the end of loyalty' (Baruch 2001; Ellig 1998). This increasingly extends across occupational groupings including managers and technicians in a phenomenon described by Brown et al. (2003, p.108) as 'the democratisation of insecurity.'

With the decline of the 'job for life', employability measures are intended to prepare individuals for transition (Tomkin and Hillage 1999). In all contexts it is important therefore to address both sides of the employability equation, which might involve acknowledging and addressing three sets of factors (McQuaid and Lindsay 2005): individual employability attributes (competences); individual circumstances (socioeconomic contextual factors, including household circumstances); and external factors (labor demand conditions and the enabling support of employment-related public services).

EMPLOYABILITY IN THE EUROPEAN EMPLOYMENT STRATEGY

The end of the era of full employment and its downgrading as a public policy goal certainly brought employment back to the trade union agenda in the last decades of the twentieth century, initially with union calls for traditional demand management to promote economic growth. The Delors White Paper *Growth, Competitiveness and Employment* (EC 1993) secured consensus between member states and social partners on the equal importance and indeed interdependence of the three objectives. By setting the framework for discussion of employment policy at European level within a context where macroeconomic policy would support job creation, as well as calling for a negotiated reform of labor markets, the White Paper encouraged trade unions to engage with the agenda of modernizing social and labor market policy, thereby addressing the supply side of the debate. Specifically, the Essen summit in December 1994 agreed on five priorities for employment policy to be implemented at national level:

- investment in human resources (education and training);
- encouraging employment intensive patterns of growth by a) changes in working time and work organization, b) wage moderation in respect to productivity and c) targeted job creation in labor intensive sectors;
- reductions in nonwage labor costs;
- shifting labor market spending from passive to active programs;
- targeting specific groups disadvantaged in the labor market (women returning to work, young people and the long-term unemployed).

Subsequently, a new draft treaty agreed at the Amsterdam summit in June 1997 included an Employment Title, committing member states and the Community to work toward a coordinated strategy for employment. This approach marked a watershed for three reasons. First, by defining employment as an issue of common concern, the treaty opened the way to coordination of national (and regional, local or sectoral) policies without seeking to determine from Brussels the exact policy mix appropriate in any given setting. Second, it emphasized the integrated nature of the EU economy and implicitly insisted that the solution to the employment problems of one country should not be to export them to another. Third, and perhaps most significantly, it reflected a redefinition of the unemployment problem in terms of a low level of employment, benchmarked in particular against the US (HM Treasury 2001). Defining the problem in terms of low employment rather than high unemployment reinforced the shift of focus from demand to supply and created the real policy space for employability.

A special *Jobs Summit* was held in Luxembourg in November 1997 at which the Commission proposed a draft EES together with underpinning employment policy guidelines (Goetschy 1999). The Employment Guidelines that emerged from this process were structured into four pillars: employability; entrepreneurship; adaptability; and equal opportunities. Member states were required to address the Employment Guidelines in their employment policies in a procedure—the so-called Luxembourg Process—that deliberately echoed the monitoring and review of economic policy commitments under the Maastricht Treaty. Member states were to report annually on their employment policies in the light of the guidelines, which were to be consistent with the Broad Economic Policy Guidelines (BEPGs). Each country was to produce a National Action Plan for Employment (NAPE) with the involvement of the social partners, which was then subject to peer review by another country, as well as evaluation by the Commission, which produced a Joint Employment Report commenting on progress.

The structure of the Employment Guidelines was fundamentally designed to address perceived weaknesses in European labor markets. The principal reason for the revision of policy goals was the perception that low employment rates, if allowed to persist, would undermine the capacity to finance the advanced social protection systems that distinguish Europe from major trading partners like the US and Japan, which had higher employment rates than the EU. Hence, the use of active labor market policies to raise employment was a key theme throughout the EES, as was an emphasis on the prevention of structural/long-term unemployment. Measures to assist the unemployed back into the labor market would therefore be brought into play *before* the loss of skills and confidence which might stigmatize individuals in the eyes of employers. It was also assumed that commitment from the social partners was necessary to guarantee the quality of the work or training initiatives, designed to reintegrate individuals into the labor market, that reintegration demanded.

At the European level, the ETUC gave firm political support to the Employment Guidelines and was involved in their elaboration and subsequent modification. Some national trade union confederations (predominantly from the Mediterranean countries) expressed fears that the approach risked stigmatizing the unemployed, but unions overall were positive, with the caveats that initiatives to support the unemployed or groups at risk should be of high quality, and that labor demand (job creation) should also be addressed. In accepting the emphasis on supply-side issues, unions effectively recognized the need to improve labor market responsiveness to ensure that any demand impulse would produce jobs rather than inflation. Negotiated labor market reform was thus seen as preferable to the market-driven flexibility that would otherwise have been paramount. As a result, trade unions became increasingly involved in developing employability policy (Foden 1999), and in implementing initiatives to support employability policy objectives (Danau et al. 2000). This occurred most notably in the UK, where union-led learning became a mainstream route for workers to upgrade their skills (Stuart et al. 2010).

In the 1999 version of the Employment Guidelines, the pillar Improving Employability was at the heart of the EES (Lefresne 1999). It comprised nine guidelines grouped under five headings: tackling youth unemployment and preventing long-term unemployment (LTU); transition from passive to active measures; encouraging a partnership approach; easing the transition from school to work; and promoting a labor market open to all. Many of the guidelines made specific reference to employability. Guidelines 1 and 2, in addressing unemployment, referred to training, retraining and work practice, noting that 'preventive and employability measures should be combined with measures to promote the reemployment of the long-term unemployed.'

In the preamble to Guidelines 3 and 4, detailing the move from passive to active measures, it was noted that 'benefit, tax and training systems . . . must be reviewed and adapted to ensure that they actively support employability.' Guidelines 5 and 6, concerning the need to engage the social partners, were designed to encourage agreements promoting 'training, work experience, traineeships or other measures likely to improve employability'. Guidelines 7 and 8 on school-work transition did not mention employability directly, but the labor market relevance of education and training is evidently an aspect of employability. Similarly, Guideline 9, which addressed integrating disadvantaged groups into the labor market, referred to 'acquiring relevant skills' that will raise their employability.

The Lisbon Summit in March 2000 established the key objective of making Europe by 2010 'the most competitive and dynamic knowledge-based economy in the world capable of sustainable economic growth with more and better jobs and greater social cohesion' (European Council 2000, para. 5). In pursuit of this high skills agenda, the Commission published an *Action Plan for Skills and Mobility* in February 2002, which emphasized the need to increase occupational mobility of workers from the poorer to wealthier regions of the EU (EC 2002). The EES was seen as a key tool underpinning the Lisbon strategy, which set targets for employment rates for 2010 (70 percent overall and 60 percent for women) and recommended new or strengthened priorities (such as skills and mobility, and lifelong learning), and these were reflected in the Employment Guidelines for 2001 through new horizontal objectives. In 2003 the European Commission (2003a) assessed the future of the EES under the Lisbon strategy and proposed to restructure the 18 guidelines into '10 commandments' (EC 2003b). Hence, from the adoption of the Employment Policy Guidelines for 2003–2005, employability disappeared as an explicit policy objective but remained a coherent and implicit theme in terms of active and preventative measures; promotion of adaptability and mobility; development of human capital; and integration of people at disadvantage. Following a midterm assessment of the Lisbon Strategy by the high-level group led by Wim Kok (2004), the Lisbon Strategy was relaunched with the objective of fostering 'stronger and lasting growth and the creation of more and better jobs' through measures to encourage firms and workers to adapt to change (EC 2005, p.1). Among the key actions were increasing adaptability to adjust to restructuring and market changes; simplifying mutual recognition of qualifications to facilitate labor mobility; and investing more in human capital by improving education and skills.

As a result, in 2005 the EES was revised and employment measures focused on the Lisbon objectives were incorporated into Integrated Guidelines for Growth and Jobs. A National Reform Programme (NRP) was to be developed annually by each member state in collaboration with the social partners. Replacing the NAPEs, each NRP report contained an employment chapter, and the Joint Employment Report became the Employment Chapter of the EU Annual Progress Report adopted by the Council. The eight guidelines relating to employment (Guidelines 16–23) focused on developing policies for full employment, improved quality, productivity, social and territorial cohesion; promoting a lifecycle approach to work; ensuring inclusive labor markets; better matching labor market needs; promoting flexibility and security; ensuring employment-friendly labor costs; increasing investment in human capital; and adapting education and training to meet new competence needs. Four priority areas were identified for employment: attracting and retaining more people in employment; increasing labor supply and modernizing social protection systems; improving adaptability of workers and enterprises; and increasing investment in human capital through improving education and raising skills.

With the onset of financial crisis, the *New Skills for New Jobs* (EC 2008) initiative reiterated the need to enhance human capital and employability, noting that the severity and unpredictability of the crisis made it essential to secure a better matching of skills supply to labor market demand. Two years later, it was evident that the center of gravity of the global economy was undergoing a major transformation and that radical action was also needed to combat the effects of climate change. The Brussels Summit in March 2010 thus endorsed Europe 2020, a new strategy for sustainable growth and jobs which placed knowledge, innovation and green growth at the heart of EU competitiveness (EC 2010a). Described as a comprehensive roadmap for the EU's economic recovery, sustainability in both a competitive and environmental sense was added to the original goals of growth based on knowledge and innovation coupled with high employment and social cohesion.

The modified processes whereby NRPs must address the new integrated BEPGs are now concerned with the five 'headline targets' of Europe 2020: raising the employment rate to 75 percent; reducing the proportion of early school leavers to 10 percent (from 15 percent) and ensuring 40 percent of young people are qualified to degree or diploma level; reducing the population living in poverty by 25 percent; raising investment in research and development; cutting greenhouse gas emissions by 20 percent and sourcing 20 percent of energy from renewable sources. The implicit centrality of employability in Europe 2020 is evident from the conclusions of the Council of the European Union in March 2011, which stated that education and training have a fundamental role to play in achieving the Europe 2020 objectives of smart, sustainable and inclusive growth, notably by equipping citizens with the skills and competences that the European economy and European society need in order to remain competitive and innovative, but also by helping to promote social cohesion and inclusion (Council of the EU 2011a). The Council conclusions noted the particular relevance of two of the proposed Europe 2020 'flagship' initiatives: the *Agenda for New Skills and Jobs* (EC 2010b), designed to upgrade skills and boost employability, and the *Youth on the Move* initiative (EC 2010c), designed to help young people improve their employment prospects.

Hence, since the early 1990s, employment policy has undergone several shifts. Under the Delors Presidency (1985–1994), it was largely focused on classic demand management—stimulating jobs to combat unemployment—but the *Competitiveness* White Paper in 1993 initiated a subtle transformation as it introduced additional supply-side human resource development initiatives to underpin productivity and competitiveness, as well as active labor market policies to facilitate reintegration of the unemployed. Toward the end of the 1990s, a clearer consensus emerged around the utility of supply-side measures in employment policy, with demand-side mechanisms focusing less on direct job creation than on removing barriers to employment by reducing nonwage labor costs and stimulating entrepreneurship. From the Luxembourg Process introduced in November 1997, through the Lisbon objectives agreed in 2000 to the Europe 2020 strategy adopted in 2010, the principal approach to raising the employment rate has been via supply-side employability initiatives even if the term employability was withdrawn from the policy vocabulary, perhaps, in response to crisis, in favor of broader (and benign) terms such as 'flexicurity'.

With this changing emphasis, NRP reports have no explicit 'employability initiatives' as was the case in the earlier NAPEs. However the Employment Guidelines remain presented (since October 2010) under four directly relevant themes: increasing labor market participation of women and men, reducing structural unemployment and promoting job quality; developing a skilled workforce responding to labor market needs and promoting lifelong learning; improving the quality and performance of education and training systems at all levels and increasing participation in tertiary or equivalent education; and promoting social inclusion and combating poverty. These represent recurrent themes throughout the period and will be used to structure the analysis of country initiatives in the following section. The focus is on active measures to combat unemployment and promote employment; training, lifelong learning and human capital development; and inclusion and the labor market integration of disadvantaged groups. Space precludes detailed quotation from the NRP reports, but in the following section, our comments relate to the countries identified in the introduction: Belgium, France, Germany and the UK among the 'old EU15'; and Lithuania, Malta, Romania and Slovenia among the 'new' EU member states.

DIVERSITY IN ACTIONS TO PROMOTE EMPLOYABILITY IN MEMBER STATES

Before considering the NAPEs and NRP reports of different EU member states, it is important to enter a number of caveats. Given the nature of the reporting and review system described above, governments are driven to present their policies in ways that appear to address the priorities of the Employment Guidelines, whether these are genuine innovations or a simple repackaging of more or less substantial interventions. In addition, the actual implementation and impact of these policies is difficult to assess. Employment rates, for example, are subject to diverse economic influences. What can be said is that where policy documents are weak on employability initiatives, there is unlikely to be much actually happening on the ground. In considering the content of the NRPs, we return to the three broad areas: unemployment and employment; training and development; and inclusion.

Unemployment

Measures to combat unemployment and promote employability are predictably ubiquitous in country approaches to addressing the Employment Guidelines. An overview of the NRPs in 2011 highlighted major concerns that are found across member states (Council of the EU 2011b). These included continuing high levels of unemployment,including long-term unemployment compounded by striking regional disparities and a concern about rising rates of youth unemployment. The social impact of joblessness in terms of poverty and family welfare remains a major worry. Overall, however, the Council offers a positive perspective on the impacts of the NRPs with progress toward the EU employment rates and bottlenecks in the labor market that hamper employment creation identified and addressed in many countries. Employment challenges remain centered on young and older people, women, the low-skilled, and migrants. The need to develop further inclusive labor markets, especially by developing effective enabling services is identified as a continuing priority. At the same time, the adequacy of social security and pensions provision is a concern, especially in countries in which the need to tackle debt is a macroeconomic priority. In sum, progress is being made in difficult circumstances, but important challenges remain, and much more must be done.

Analysis of the national NRP reports suggests a number of categorizations of country approaches to employability. An obvious distinction is between older/larger EU member states and the newer, mostly smaller countries. The former detail initiatives based on more developed policy and resource foundations, whereas the latter tend to report developments that are foundation-building and at an earlier stage of adjustment to the requirements of the EU and adaptation to labor market needs. Thus, for, example, Slovenia reports initiatives to ensure its Employment Service meets demand; Romania reports similar upgrading of its Public Employment System in labor market forecasting; Lithuania reports the need to develop a skill base in labor market analysis. While these differences are explicable in terms of national economies and degrees of EU integration, they reinforce the need for capacity-building activities around labor market policy design and implementation.

The priorities established by the Lisbon Summit provided an organizing principle for the NRPs, but inevitably, countries adopted different approaches and emphases within their responses. Thus, for example, the 2005–2008 NRPs took the five 'headline targets' noted above as a useful organizing principle. Subsequently, for the 2008–2010 NRPs, countries adapted changing EU priorities to include, for example, revisions to the Integrated Guidelines for Growth and Jobs, and country-specific Economic Committee recommendations and 'points to watch' that emerged from assessment of the 2005–2008 phase. A first set of initiatives emerging from the two NRP phases responds to the need for active measures to combat unemployment and promote employment. Here, contextual factors are important. The provision of macroeconomic stability, coupled with a return to growth, is universally seen as a precondition for reduced unemployment and new jobs. Reduced or stable public sector expenditure is a common focus, as is reform of tax and pension regimes. In this context, many countries report related emphases in, for example, increased labor market flexibility, productivity enhancement, ICT development, innovation strategies, R&D, support for and training in entrepreneurship, and reducing the cost of a job for business. In a number of countries (Romania and Slovenia, for example), the problems created by the informal economy and 'undeclared work' are also policy targets. Thus, across the NRPs, both macroeconomic and microeconomic measures are promoted as a foundation for future employment.

Employment-related initiatives can be ordered in terms of infrastructure, preferred interventions and target groups. In terms of infrastructure, many countries have initiated significant reorganization and capacity building in labor market services to tackle employment issues. More commonly (but not exclusively) in the newer member states, it is clear that a combination of challenges—growth, productivity, long-term unemployment, vulnerable groups, social inclusion and demographic change—has moved governments to upgrade their employment services. The idea of integrated services is also widespread, as can be seen in the UK's move to combined employment and skill provision.

The NRPs also reveal a wide range of preferred interventions. Targeted interventions are very common, focusing on specific groups such as LTU or those living in rural areas. Others have turned to SMEs as a focus for job creation, and/or tried to identify 'job-creating' sectors in which employment opportunities might emerge more quickly. The identification of bottlenecks in the labor market, and policies to remove them, is common, often by relaxing employment protection legislation and reducing rigidities in working-time arrangements. Subsidies to companies to promote training and retain employment also occur. Migration is also a concern for several countries. For example, Lithuania has established a labor market analysis facility to identify factors affecting emigration and develop measures to 'repatriate national skills', while Romania is developing a management system for labor migration.

Training

A second set of initiatives addresses training, lifelong learning and human capital development. A pervasive theme is that institutional arrangements require renovation or restructuring to meet contemporary needs whether in formal education (from pre- to postcompulsory), in vocational education and training (VET), in lifelong learning, or in specialist programs. This may involve configuring basic provision, as is often the case for newer member states, or more sophisticated, integrated approaches. The compulsory education system comes under scrutiny in many countries and measures proposed to raise performance include improved physical infrastructure, curricula reform (sometimes emphasizing development over exam-driven achievement), entrepreneurship training, improved ICT skills, more sophisticated teacher training and a clear focus on improved school-to-work transition in preparing students for the modern labor market. Linked to this is the ambition to reduce the numbers of early school leavers, as well as improving the quality and relevance of higher education in terms of the labor market.

National qualification systems are also targeted for rationalization or renovation, with core competences such as literacy and ICT as key areas for action, including VET. Areas commonly identified for development include improved funding, engagement with sectoral needs, and better integration with labor market requirements, including the need to respond to new occupational skills in ICT and the service sector. Also addressed is the issue of incentives for business to adopt a more active training role, including tax advantages and subsidies for training. Developments in apprenticeships, in 'on the job' experience, and in flexible skills are common concerns in these strategies, often targeted to particular groups in the labor market, such as 'women returners' and the LTU. There is also a high-skills focus on promoting emerging sectors such as biotechnology. A recurring leitmotif is also 'lifelong learning', which is presented as for an integrated life-cycle approach to training and development. However, like employability, the concept is all too often linked to a shift of responsibility from the state and employers to the learning motivations and capabilities of the individual (Keep 2000).

Inclusion

A related, third set of initiatives addresses inclusion and the labor market integration of disadvantaged groups. Target groups are universal, reflecting generalized labor market pressures across Europe as well as EU policy priorities, and comprise young people; the LTU; the low skilled; women; identified minorities; older workers; people with disabilities; migrant workers; people in particular regions and sectors; and other disadvantaged groups. Women are a particular focus for intervention and issues relate to work-life balance and family-friendly considerations, flexible work arrangements, and child-care and preschool education provision. One example is Malta, which has the lowest female employment rate in Europe. In 2005–2008, it funded (via the European Social Fund) childcare facilities at work, and broader family-friendly measures throughout the public sector; it also reviewed its tax and benefits systems to reduce disincentives for women to work. Similarly, for 2008–2010, Malta implemented training initiatives for women, particularly women returners, and further improved childcare services including the introduction of tax breaks for parents using such facilities. However, it was also recognized that the major obstacle to women's employment remained culture and attitudes—hence, a growing emphasis on full-time education.

The modernization or reform of welfare and pensions systems is another area impacting on discussions about inclusion, although these matters are sometimes opaque in the NRPs. Affordability questions driven by demographic changes and austerity have led to considerations such as raising the retirement age. Analysis of the NRPs suggests that these debates are likely to continue, and will be driven by macroeconomic settings across Europe. While labor market inclusion and training provision may be driven by domestic priorities, taken in conjunction with EU priorities and advice, the configuration of welfare and pension provision will be more likely driven by shifts in the global economy, mediated by EU priorities and national economic performance.

Looking across the member states considered, all NRP reports are aligned with the EU policy framework in general and address the Lisbon/Europe 2020 objectives in particular, though member states are of course thus obliged. Inevitably most action is focused on reintegrating the LTU, disadvantaged and excluded into the labor market and to raising the employability of school leavers and workers 'at risk' of joining the unemployed. Governments are clearly aware of the dangers of neglecting the *inclusion* agenda, and rightly so, but in so doing, the *high-skills* agenda appears somewhat marginalized. Europe 2020 presents a roadmap for building EU competitiveness through raising intermediate and higher-level skills, yet the NRPs appear to be preoccupied with basic skills. There is surprisingly little deviation from this prioritization, even in 'high-skill equilibrium' countries like France and Germany, and this is probably because unemployment disproportionately affects youth (lacking work experience) and older workers (with fewer relevant qualifications).

CONCLUSIONS

Analysis of the NRP reports reveals significant variation with respect to particular supply-side interventions, and this often reflects differences both in labor market conditions and in preexisting infrastructure and capacity for intervention. That said, the challenge of realigning existing institutions may in some cases be greater than that of establishing new purpose-built capacity, providing there is adequate stakeholder engagement. Notwithstanding the difficulty of separating intentions from actions in NRPs, there is also substantial variation between member states in the financial, legal and administrative resources committed. Most of the transition economies lack resources commensurate with the scale of the problems faced, although in smaller countries (in general) problems do not appear to be overwhelming.

The need to 'modernize' social dialogue is seen as important in a number of countries. In France, a national intersectoral agreement led to the Law of 31 January 2007 on modernizing social dialogue. In the six months leading up to the presidential campaign in March 2012, an unprecedented number of national intersectoral agreements were negotiated: four concerned social protection measures, including pensions and unemployment insurance, while another four adressed the employment of young people. The subtext here appears to be that existing social dialogue is not necessarily attuned to the challenges of contemporary labor markets or the wider economy. Hence, while European commitment to social dialogue is reemphasized, the requirement that it adapts to, for example, the need for greater labor market flexibility and adaptability, is also at the fore. The question is compounded by different national traditions of social dialogue. One issue that arises in a number of countries is the need for improved wage determination along with wage moderation, as foundations for future growth. This is broadly in tune with the macroeconomic commitments common across all countries. The differences between most of the new member states (except Slovenia, Malta and Cyprus) and the old EU15 are particularly apparent with respect to social dialogue and in particular the weakness of trade unions. In the NMS the issues are about establishing sustainable social partner institutions and social dialogue structures beyond the fragile Economic and Social Committees that were established in line with EU entry conditions. This is in contrast to, say, France, where low union density does not preclude significant social dialogue at all levels (Winterton and Strandberg 2004; Winterton 2007). Yet, while governments in the new member states are grappling with developing economic growth, institutional arrangements for social dialogue are likely to remain a low priority in the absence of external pressures to bear.

In conclusion, we offer some observations on the journey that employability appears to have taken since the concept rose to prominence in European discourse, dealing respectively with theory, policy and practice. First, as a concept, employability is seen to suffer from a considerable degree of confusion and ambiguity, which is partly explicable by the tendency to focus on supply-side issues in pursuit of global competitiveness. Yet raising the employability of individuals may be a distraction, or even counterproductive, if one ignores the insufficiency of demand for (quality) labor. Faced with this theoretical ambiguity, it is possible to critique the notion and terminology as a mechanism for 'blaming the victims': whereas unemployment is caused by a shortage of job opportunities, 'unemployability' is attributed to deficiencies in the competence of individuals. In these times of high unemployment, 'employability' has also become less a high-skills strategy than a concept associated with the LTU, workers at risk and difficulties in school-to-work transition.

This might explain why, in policy terms, employability has passed from the first, and most important, pillar of the EES to the ghost at the banquet in current NRP reports. While many of the initiatives discussed above (active measures, training and inclusion strategies) are clearly designed to address employability concerns, the absence of employability as an explicit headline term is in stark contrast with its pervasiveness a decade ago. To some extent this represents mainstreaming of employability, which has become so thoroughly embedded that it is driving the Lisbon and Europe 2020 objectives and associated strategies for education and training. At the same time, it is apparent that adopting alternative vocabularies deflects criticism of employability interventions that might be interpreted as attempts to blame or stigmatize the victims of unemployment in a time of severe economic crisis.

In terms of practice, or at least practice as outlined in NRP reports, inevitably the actions put in place in each member state are context-specific and driven by their macroeconomic setting. While all member states are addressing a common agenda in the BEPGs, there is substantial diversity in practical initiatives and outcomes reflecting, say, the length of EU membership and specific labor market context. Initiatives need to be culturally and institutionally specific. Are, for example, employability measures deemed appropriate for addressing the low level of labor market participation of women in Malta, which is rooted in deep cultural traditions and social norms, appropriate elsewhere? Is the UK's attempt to establish a highly integrated supply-side approach to training and labor market inclusion also readily transferable?

The fundamental question remains as to how far supply-side employability interventions can stimulate demand for labor by demonstrating that human capital is available, especially in support of a 'high-road' approach to restructuring European economies. In the current context of global structural shift, Eurozone financial crisis and national sovereign debt, there is little evidence that employability initiatives offer more than a marginal impact on employment rates, and there is no reason for assuming that this will change in the near future. What is clear, however, is that there is an urgent need, not seen since the Great Depression, for action to create employment and thereby to support employability in Europe.

REFERENCES

Ashton, D., Maguire, M., and Spilsbury, M. 1990. *Restructuring the Labour Market: The Implications for Youth*. London: Macmillan.
Baruch, Y. 2001. 'Employability: A substitute for loyalty?' *Human Resource Development International*, 4:4. 543–566.
Brown, P., Hesketh, A. and Williams, S. 2003. 'Employability in a knowledge-driven economy', *Journal of Education and Work*, 16:2. 107–120.

Campbell, M. 2000. 'Employability, adaptability and flexibility: Changing labour market prospects', *Regional Studies*, 34. 655–668.

CBI 1999. *Making Employability Work: An Agenda for Action*. London: Confederation of British Industry.

Council of the European Union 2011a. 'Council conclusions on the role of education and training in the implementation of the "Europe 2020" strategy' (2011/C 70/01). Brussels, 3 April. Available at: <http://eurlex.europa.eu/JOHtml.do?uri= OJ:C:2011:070:SOM:EN:HTML>

———. 2011b. 'Examination of the National Reform Programmes 2011—Joint Opinion of the Employment Committee and the Social Protection Committee', 10664/11, Brussels, June.

Danau, D., Koutsivitou, A., Tortopidis, A. and Winterton, J. 2000. *Factors for Success: A Compendium of Social Partner Initiatives Relating to the Employment Guidelines of the European Employment Strategy*. Brussels: CEEP, ETUC and UNICE/UEAPME.

Ellig, B. R. 1998. 'Employment and employability: Foundation of the new social contract', *Human Resource Management*, 37. 173–175.

European Commission 1993. *Growth, Competitiveness, and Employment: The Challenges and Ways Forward into the 21st Century*, COM (93) 700 final. Brussels, 05.12.1993.

———. 2002. 'Commission's Action Plan for Skills and Mobility', COM (2002) 72 final. Brussels, 13.2.2002.

———. 2003a. 'The future of the European Employment Strategy (EES): A strategy for full employment and better jobs for all', COM/2003/0006 final.

———. 2003b. 'Proposal for a Council Decision on Guidelines for the Employment Policies of the Member States', COM/2003/0176, 8 April.

———. 2005. 'Restructuring and Employment: Anticipating and Accompanying Restructuring in Order to Develop Employment: The Role of the European Union', COM (2005) 120 final. Brussels, 31/03/05.

———. 2008. 'New Skills for New Jobs: Anticipating and Matching Labour Market and Skills Needs', COM(2008) 868 final. Brussels, 16/12/08.

———. 2010a. 'Communication from the Commission to the European Parliament, the Council, the European Economic and Social Committee and the Committee of the Regions, *Europe 2020: A strategy for smart, sustainable and inclusive growth*', COM (2010) 2010 final. Brussels, 03/03/10.

———. 2010b. 'Communication from the Commission to the European Parliament, the Council, the European Economic and Social Committee and the Committee of the Regions, *An Agenda for New Skills and Jobs: A European Contribution towards Full Employment*', COM (2010) 682 final. Strasbourg, 23/11/10.

———. 2010c. 'Communication from the Commission to the European Parliament, the Council, the European Economic and Social Committee and the Committee of the Regions, *Youth on the Move: An Initiative to Unleash the Potential of Young People to Achieve Smart, Sustainable And Inclusive Growth in the European Union*, COM(2010) 477 final.

European Council 2000. Presidency Conclusions, Lisbon, 23 and 24 March 2000: Council of the European Union. Brussels: Nr: 100/1/00.

Evans, C., Nathan, M. and Simmonds, D. 1999. *Employability through Work*. Manchester: Centre for Local Economic Strategies.

Evans, M. 2001. 'Britain: Moving towards a work and opportunity-focused welfare state?' *International Journal of Social Welfare*, 10:4. 260–266.

Finn, D. 2000. 'From full employment to full employability: A new deal for Britain's unemployed?' *International Journal of Manpower*, 21:5. 384–399.

Foden, D. 1999. 'The role of the social partners in the European Employment Strategy', *Transfer*, 5:4. 522–541.

Gazier, B. (ed.) 1998. *Employability: Concepts and Policies*. Berlin: European Employment Observatory.

Gazier B. 2001. 'Employability: The complexity of a policy notion' in P. Weinert, M. Baukens, P. Bollérot, M. Pineschi-Gapènne and U. Walwei (eds.) *Employability: From Theory to Practice*. New Brunswick, NJ: Transaction Books. 3–23.

Goetschy, J. 1999. 'The European Employment Strategy: Genesis and development', *European Journal of Industrial Relations*, 5:2. 117–137.

Hemerijck, A. and Kuin, R. 1999. 'Entrepreneurship policy in an employment-friendly welfare state—the case of the Netherlands' in D. Foden and L. Magnusson (eds.) *Entrepreneurship in the European Employment Strategy*. Brussels: ETUI. 98–131.

Hespanha, P. and Møller, I. H. 2001. 'Activation policies and social inclusion in Denmark and Portugal', *Transfer*, 7:1. 54–73.

Hillage, J. and Pollard, E. 1998. *Employability: Developing a Framework for Policy Analysis*. Research Briefing No. 85. London: Department for Education and Employment.

HM Treasury 1997. *Treasury Press Release 122/97, 13th October: Gordon Brown Unveils UK Employment Action Plan*. London: HM Treasury.

———. 2001. *European Economic Reform: Meeting the Challenge*. London: HM Treasury.

Hollywood, E., Lindsay, C., McQuaid, R. and Winterton, J. 2000. *Changing Perceptions: A Study of the Long-Term Unemployed in Five Areas of Edinburgh*. Edinburgh: City of Edinburgh Council.

Jessop, B. 1992. 'Towards a Schumpeterian workfare state? Preliminary remarks on post-Fordist political economy', *Studies in Political Economy*, 40. 7–40.

Keep, E. 2000. 'Learning organizations, lifelong learning and the mystery of the vanishing employers', *Economic Outlook*, 24:4. 18–26.

Kleinman, M., West, A. and Sparkes, J. 1998. *Investing in Employability: The Roles of Business and Government in the Transition to Work*. London: London School of Economics.

Kok, W. 2004. 'Facing the Challenge: The Lisbon Strategy for Growth and Employment'. Report from the High Level Group chaired by Wim Kok, November.

Lefresne, F. 1999. 'Employability at the heart of the European employment strategy', *Transfer*, 5:4. 460–80.

Lindsay, C. 2002. 'Long-term unemployment and the "employability gap": Priorities for renewing Britain's New Deal', *Journal of European Industrial Training*, 26:9. 411–419.

Lindsay, C., McCracken, M. and McQuaid, R. W. 2003. 'Unemployment duration and employability in remote rural labour markets', *Journal of Rural Studies*, 19:2. 187–200.

Lindsay, C. and Serrano Pascual, A. 2009. 'New perspectives on employability and labour market policy: Reflecting on key issues', *Environment and Planning C: Government and Policy*, 27:6. 951–957.

McQuaid, R. W. and Lindsay, C. 2002. 'The employability gap: Long-term unemployment and barriers to work in buoyant labour markets', *Environment and Planning C: Government and Policy*, 20:4. 213–268.

———. 2005. 'The concept of employability', *Urban Studies*, 42:2. 197–219.

OECD 1994. *The OECD Jobs Study: Evidence and Explanations. Part I: Labour Market Trends and Underlying Forces of Change*. Paris: Organization for Economic Cooperation and Development.

Peck, J. and Theodore, N. 2000 'Beyond employability', *Cambridge Journal of Economics*, 24:6. 729–749.

Philpott, J. 1999. *Behind the 'Buzzword': Employability*. London: Employment Policy Institute.

Serrano Pascual, A. (ed.) 2004. *Are Activation Policies Converging in Europe? The European Employment Strategy for Young People*. Brussels: ETUI.

———. 2009. 'The battle of ideas in the European field: The combat to defeat unemployment and the struggle to give it a name', *Transfer*, 15:1. 53–70.

Streeck, W. 1989. 'Skills and the limits of neo-liberalism: The enterprise of the future as a place of learning', *Work, Employment and Society*, 3:1. 89–104.

Stuart, M., Cook, H., Cutter, J. and Winterton, J. 2010. *Assessing the Impact of Union Learning and the Union Learning Fund: Union and Employer Perspectives*. Centre for Employment Relations Innovation and Change, Policy Report No. 4. Leeds: Leeds University Business School.

Tomkin, P. and Hillage, J. 1999. *Employability and Employers: The Missing Piece of the Jigsaw*. Report 361. Brighton: Institute for Employment Studies.

Winterton, J. 2007. 'Building social dialogue over training and learning: European and national developments', *European Journal of Industrial Relations*, 13:3. 281–300.

Winterton, J. and Strandberg, T. 2004. 'European social dialogue: Evaluation and critical assessment' in B. Galgóczi, C. Lafoucriere and L. Magnusson (eds.) *The Enlargement of Social Europe: The role of Social Partners in the European Employment Strategy*. Brussels: European Trade Union Institute. 21–76.

11 The 'State of Affairs' of Flexicurity in Industrial Relations

Assessing Country Performance Using Transition Indicators

Ton Wilthagen, Ruud Muffels and Heejung Chung

INTRODUCTION

Labor markets and industrial relations systems have dramatically changed since the early 1990s due to cultural (e.g., individualization) and structural (e.g., globalization, aging) developments. In its influential 1997 Green Paper on 'Partnership for a New Organization of Work', the European Commission emphasized the importance of improving flexibility on the one hand and safeguarding security on the other, while acknowledging difficulties due to these ongoing cultural and structural shifts. Hence, the distinct concept of flexicurity entered into Europe's policy agenda, notably within the framework of the European Employment Strategy (EES). In 2007 the European Parliament endorsed a resolution entitled 'Common Principles of Flexicurity' in response to a Commission Communication, and the Council then adopted eight common principles of flexicurity emphasizing the need for contractual flexibility, active labor market policies and lifelong learning. The policy framework now consists of Common Principles, Employment Guidelines, components and typical pathways, agreed upon by the European Council but stressing the need to adapt to local circumstances and include the social partners. Within the new EES for 2020, and also within the EU's response to the impact of the economic crisis on employment (the so-called Employment Package; European Commission 2012), flexicurity is maintained as the dominant policy framework, encompassing social dialogue, which is seen as a key condition for developing integrative and balanced reform packages.

Much of what has been achieved or will be achieved in terms of flexicurity policies at the national level depends upon developments at the company and business sector level. One example is the extensive use of short-time practices in German companies following the 2008 crisis, involving 1.2 million workers (Schmid 2011). On the other hand, there are examples showing a different picture. Most particularly, the recent crisis showed the growing importance of temporary labor for swift adjustment to adverse economic shocks (IMF 2010). The increase in temporary work in Europe since the 1990s (Arrowsmith 2006) reflects both increasing competition and uncertainty, combined with the so-called 'honeymoon' effect in labor markets with strong mechanisms of protection (Boeri and Garibaldi 2007). This means that employers are generally more reluctant to hire permanent workers due to the high transaction costs in terms of time and money involved in the event of layoffs. The temporary workforce operates under these conditions as a flexible buffer in modern industrial relations systems. This so-called numerical flexibilization of the worforce seems to have accelerated in a number of countries in Europe after the wake of the financial crisis in 2008 and the subsequent debt crisis in 2010. At another level, flexicurity can also entail company training and lifelong learning practices, varieties of 'employee-friendly' flexible working-time arrangement and other employee-centered measures, which may be negotiated with the social partners (see Chung et al. 2007 for more on company practices).

Reflecting perhaps the diversity not only of the types of policies but also with regard to the levels in which flexicurity can be implemented, no clear framework has been developed yet that enables a comparison of flexicurity policies across countries (Chung 2012). This lack of a framework, and even more so a lack of a commonly defined concept of flexicurity, means it is difficult to monitor or assess the effectiveness of flexicurity policies (especially in times of crisis or other socioeconomic change). Thus, the focus of this chapter is to develop a framework for the evaluation and monitoring of flexicurity policies and practices operating at various levels of authority—the European, the national and more decentralized levels, in particular the company level. This conceptual and evaluative framework is then used to map countries on the basis of their flexibility-security performance and to empirically assess the state of affairs of flexicurity and work-life balance policies and (company) practices in the European Union. Although the empirical timeframe under investigation is limited to the period 2005–2007/2008, due to availability of data, the results found in the paper allow us to test the viability of the framework as well as to make wider inferences concerning the outcomes of flexicurity policies in different socioeconomic conditions.

METHODOLOGICAL FRAMEWORK

A Dynamic Framework for Monitoring Flexicurity

Flexicurity has been heralded as one of the underlying key concepts in the ongoing transformation of employment relations, reconfirmed in the Europe 2020 agenda that is focused on endorsing smart, sustainable and inclusive growth (European Commission 2010). A constructive social dialogue is considered a crucial precondition for developing integrative and well-balanced reform packages at the national and sector level, and the social partners are expected to actively engage in an 'industrial relations of flexicurity'. The European-level social partners made a significant contribution with a joint analysis of flexicurity and labor market challenges in 2007, and a recent study shows that 'though not always in direct reference to the flexicurity concept and often driven by different concerns and priorities—social partners are actively contributing to reform processes and solutions', thus supporting the implementation of the key dimensions of the EU's Common Principles on Flexicurity (Voss and Dornelas 2011, p.68; see also Pedersini 2008 and Wilthagen 2007).

However, the way flexicurity is implemented is not necessarily sufficiently balanced in terms of promoting security as well as flexibility across different countries. This imbalance in the actual implementation of the flexicurity concept (rather than in the original design; see Wilthagen 1998; Wilthagen and Tros 2004; European Expert Group on Flexicurity 2007) is reported in various studies and critical commentaries (e.g., Pedersini 2008; Keune 2008; Keune and Jepsen 2007). The design and implementation of flexicurity policies in the member states is, therefore, not uncontested in the social dialogue at European and national levels.

It is for these reasons of ambiguity—as well as the importance of the issue—that any assessment of the empirical developments of the components of flexicurity requires a sound methodology. This chapter starts from the premise that process-oriented institutional and dynamic outcome indicators at various levels are a prerequisite for the stocktaking of countries' progress in improving the balancing of flexibility and security goals. This is clearly expressed by the director of the Lisbon Council who, referring to Europe 2020, the current ten-year strategy for the EU, stressed the need for 'a concerted effort to find measurements that can capture the notion of change, of dynamics, of movements in the economy and society' (Mettler 2009, p.647).

Flexicurity as State of Affairs

Following Wilthagen (2005), the concept of flexicurity can be understood both as a 'state of affairs' and as a 'policy strategy', where policies also refer to practices at lower levels of authority such as sector and company (see also Chung 2012). To assess and monitor the way flexicurity is implemented at the country level a 'stocks-flows-outcomes' or 'capabilities-transitions-outcomes' (CTO) approach is proposed. The capabilities or stocks refer to the various forms of capital a country has built up, considered as capacities constituting the basic conditions for implementation of flexicurity. The transitions or flows part refers to the labor market transitions that people experience, or labor market dynamics. Outcomes measure the implementation results in terms of attaining a proper balance of flexibility and security. This balance is indicated as a 'state of affairs' because it is not a static but a dynamic concept, which refers to a continuous monitoring of implementation outcomes. The CTO approach fundamentally rests on an 'agency-structure' perspective, where agency refers to the behavior of individual actors like employers and workers in the labor market, and structure to labor market institutions and (company) practices. The monitoring of flexicurity outcomes therefore concerns the attained level of different types of flexibility (numerical, functional) and the various types of security such as income and employment security and work-life balance. In terms of defining indicators, the *agency* part asks for indicators measuring the capabilities or stocks, the transitions or flows, and the outcomes and the *structure* part for institutional and policy indicators.

The conceptual model is shown as Figure 11.1. Indicators are developed for each of the four domains of flexicurity policies (European Commission 2007): Lifelong Learning (LLL); Flexible Contractual Arrangements (FCA); Active Labour Market Policies (ALMP) and Modern Social Security Systems (MSS). *Outcomes* deal with a variety of dimensions—that is, economic, social and environmental (the three overarching goals of the EU)—and the overall approach is theoretically inspired by the capability approach of Sen and resembles recent work for the French Presidency of the EU in the field of economic welfare (Stiglitz, Sen and Fitoussi 2009). *Capabilities* refer to

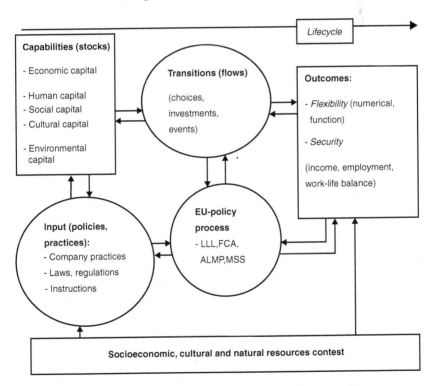

Figure 11.1 Flexicurity as a 'state of affairs': A capabilities-transitions-outcomes (CTO) or stocks-flows-outcome approach

Notes: LLL = Lifelong learning; FCA = Flexible contractual arrangements; ALMP = Active labor market policies; MSS = Modern social security systems

the freedoms or opportunities people have to achieve the things in life they have reason to value most (e.g., Sen 1993). These reflect the 'free choices' of people, which are hard to measure, so for indicator purposes the idea is to use proxies for capabilities as indicating amounts of economic capital (GDP per capita), human capital (education, work experience), social capital (contacts, social networks), cultural capital (preferences, values, attitudes) and environmental capital (sustainable resources and institutions). However, for the transitions and outcomes direct yardsticks can be defined derived from various data sources.

Evaluating Country Performance Using Flexicurity Transition Indicators

The idea here is to use a limited set of flexicurity indicators to assess the way countries implement flexicurity policies and thereby map the countries using these flexibility and security indicators. Compared to existing approaches in the literature, we argue for defining transition flexibility and security indicators at the various national, sector and company levels of industrial relations systems. To clarify the approach in more detail we explain for the national level the type of indicators proposed (as listed in Table 11.1) and how they are defined and calculated. The set of indicators derived from the CTO framework distinguishes outcome from institutional indicators and static from transition indicators. Capabilities (stocks) are measured by static indicators, the choices and events (flows) by dynamic or transition indicators and the policies and practices by institutional indicators. Eventually, the outcomes are measured by either static or dynamic outcome indicators. Various indicators are defined for the four domains of Flexible Contractual Arrangements (FCA)—i.e., MSS, including work-life balance security (WLB), LLL and ALMP. We only discuss the set of transition indicators because the treatment of static and institutional indicators on these domains would not add much to the existing literature (see Manca et al. 2010; Bachmann et al. 2011). These transition outcome indicators aim to measure the level and change of labor market mobility on the one hand and the level and change of income and employment security and work-life balance security on the other. Taken together, the sets of transition outcome indicators measure the achievement of a country in safeguarding a balance between transition-flexibility and transition-security. The idea here is not to set up a new system of indicators as there are already many attempts to design such a comprehensive system (e.g., Bachmann et al. 2011), but rather to show the added value of transition indicators on the various policy domains.

There are several data sources that can provide information on these transition outcome indicators. The two most important are the European Labour Force Survey and the EU Statistics on Income and Living Conditions Survey (SILC). In this chapter we use in particular the longitudinal SILC data covering the period 2005–2007/2008 to examine the performance

Table 11.1   Transition flexibility and security indicators on the four EU flexicurity domains

---

I. *Flexible and Contractual Arrangements:*

A. *Transition-flexibility indicators*

 – transitions between jobs (job mobility)

 – transitions between contract statuses (contract mobility)

 – transitions between wage levels (wage mobility)

B. *Employment transition security indicators*

 – transitions between different statuses of 'employment security' to show the differences across countries in the way they achieve employment transition security

 – transitions between different working time patterns (part-time; fulltime)

II. *Life-long Learning (LLL) and Active Labour Market Policies (ALMP)*

 – transitions by employment status and pay level

 – transitions into permanent and temporary jobs after participation in education or training courses

 – transitions between unemployment and employment statuses (job gain/ re-entry, job loss/exit)

 – the probability to re-enter employment conditional on the length of stay in unemployment (based on monthly status information in SILC) for different social groups (using the calendar information for 2005–2006) being a duration measure of employment transition security

III. *Modern Social Security Systems (MSS): Transition income security*

 – upward or downward income transitions, transitions in low-wage mobility and transitions in income security (moving in and out of income poverty) indicating transition income security (the so-called YSD measure).

IV. *Combination security or Work-life Balance (WLB) security*

 – percent of women in employment and working time arrangements disaggregated by life-course stage (from being at school, forming a family, empty nest to retirement)

 – time spent to work and caring duties for different families and work-care combinations

 – percent of persons in work-care combinations for different types of households

 – transitions between work-care combinations across two years aimed at defining a measure for WLB transition security using the SILC data.

Source: Muffels et al. (2011).

of countries in balancing flexibility and security and changes therein over time (see also Muffels et al. 2011). In a few instances we supplement these with the European Community Household Panel (ECHP) survey covering the period 1994–2001; in the third section we discuss the situation for the mid-2000s compared to the mid-1990s; unfortunately, there is a lack of longitudinal information stretching over the entire period between the early 1990s and the late 2000s.

These transition indicators need of course to be supplemented with static outcome and static and dynamic institutional indicators, in which the latter show the improvement in outcomes at the various levels including the company level due to particular policies and practices. Longitudinal data on institutional indicators and effects at the national level are not readily available (due to lack of data); hence in most studies static indicators are used. The longitudinal information available at the company level is scarce and isolated. There is, however, ample static information at national and company levels such as that included in the 2009 European Company Survey (ECS) of the European Foundation (Eurofound) in Dublin. We will present some indicators on wage bargaining and flexible working-time arrangements using the ECS in the fourth section.

Evaluating Country Performance Using Indicators at Sector and Company Level

In addition to outcome indicators at the country level, the outcomes of flexicurity practices are also relevant as part of the industrial relations systems implemented at sector or company level. In a 2008 report by the European Foundation entitled 'Flexicurity and Industrial Relations' (Pedersini 2008), a distinction is made between the political, regulatory and unilateral dimensions of the social partners' role in the flexicurity domain. The first dimension refers to the social partners' national-level role in the design of flexicurity policies, the second to the role in the collective bargaining processes at sector and company levels, and the unilateral role to the services (e.g., training, job placement, social security) provided by trade unions and employers organizations to their members. The Eurofound report also classified countries according to these three dimensions (Table 11.2). Most countries score high on their involvement at the political dimension or central level, but at the same time many countries score significantly lower at the regulatory (14) and especially the unilateral dimension of flexicurity involvement (20). Only five countries score high at the regulatory and unilateral dimension at the same time. Germany and the UK score low on involvement at the national level but high at either the regulatory wage-bargaining level (Germany) or the unilateral level (UK).

The role the social partners can play is shaped by their influence or power, and a proxy often used for the balance of power in industrial relations is trade union density (TUD). Visser (2008) showed that average TUD in EU27 declined from more than 30 percent in 1995/1996 to around 25 percent in

Table 11.2   Analysis of the social partners' role in flexicurity

		Regulatory dimension			
		High		Low	
		Unilateral dimension		Unilateral dimension	
		High	Low	High	Low
Political dimension	High	Ireland, Luxembourg, Portugal, Sweden	Austria, Belgium, Denmark, Finland, France, Italy, Netherlands, Norway, Slovakia	Bulgaria, Malta	Estonia, Hungary, Latvia, Spain, Romania, Slovenia
	Low	Germany		United Kingdom	Cyprus, Czech Republic, Greece, Lithuania, Poland

Source: Pedersini (2008).

2009. The drop is especially strong in Eastern and Baltic countries dropping from 60 percent to less than 20 percent in Lithuania and from more than 30 percent to 15 percent in Poland. A further consideration is Human Resource Management (HRM) policies at the company level. To give one example, training is considered of paramount interest for improving employability and is therefore one of the cornerstones of flexicurity. Using Eurofound's Company Survey data for 2009, the share of companies giving employees time off for training is very different across sectors and across the various regions in Europe. In the public sector this is offered by 75 percent of organizations against 59 percent in the private sector (see Muffels and Wilthagen 2011). The percentage for the public sector is only 42 percent in the Baltic States against 76 percent in the Northwestern part of Europe (the UK, Ireland). For this reason, indicators at the sector and company level will be briefly reviewed in the fourth section of this chapter.

TRANSITION-FLEXIBILITY AND TRANSITION-SECURITY INDICATORS IN FOUR POLICY DOMAINS

Flexible and Contractual Arrangements (FCA): Transition-Flexibility Indicators

The level of job and contract mobility indicates the turnover and volatility in the labor market and is affected by institutions and regulations such as minimum wage schemes, pay systems, unemployment insurance, activating labor market policies, wage bargaining and employment protection laws. Mobility can be voluntarily, where people move because they find a better job match or involuntarily, as when they lose their job due to redundancies, layoffs and business closures. The mobility from a temporary job into a permanent job (part of contractual mobility) provides essential information on the flexibility of the labor market because a low transition rate indicates a poorly operating or even segmented labor market in which there is a shortage of job openings. The EU-SILC data[1] allows us to derive job mobility indicators for most European countries by using a question about whether or not the respondent changed jobs (also involving a change of employer) in the past year. The job mobility indicator we use here is calculated as the percentage of employed people aged 16–64 that changed jobs last year weighted by the share of permanent or temporary contract in employment to arrive at a population-wide estimate. The information is available for twenty-three EU-SILC countries only (see Figure 11.2). The lowest job mobility rates are observed in Luxembourg, Poland, Slovakia, the Czech Republic, Slovenia and Belgium, and the highest in Spain, Norway, Hungary, the UK and Sweden. Spain has a remarkably high level of job mobility that is especially due to a high incidence of temporary contracts. Denmark has lower total job mobility rates than anticipated, for Denmark is known for its relatively lean employment protection (though the figure is downwardly biased due to lack of information on the mobility of workers on temporary contracts). On balance, we consider voluntary mobility in open-ended contracts to be a better measure of flexibility than the sum of hirings and firings or total job mobility in which also fixed-term contract mobility is included.

In Figure 11.3 we present the results for twenty-five EU-SILC countries. Spain now has average mobility since a large part of total mobility was due to extensive fixed-term contracting. The findings show that voluntary job mobility is much larger than involuntary job mobility. The lowest levels of voluntary and involuntary mobility are registered in Poland, Slovenia,

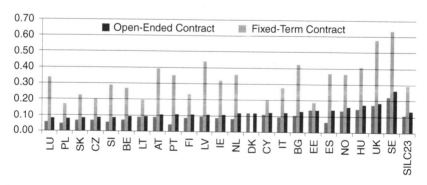

Figure 11.2 Job Mobility of workers in fixed-term and open-ended contracts plus total job mobility, 2007–2008

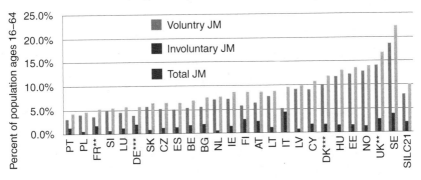

Figure 11.3 Voluntary, involuntary and total job mobility into permanent contracts, 2007–2008 (weighted data)

Germany, Portugal, Luxembourg and France. The UK and Sweden show the highest rates of voluntary as well as involuntary mobility; the UK figures reflect the typical features of an efficiently operating unregulated labor market showing high mobility and turnover, whereas the high figures for Sweden may mirror the preoccupation of Swedish social democracy with employment (e.g., through use of sector-based transition funds).

For Germany and the UK we also have information from socioeconomic panel surveys on the evolution of voluntary job mobility since the early 1990s. Voluntary job mobility (for people aged 16–64) decreased from 14 percent in 1992–1993 to 11 percent in 2007–2008 in the UK and from 8 percent in Germany in 1992–1993 to 4 percent in 2007–2008. We also found that average job tenure did not change much in either country; in Germany from 10.4 years in 1993 and 10.5 years in 2008, and in the UK from 8.1 years in 1993 to 8.7 years in 2008. There is, therefore, no evidence of a strong effect of globalization or increased flexibility on job mobility; on the contrary we observe a significant decline especially in Germany, possibly caused by extensive job growth and the negative effect of aging.

In the next step we used the EU-SILC panel for 2005–2008 and the ECHP for 1994–2001 to view the mobility rates from a temporary job into open-ended contracts and the change in transition rates for some countries over the last decade (since 1997–1998). Segmented labor markets show more volatility because of a high proportion of temporary jobs combined with high entry barriers to permanent work. The mobility rates from temporary jobs into permanent jobs are therefore important and suggest to what extent temporary jobs act as a 'stepping stone' or vehicle for marginalization. Figure 11.4 shows the results. The relatively unregulated labor markets of Ireland and the UK show the highest mobility rates into permanent jobs as do some Eastern and Baltic countries such as Slovakia, Latvia and especially Estonia. Very low mobility rates are found in the Southern countries (Italy, Spain, Cyprus) but also in the Netherlands and especially in Finland

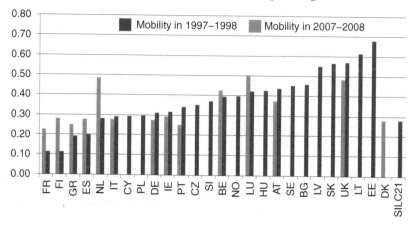

Figure 11.4   Mobility from fixed-term to open-ended contracts in 2007–2008 and change in mobility rates since 1997–1998

and France. The picture for the change in transition rates between the 1990s and the 2000s is mixed; in some countries, notably the Netherlands but also Spain and Greece, the transition rates have dropped, while in others they have risen—though less so in Austria, Portugal and the UK.

The evidence from these data sources shows that there is a negative relation between the incidence of temporary work and the transition into a permanent job. The higher the share of workers in non-standard contracts, the more difficult it is to move into an open-end contract. In Figure 11.5 the relationship is depicted. The evidence also suggests a negative relation between these transition rates and employment protection (see OECD 2010). The 'stricter' the protection of the 'insider' means fewer chances for the outsiders (such as temporary workers) to enter a standard tenured job.

In Figure 11.1 we also listed transition indicators for wage/income mobility and employment transition security. The former refers to transitions into a higher/lower wage job or into or out of income security (or poverty), and the latter to year-to-year changes in employment security due to changing status. Wage transitions are associated with job changes in the internal and external labor market. Employment transition security is defined as the change in employment security due to the change in employment status across two years. Because employment security concerns the nucleus of the flexicurity concept, we developed an employment transition security indicator that is defined as the percentage of people improving their employment security status from year $t - 1$ to t (upward transitions) minus the percentage of people who saw their employment security status reduced (downward transitions) (see Muffels and Luijkx 2008). Figure 11.6 shows the percentage of people improving or worsening their employment transition security status from 2005 to 2006 (ETS-Up versus ETS-Down). We use the SILC 2005–2006 data because it gives a similar picture as for later years but covers twenty-six countries including Denmark, Germany and France, which are not included in the data for later years.

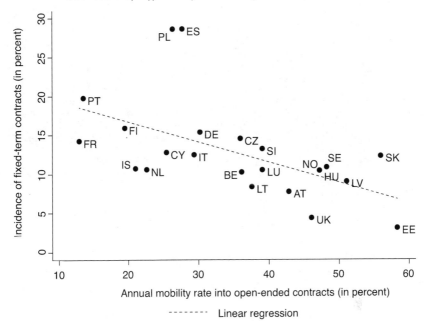

Figure 11.5   The relationship between incidence of fixed-term contracts and job mobility rates into tenured contracts based on SILC data for 2004–2007

Source: Eurostat, EU-SILC Longitudinal Data 2004–2007.

Note: The sample consists of people in temporary contracts in 2004, 2005 and 2006 moving into open-ended contracts one year later. The country score represents the average percentage over the three years for each of the twenty-three EU-SILC countries (no information available for Denmark, Greece and Bulgaria).

Each employment status is assumed to reflect a particular employment security level and the further the distance to the labor market the lower that level of employment security arguably is. In 2009 the indicators group of the Employment Committee of the European Commission (EMCO) agreed on a similar transition security indicator. The highest employment transition security levels are attained by the Nordic countries Sweden, Norway, Denmark and Iceland but with the UK, at a time of relatively buoyant economic performance, very nearby. This shows that high levels of employment security can be achieved in rather different ways.

LIFE LONG LEARNING AND ACTIVE LABOR MARKET POLICIES (LLL/ALMP)

One of the most important components of flexicurity policies is investment in the education and training of workers, as this raises employability and transition security. One indicator therefore concerns the participation in education and training programs either organized outside the firm or

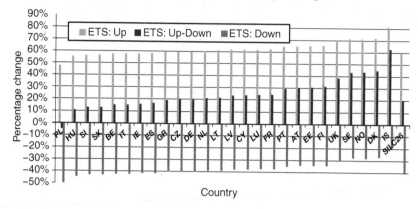

Figure 11.6 Employment transition security (ETS) by country, 2005–2006

offered within firms by employers. Other indicators deal with the duration, the costs, the age-specific participation rate, the kind of qualifications obtained or the type of training (firm-specific or general) and the level of education offered (Mascherini 2008). Here we are concerned with dynamic or transition (rather than institutional) indicators, such as the movement of trainees into better paid or more secure (open-ended) work after training, or the movement of nonworking people into a temporary job or other forms of work. We believe that the larger the share of people moving after training into a fixed-term job and the lower the percentage of people moving into a job with tenure, the worse the labor market performs with a view to rewarding investments in training. From a flexicurity perspective, though, what matters more for an efficiently operating labor market is that people after training are more employable and therefore more employment-secure (instead of more job-secure), meaning that they stay employed but not necessarily with the same employer or in the same job. SILC contains information on training where training is considered the main activity of the person. In Figure 11.7 we depict the results on this particular indicator for the transitions between 2005 and 2006 for the twenty-six EU-SILC countries.

The mobility rates into tenured jobs or open-ended contracts after training are largest in Latvia, the Netherlands, Norway, Denmark and the UK, and lowest in the Southern countries Italy, Spain, Greece and Portugal, but also in Poland, Luxembourg, Belgium, Germany and France. The more regulated countries show the lowest mobility rates into tenured jobs, suggesting that training does not close the entry barriers that 'outsiders' experience in such regimes. In Spain, many people, probably most of them young, move into fixed-term jobs after training.

For active labor market policies a number of static institutional indicators are also are available and used in the EES context, such as the percentage of GDP spent on active and passive LMP arrangements and the number of people covered in particular labor market programs (Mascherini and

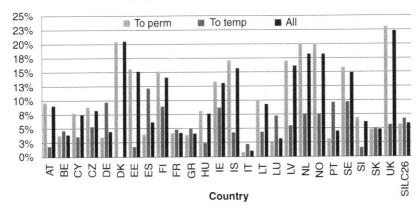

Figure 11.7   Job mobility after training into permanent and temporary contracts, 2005–2006

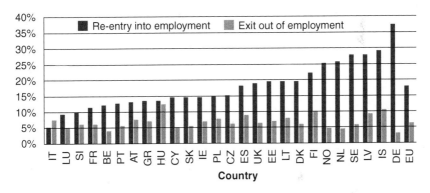

Figure 11.8   Re-entry into work and exit out of employment of people ages 16–65, by country, 2005–2006

Manca 2009; Manca et al. 2010; Bachmann et al. 2011). Dynamic indicators include the number of people reentering employment after some time in training or other employment reintegration program (public employment services). Dynamic outcome indicators might be defined as the exit rates out of a job into unemployment and the reentry rates out of unemployment into employment (Figure 11.8). These exit and reentry rates can be defined as conditional on the duration of previous (un)employment. Figure 11.8 shows that reentry is largest in Germany and the Nordic countries, including Iceland. Exit is large in Hungary and Finland.

Figure 11.9 shows the reentry rates into employment conditional on the duration of unemployment in the last year. As might be expected, where people are unemployed for the twelve-month period, their reentry chances are lower. The highest reentry chances for the long-term unemployed after

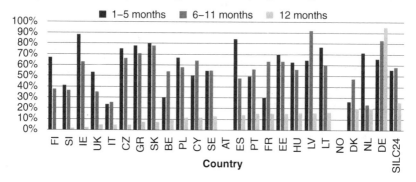

Figure 11.9   Re-entry into employment of people ages 16–64 after 1–12 months of unemployment, 2005–2006

being unemployed for at least one year are observed in Germany and the Scandinavian countries, and the lowest in Finland, Ireland and the UK, and the Southern and Eastern countries.

MODERN SOCIAL SECURITY SYSTEMS (MSS)

Transitions in Wage and Benefit Incomes

There are a number of institutional indicators in the domain of modern social security systems (MSS) that have been jointly developed in the EES framework by the Commission and the OECD. These include expenditure on and coverage of benefits, financial incentives to take up work (unemployment and inactivity 'traps'), the level and duration of benefits (replacement rates for short- and long-term unemployment) and the availability of childcare places in companies and in public services, the latter indicating elements of work-life balance (WLB). Here we focus on defining dynamic outcome indicators. Modern social security schemes 'make transitions pay' and allow people to switch more easily between employment and nonemployment or benefit statuses (retraining, care leaves, sabbaticals) and render in-work income support to, for example, part-time workers. Our measure views changes in income earned from wage or social security income across two years. It might be that as people change from unemployment into employment, benefit income drops and wage income rises, but people's income might also change for various reasons related to family formation events (divorce, separation), social security or benefit related events, but also a variety of other labor market related events (e.g., health shock, part-time work, short-term work). We calculated the number of people experiencing a more than 10 percent upward or downward change in wage plus social security income (unemployment, disability, pensions, education benefits) across two years (Figure 11.10). People staying within this range are considered to be experiencing lateral

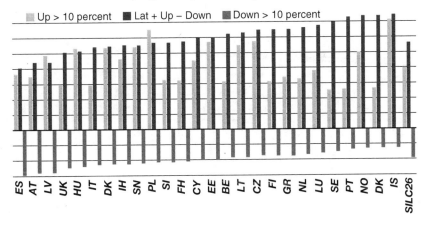

Figure 11.10 Upward and downward labor mobility (<10 percent) plus net income improvement (Lat + Up – Down) of people ages 16–65 years on wage and/or benefit income, 2005–2006

mobility (Lat). We show the upward (Up) and downward (Down) mobility rates and net income improvement that can be seen as a transition into more income security (Up + Lat – Down). The Nordic countries Denmark, Norway and Iceland show the largest average net income improvement but with low upward and downward mobility. Portugal and Greece scored surprisingly high, whereas Spain, Austria and the UK show the lowest level of upward and highest level of downward income mobility.

The net income change or transition income security indicator can be disaggregated by sex or by social group to compare the income security between various groups such as the employed versus the unemployed. With more years available, this provides a measure for changes in income security. More specific measures on income security can further be constructed by viewing particular risk groups such as the in-work poor or workers on low wages (for more details and outcomes on these indicators, see Muffels et al. 2011).

Work-Life Balance (WLB) Security Indicators

In the literature on indicators only static measures have been developed for WLB security. These measures deal with labor market participation rates and the share of part-time employment. Another way of focusing on WLB is to examine to what extent mothers in different life-course stages change their participation across time and withdraw from the labor market or reenter employment (Figure 11.11). These (re)entry patterns indicate the performance of the labor market in allowing women to find a job but also the potential generosity of WLB support in each country, from both public and private sources. Here we look into the proportions of single parent and

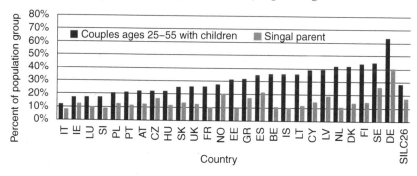

Figure 11.11   Re-entry mobility by life course stage, single parents and couples ages 25–55 with children

coupled mothers (between twenty-five and fifty-five years old) who reenter the workforce across two years. The picture appears very different between the two groups and across countries. For example, reentry rates of single mothers are very low in Italy, Ireland, Luxembourg and Iceland and relatively high in the Nordic countries, the Netherlands and in Germany.

Mapping Countries on Flexicurity Using Transition Indicators

For mapping countries on both the level of attained flexibility and security, we can combine the measures developed before by calculating composite measures. For flexibility we calculated a mobility measure M being the sum of job (JM), contract (CM) and wage mobility (WM) and for security the security measure S being the sum of employment (ESI) and income security (YSI). We first created indices for each of the five underlying dimensions (JM, CM, WM, ESI, YSI), meaning that the country scores on each item are divided by the average score of all countries, and the index for the EU26 is set at 100. Then we summed the various indices using equal weights for each separate index. The country's score therefore provides a relative position to the European overall average. In Figure 11.12 we combine the job, contract and wage mobility indicators into one composite measure (M). The same is done for employment and income security (S).

The lowest mobility figures are for the Netherlands, France, Portugal, Greece, Luxembourg, Germany and Slovenia. However, in terms of income and employment security France and the Netherlands are performing much better, though not as well as Denmark or the other Nordic countries, Iceland, Norway, Finland and Sweden, and slightly worse than the UK. The graph further shows the position of the countries in the so-called flexicurity quadrant with the upper right hand side indicating countries that perform better than the EU average on both flexibility and security (flexicurity). The countries in the other quadrants show tradeoffs (e.g., flex-insecurity). The Nordic countries perform best with a view to both dimensions of transition

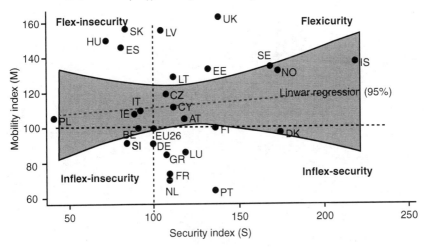

Figure 11.12 Mapping countries using composite indices for transition-flexibility (job, contract plus wage mobility) and transition-security (income, employment), 2005–2006

Source: Eurostat, EU-SILC 2005–2006.

flexibility and security. The linear regression line (at 95 percent reliability), also shown in Figure 11.12, indicates a weak positive relationship between transition-security and flexibility.

INDICATORS FOR MEASURING FLEXICURITY PRACTICES AT THE COMPANY LEVEL

For a more rounded assessment of country performance, the indicators defined at national level need to be supplemented with institutional and outcome indicators at sector and company level. However, the firm-level data needed to capture the performance of companies with respect to flexicurity are not readily available. Most of the time information on firms is derived from employee surveys or firm-level data covering only a small portion of firms. Here we will make use of the Eurofound's ECS data for 2009 covering twenty-three European countries. The survey contains information on 1) membership of a trade union (providing information on TUD); 2) collective wage bargaining coverage (percent of workers covered by a collective labor agreement, or CLA) and 3) the degree of centralization of the wage bargaining arrangements. We utilized the data on a number of other institutional indicators at the company level such as part-time work and flex-time arrangements, the availability of time off for training, the share of workers attaining continuation of their fixed-term contract after expiration and the share of workers in performance pay systems. We used this company data on the HRM context in which companies operate, such as absenteeism or sickness, recruitment problems of skilled personnel, low motivation of staff, or the need to reduce staff for economic reasons. Such problems hinder firms in attaining a proper balance between flexibility and security. Labor productivity issues are also considered important in this respect as a basis for decent remuneration, training investments and greater employment security.

We provide examples of indicators below that correspond to flexicurity implementation at sector and company level, presented by broad sector (public versus private) and country clusters. The information selected pertains to flex-time arrangements (long-term working-time accounts) and training and lifelong learning practices. These two practices were chosen because they are important components of future flexicurity policies, they vary widely between companies and the information is not already contained in the indicators presented before.

Flexible working-time arrangements belong to the first flexicurity component. Workers in many companies can accumulate or save hours over time to draw-down in later periods. These flex-time arrangements are often called *working-time accounts*, and a distinction can be made between short-term (working hours being flexible per day or over the week) and longer-term accounts (covering periods of more than one year). Figure 11.13 provides information on the prevalence of longer-term accounts across sector and regions. These long-term working-time accounts (LT-WTA) exist especially in the Nordic and the Continental countries but hardly feature in the new member states in the Eastern part of Europe. In these regions though, working-time accounts are more prevalent in the private than the public sector.

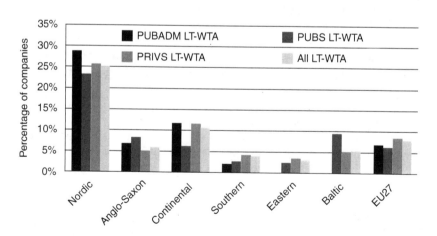

Figure 11.13   Percentage of workers in long-term working time accounts by sector and regime, ECS 2009

Source: European Foundation, ECS, 2009 (own calculations).

Notes: PUBADM = public administration; PUBS = public sector; PRIVS = private sector; ALL = all companies.

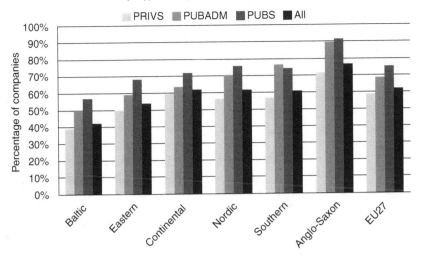

Figure 11.14 Proportion of companies with more than ten employees offering time off for training by sector and regime

Source: European Foundation, ECS, 2009 (own calculations).

Note: PUBADM = public administration; PUBS = public sector; PRIVS = private sector; ALL = all companies.

The ECS survey also contains information on lifelong learning, the second policy domain, in particular concerning the availability of facilities for workers to receive time off for further training in the company (Figure 11.14). In all countries public sector companies invest more in training by allowing time off for further training than do private sector companies. Private sector companies in the Anglo-Saxon countries invest most in training and companies in the Eastern and Baltic countries the least. Private sector companies in the Nordic and Continental countries perform average in this respect.

CONCLUSIONS

The starting point of this chapter was that the institutional and static indicators generally used for evaluating a country's achievement on flexicurity are inadequate given that flexicurity policies have to deal with labor market dynamics. We first explained our conceptual model, which we called the 'capabilities-transitions-outcomes' (CTO) or 'stock-flows-outcomes' model on flexibility and security. In this approach, capabilities (forms of human, social and cultural capital) together with transitions (choices and events) determine outcomes in terms of flexibility and security. These transition indicators at the country level need, however, to be supplemented with (transition) indicators at the sector and company level to complete the picture for monitoring a country's performance in the flexicurity domain.

We calculated a number of single outcome indicators on transition flexibility (job, wage and contract mobility) and transition security (income and employment security) and viewed how well the various labor markets perform according to these. We then constructed two composite indicators on flexibility and security, combining the information embedded in the single indicators. The picture from these transition outcome indicators at the national level was in the last part supplemented with institutional and outcome indicators at the sector and company levels. It was shown that the state of affairs of flexicurity in the years 2005–2008 appears very different across countries and country clusters. It also appeared that very different flexicurity policies may lead to more or less similar results. The evidence we had on the changes during the last decade show no clear trend except for a declining union density in most countries. No strong evidence was found for convergence. This remains our most important conclusion regarding the actual state of affairs of flexicurity.

The findings on the Eastern and Southern countries translate strongly into the relative poor outcomes of these segmented labor markets with respect to exhibiting low levels of mobility in terms of job, contract and wages and simultaneously achieving low standards of income and employment security. The company-level results on flexible working times and lifelong learning practices support these results. The Scandinavian countries, but also the UK and Ireland, seem to attain fairly high levels of employment-transition security and transition-income security, notwithstanding major differences in industrial relations and labor market governance systems. Southern and Eastern countries, on the other hand, appear challenged to increase labor market mobility and income and employment-transition security in order to escape from relatively low levels of flexicurity. The Continental countries show a mixed picture. Some (the Netherlands, Austria and Germany) have relatively low rates of job mobility but manage to maintain relatively low unemployment levels, thereby relying on a growing share of nonstandard jobs. Here the risk is of growing dualism in the labor market. Other Continental countries (France, Belgium) also show low levels of mobility but maintained decent levels of income-transition security for people not working.

An important proviso needs to be made. The information presented here covers the years 2005–2008, a period in which the labor market was flourishing in most European countries—certainly when compared to post-2008. The question therefore is whether these apparently generous systems are sustainable in the future due to the high costs involved. The debt crisis in Europe has already showed that governments have had to reduce social protection benefits, and the same holds for companies with respect to their HRM practices. It needs further scrutiny with more recent data to examine the different performance of countries during the recent crisis with a view to safeguarding income and employment security.

We might infer from our analysis over the years immediately prior to the crisis that countries with a high transition-flexibility but low transition-security like some Eastern and especially Baltic countries, including to some extent the

UK, are likely to show a poorer record in balancing flexibility and security goals. Equally, countries with low transition-flexibility and low transition-security can be expected to perform relatively poorly in terms of maintaining flexicurity performance, such as some Eastern and especially Southern countries. But countries with an intermediate level of transition-flexibility and a high level of transition-security, endorsed by particular flexicurity measures such as short-time arrangements, seem to perform best in terms of balancing flexibility and security goals (e.g., Germany, the Netherlands). To conclude, the various coordination mechanisms—states, markets, associations (social partners), hierarchies (firms), networks and communities—can all contribute to a well-balanced flexicurity. Within this configuration, mature and highly articulated industrial relations systems no doubt have a larger chance of success, assuming (as the OECD has recently indicated in the case of Austria; OECD 2011) that the social partners continue to take joint responsibility for necessary reforms. Whether they will manage to do so strongly depends on the direction the continued transformation of industrial relations will take.

NOTE

1. The sample of the EU-SILC (Statistics on Income and Living Conditions) longitudinal data contains as of 2005, twenty-four EU countries (EU27 minus Germany, Ireland and Romenia) plus Norway and the candidate member state Iceland. The cross-sectional SILC data contains twenty-eight countries in 2008 (EU27 minus Malta plus Iceland and Norway).

REFERENCES

Arrowsmith, J. 2006. *Temporary Agency Work in Europe*. Luxembourg: CEC.

Bachmann, R., Bechara, P., and Schaffner, S. 2011. 'Paper on the Identification of of the Flexicuirty Profile of Member States Using Micro-Economic Data'. Essen: RWI.

Boeri, T. and Garibaldi, G. 2007. 'Two Tier Reforms of Employment Protection: A Honeymoon Effect?' Working Paper, Fondazione Collegio Carlo Alberto-University of Turin, No. 37, Turin.

Chung, H. 2012. 'Measuring flexicurity: Precautionary notes, a new framework, and an empirical example', *Social Indicators Research*, 106:1. 153–171.

Chung, H., Kerkhofs, M. and Ester, P. 2007. 'Working Time Flexibility in European Companies'. European Foundation. Luxembourg: Office for Official Publications of the European Communities.

European Commission 2007. 'Towards Common Principles of Flexicurity: Communication on Flexicurity.' COM(2007) 359. Brussels, 27.6.2007.

———. 2010. 'An Agenda for New Skills and Jobs: A European Contribution towards Full Employment'. COM(2010) 682 final/2. Strasbourg, 26.11.2010.

———. 2012. "Towards a Job-Rich Recovery'. COM(2012) 173 final. Strasbourg, 18.4.2012.

European Expert Group on Flexicurity 2007. 'Flexicurity Pathways: Turning Hurdles into Stepping-Stones', Brussels: Expert Report for European Commission, June.

IMF 2010. *World Economic Outlook—Rebalancing Growth*. Washington, DC: International Monetary Fund, April, 216.

Keune, M. 2008. 'Flexicurity: A contested concept at the core of the European labour market debate', *Intereconomics*, 43:2. 92–98.

Keune, M. and Jepsen, M. 2007. 'Not balanced and hardly new: The European Commission's quest for flexicurity' in H. Jørgensen and P. K. Madsen (eds.) *Flexicurity and Beyond*. Copenhagen: DJF Publishing. 189–211.

Manca, A. R., Governatori, M. and Mascherini, M. 2010. *Towards a Set of Composite Indicators on Flexicurity: A Comprehensive Approach*. Luxembourg: Publication Office of the European Union/JRC.

Mascherini, M. 2008. *Towards a Set of Composite Indicators on Flexicurity: The Dimension of Life Long Learning*. JRC 47627, European Communities. Luxembourg: Office for Official Publications of the European Communities.

Mascherini, M. and Manca, A. R. 2009. *Towards a Set of Composite Indicators on Flexicurity: The Composite Indicator on Active Labour Market Policies*. JRC 53183, European Communities. Luxembourg: Office for Official Publications of the European Communities.

Mettler, A. 2009. 'Innovating indicators: Choosing the right targets for EU2020', Lisbon Council E-brief, Commission Working Document: Consultation on the Future, "EU2020" Strategy, Brussels, COM (2009), 647. 1–16.

Muffels, R. and Luijkx, R. 2008. 'The relationship between labour market mobility and employment security for male employees: Trade-off or flexicurity?' *Work, Employment and Society*, 22:2. 221–242.

Muffels R. and Wilthagen, T. 2011. 'Defining Flexicurity Indicators for the Public Sector'. Tilburg University, ReflecT Research Papers, No. 11/005: 38.

Muffels, R., Wilthagen, T., Chung, H. J. and Dekker, R. 2011. 'Towards a Methodology to Monitor and Analyse Flexicurity (FLC) and Work-Life Balance (WLB) Policies in the Member States of the EU'. Tilburg University ReflecT Research Paper No. 11/003:92.

OECD 2010. 'Economic Outlook'. Paris: OECD.

OECD 2011. 'Economic Survey of Austria'. Paris: OECD.

Pedersini, R. 2008. *Flexicurity and Industrial Relations*. Dublin: European Foundation for the Improvement of Living and Working Conditions (Eurofound).

Schmid, G. 2010. 'The Future of Employment Relations: Goodbye "Flexicurity"—Welcome Back Transitional Labour Markets?' Working Paper WP106, AIAS. Amsterdam: University of Amsterdam.

Sen, A. K. 1993. 'Capability and well-being' in M. Nussbaum and A. K. Sen (eds.) *The Quality of Life*. Oxford: OUP.

Stiglitz, J., Sen, A. and Fitoussi, J. P. 2009. 'Report by the Commission on the Measurement of Economic Performance and Social Progress'. Brussels: European Union.

Visser, J. 2008. *Institutional Characteristics of Trade Unions, Wage Setting, State Intervention And Social Pacts (ICTWSS): An International Database*. Amsterdam: Amsterdam Institute for Advanced Labour Studies (AIAS).

Voss, E. and Dornelas, A. 2011. 'Social Partners and Flexicurity in Contemporary Labour Markets'. Synthesis Report. Brussels, May (European Social Dialogue 2009–2011).

Wilthagen, T. 1998. 'Flexicurity: A New Paradigm for Labour Market Policy Research?' *WZB (Wissenschaftszentrum Berlin) Discussion Paper* FS I 98–202, March.

———. 2005. 'Striking a balance? Flexibility and security in European labour market' in T. Bredgaard and F. Larsen (eds.), *Employment Policy from Different Angles*. Copenhagen: DJØF Publishing. 253–268.

———. 2007. 'Flexicurity Practices'. Brussels: Report to DG Employment.

Wilthagen, T. and Tros, F. 2004. 'The concept of "flexicurity": A new approach to regulating employment and labour markets', *Transfer, European Review of Labour and Research*, 10:2. 166–186.

12 Conclusions

The Transformation of Employment Relations within the European Union: A Common Process of Fragmentation

Valeria Pulignano and James Arrowsmith

The contributors to this book have analyzed some of the main changes in employment relations in the first two decades of the EU with a retrospective and thematic perspective. Rather than comparing developments on a case by case basis with the country as the unit of analysis, this approach offers analytical consistency in that the chapters collectively contribute to a deeper understanding of the bigger picture over time, as well as addressing important topics in their own right. Of course, not all countries or important issues can be addressed but the contributions offer insightful analyses of the broader dynamics and patterns of change across different national-institutional contexts.

One of the key overall messages from this collection is that the ostensibly integrative processes involved in the 'widening' and 'deepening' of the European Union have had the effect of fundamentally fracturing employment relations across and within member states. The recent financial crisis has revealed deep *economic* fissures within the EU, but successive enlargements, the introduction of the euro, as well as the crisis itself have also had profound disintegrative implications for employment relations. Institutions have had to contend with the rapid intensification of competition; the growth of multinational companies; financial deregulation and heightened capital mobility; intense technological change; as well as changes in the labor market associated with the growing importance of the service sectors, all of which places a new premium on 'flexible' forms of pay and working time, labor market regulation and work organization, at the same time weakening the representative scope and authority of organized labor. At the political level too, the Delorsian conception of the 'social dimension' with its 'upward harmonization' of employment rights eventually gave way to loose forms of coordination in pursuit of more ambiguous goals. 'Hard' regulation persisted in the elaboration of minimum standards concerning areas such as nondiscrimination, but employment policy increasingly became geared toward efficiency outcomes around 'employability' and 'flexicurity'. At the same time, national social concertation was reinvented to serve a competitiveness agenda based on wage restraint and the decentralization of collective bargaining.

The conclusion of this volume is that despite a high degree of formal continuity in institutional terms, with social dialogue embedded in EU policy making and multiemployer and multilevel bargaining still the norm in the major EU economies, the dramatic shift in power relations that the EU unleashed in favor of employers means that the discourse, practice and outcomes of employment relations in Europe have more or less been transformed. This transformation was clearly revealed in the aftermath of the economic crisis that began in 2008. Social dialogue at the European level was shown to be bankrupt, with 'a deepening of preexisting differences' at cross-sector level and a failure 'to provide any concrete or specific actions' at the European sector level (Demetriades and Welz 2012, pp.2–3). At the national level, where agreements were able to be reached (mainly in manufacturing), these were geared to managing rationalization with trade unions clearly on the defensive. Frustrated by this institutional failure, and in the face of often severe state-driven austerity, unions in many countries adopted an 'outsider' stance to lead the mobilization of political and industrial protest.

Our contributors explain the subtle and incremental nature of the transformation processes that culminated in this limited and dysfunctional response to the biggest postwar economic crisis witnessed in Europe. In chapters 2, 3 and 4, Sisson, Martínez Lucio and Gonzalez Menéndez, and Della Rocca analyzed the steady disintegration of collective bargaining and worker representation in the private and public sectors, which, as Meardi explains in chapter 5, never effectively took root in any case in the new member states. The effects of this were an increasing marginalization of organized labor and a growing 'flexibility' of processes and outcomes in relation to the central defining aspects of the employment relationship—pay (Keune and Vandaele, chapter 6), working time (Arrowsmith, chapter 7) and work organization (Pries, chapter 8). The final set of chapters show how, at the EU-policy level, market goals (such as participation rates) displaced social goals (such as quality of working life), in part as governance of the EU became increasingly complex and subject to 'soft' forms of coordination (Pulignano, chapter 9). This is explicitly confirmed by the hegemonic status accorded to largely supply-side policy concerns around 'employability' (Winterton and Haworth, chapter 10) and 'flexicurity' (Wilthagen, Muffels and Chung, chapter 11).

On the whole, our contributors identify commonalities in terms of change pressures, dynamics and trends, but they also highlight a growing fragmentation of employment relations systems across countries. This reflects a weakening of organized labor and the institutional arrangements for its representation; a reorientation of the collective bargaining and policy agenda towards 'competitiveness' (i.e., employer interests); and more variegated outcomes, as well as processes, as a result. In large part, then, as we briefly explore below, the political economy of the employment relationship has shifted in favor of a recommodification of labor.

THE CHANGING POLITICAL ECONOMY OF
THE EMPLOYMENT RELATIONSHIP

The employment relationship is governed by a complex, dynamic and multilevel set of institutions, rules and understandings that vary within and between countries in both procedural and substantive terms (Sisson 2009). In recent decades the different social and employment models in Europe—whether Nordic, Mediterranean, Continental, Anglo-Saxon or new member states—have faced similar pressures to 'reform' to reduce costs and increase flexibility in their employment, welfare and labor market regimes. As indicated throughout this text, this is a product of factors such as increasingly integrated and competitive product markets, 'financialization' and capital mobility, tertiarization and the changing demography of the labor market and the development of new technologies and new forms of work organization. Much of this has served to weaken organized labor, thereby accelerating the pace of change. Also challenging existing established labor market and social welfare models is the cost of sustained high levels of unemployment and population aging (Trampush 2009). Such developments potentially erode the traditional comparative advantage of distinctive national models of employment relations (Sapir 2006).

As well as common pressures, there are shared sets of outcomes, and both of these convergence tendencies seem to have intensified with the current enduring economic crisis. A most obvious feature is public-sector austerity; in a sense, the crisis offers national governments not simply an obligation but also an opportunity to respond to ongoing fiscal pressures by rapidly cutting costs and scaling back social programs geared toward market protection. Similarly, at firm level, recession provides employers with a renewed justification to drive employment externalization (e.g., through subcontracting, outsourcing, contingent employment) and internal flexibility (e.g., new forms of work organization, high performance work systems, variable pay and working time), though these tendencies have been strongly observed for some time—even in Germany, concession bargaining over employment security had become normalized well before the recession (Lehndorff and Haipeter 2011). Similarly, trends to deregulate labor markets and decentralize collective bargaining corresponded with the international resurgence of liberal-market ideology from the 1980s (Streeck 2009; Howell 2006). Thus, for many years prior to the current crisis, there was strong political support for employers' 'flexibility' and cost-cutting demands, which had a corrosive effect on coordination and social solidarity in various national systems (Hassel 2009; Baccaro and Howell 2011).

However, as the contributions to this volume also show, the common pressures associated with state-driven liberalization, international market forces and demographic change do not imply a cross-national standardization or even loose coherence in terms of employment relations practices. In part, this reflects a natural evolutionary tendency—outside of crisis—to institutional path dependency (Teague 2009). Certainly, the contrast between 'liberal' and 'coordinated' market economies remains in many ways resilient even as institutions have adapted and changed (Iversen and Soskice 2009; Martin and Swank 2012). It is also the case that, in the political and policy space, there is not one uniform dynamic but instead different 'varieties of liberalization' that institutions have to contend with, each of which has different effects in different contexts (Thelen 2012). It is clear from all of this that there is a need to consider sociopolitical as well as economic dynamics if we want to understand the transformations that have occurred in employment regimes, industrial relations and labor market institutions and social policy within and across different national economies. The governance of the employment relationship (i.e., the regulation of relations between workers and their employers), is a central concern for the social sciences whether from political, legal, economic or sociological perspectives.

This volume has modestly attempted to contribute to this multidisciplinary understanding by analyzing some of the main drivers of change, and their principal outcomes, in a retrospective, comparative and thematic perspective. The changing political economy of the employment relationship is explored in terms of a more or less incremental transformation of processes (institutions) and, especially, outcomes that reflect a profound shift in the economic and political balance of power away from organized labor. Of course, in such a wide-ranging but singular text there is much that has to be omitted, and we would have liked to explore in more depth issues such as the role of the (national-level) state in the liberalization process, or the growth and implications of contractual flexibility in different national contexts. Such a project as this is also, of necessity, inconclusive. Given the scale and complexity of change, it is difficult enough to understand what has gone before, let alone consider what lies ahead. As Kaufman (2011, p.41) points out, the most certain verdict at the present stage is that 'the future of employment relations is uncertain'.

At the same time, it is legitimate to ask what can be done to further inform analysis and debate at the current time. For much of the remainder of this concluding chapter we therefore draw on our contributions to identify some of the principal tensions and contradictions that have informed transformation within advanced capitalist societies in Europe in the past two decades. Our key theme is the *recommodification of labor* in the context of economic and political internationalization. Specifically, it is argued that the process of regional economic integration has progressively undermined the fundamental tenets of European social democracy, and the EU has therefore failed with regard in its original founding principles and goals. In this light we draw some conclusions regarding ongoing effects for the regulation of the employment relations and some indicative implications for future research.

RECOMMODIFICATION AND 'MARKET-VALUES' UNDER THE GLOBAL MARKET ECONOMY

The present epoch may be seen as a reaction to the ascendancy of social democracy, broadly defined, which was established in the third quarter of the twentieth century in Western Europe. It followed the brutal experience of depression and war and was sustained by the 'long boom' (*'les trente glorieuses'*) of reconstruction governed by the Keynesian welfare state. In a sense, it marked the culmination of Polanyi's (1944) idea of the 'Great Transformation'; i.e., associated with the need for an active state to correct the destructive social tendencies of the market (see also Pulignano 2012). In the first Great Transformation mechanisms of protection, regulation and redistribution were used to embed the economy in society. It was a very specific form of embeddedness, in which the main policies and institutions focused on labor rather than on wider notions of citizenship, but it was driven by a certain decommodification through the assertion of generic social and not just market rights.

However, the economic and financial globalization that proceeded apace after the collapse of the Keynesian consensus in the 1970s involved a clear recommodification ('disembedding') of labor driven and legitimized by neoliberal ideology. The state was not merely complicit in an employer-led reaction but actively drove the process. National welfare and labor market institutions were gradually, but sometimes radically, 'reformed' and social protection reconceptualized in increasingly bounded terms subservient to the market. This was justified with reference to the seemingly inevitable demands of globalization, which promised economic growth if at the cost of growing inequality. In Europe, the EMU project reinforced the process from the 1990s. For example, as Schwab (2012, p.14) observes, the euro 'brought currency stability but most importantly it took the tool of devaluation away from politicians who wanted an easy fix and refused to implement structural reforms. It forced each economy to be more flexible and more productive because it was much easier to implement free-market principles than when decisions belonged to each nation'.

This process of international economic integration and neoliberal reformism constitutes the second Great Transformation, which is observed in Europe and beyond. It manifests itself in three related ways. The first is an ever-closer relation between trade and labor flexibility. Unlike in the period of the first Great Transformation, the current epoch is defined by intraproduct not just interproduct trade, along with strong intrafirm trade dominated by MNCs. One effect of this is the transfer of economic risk from contractors, or major corporations, to subcontractors such as small or medium-sized firms and nominally self-employed suppliers in global production chains. This grants enhanced power to MNCs and has intensified the transfer of risk to workers through 'social dumping' and employment insecurity (Bieler and Lindberg 2010).

The rapid growth in the number and power of MNCs is the second key feature of the current Transformation, marked by a corporate social irresponsibility utilizing regime shopping, internal 'coercive comparisons' and taxation avoidance through capital outsourcing, transfer pricing and registration in 'tax havens'. At the same time, in a further demonstration of the inter-relationship of the political and economic nature of the Transformation, national governments have indulged in 'tax dumping' to produce a situation by which not only have taxes on capital fallen, but subsidies to capital have risen (in the competition for foreign investment), while employment and welfare subsidies to workers have been reduced.

The third feature of the Second Great Transformation is the withdrawal of the state from large swathes of its previous responsibilities for economic governance. This is most visible in terms of privatization, but even under public forms of ownership, more and more activities are subject to market forces and commercial ventures. Again, this liberalization and privatization process, which impacts a range of industries from the utilities to social services and which is increasingly obligatory under EU competition law, promotes a mimicking tendency towards 'social policy dumping' by nation states.

The foundations of the First Great Transformation were distinguished by extensive nonmarket social protection and welfare; employment regulation inclusive of robust and encompassing institutions of collective bargaining; and a clear 'model employer' obligation on the part of the interventionist state. Today, there is something of a scramble to the bottom, with each of the pillars dismantled even before the financial crisis on the grounds of national competitiveness (Bohle 2011).

An important indicator of this social disintegration is the generic rise of the 'precariat' (Standing 2011) which clearly signals an increasingly transactional employment relationship governed by short-term, market-based contracting (Seifert and Tangian 2008; Kallenberg 2009). At the same time, the beleaguered 'core workforce' has been subject to intensive marketization with increasingly variable wages, hours of work dictated by employer needs, and traditional benefits such as occupational pensions ever more restricted.

Hence, the state has played a continuously active role in the transformation process. This occurred in three main ways: through the changing nature of its regulation of markets; the restructuring of its own functions and services; and perhaps most fundamentally by the embrace of neoliberal ideologies, which legitimized the self-serving demands of employers as well as the reinvention of the purpose and obligations of the state itself (Levy 2006; Le Gales 2012). In a somewhat contradictory process, this deference to markets may coincide with tendencies toward a more centralized and authoritarian state (Faucher-King and Le Gales 2010). The state may be smaller, but it is also authorized to act decisively on the demands of capital—hence the socialization of private debt in the immediate aftermath of the financial crisis.

The subjugation of the state to the market was an essentially voluntary process structured by the asymmetric process of economic but not political integration in the EU. In particular, the risk of capital flight meant that national governments were constrained by the whims of financial markets and the strategies and demands of large companies, and the unstated reality was of a growing inability to govern society at the national level (Streeck 2011). Yet there was no real countervailing power established at the supranational level, and not just because of the jealousies of national elites concerned to protect their own power, nor the parochialism or (if preferred) the democratic instincts of national electorates. It was in part a consequence of economic integration itself, which unleashed forces that compounded the complexity of governance at the same time as empowering international capital. Hence 'the strange nondeath of neoliberalism' in the aftermath of the international crisis that it created (Crouch 2011).

Furthermore, the recommodification of labor is driven not just by market forces but purposively by the national and supranational state in its efforts to make social protection a productive factor, and therefore a commodity in itself. This idea gained popularity at the European level in the 1990s as a way of defending social spending by giving it market appeal. But it has done less to arrest the trend to commodification than to actually subvert the idea of social policy with a competitiveness agenda geared toward lower labor costs and labor market 'flexibility'. The revitalization of market values under the project of European regional economic integration thus hollows the social dimensions of Europe.

EUROPE AND ITS FAILURES

This dual process of integration and disintegration in EU employment regulation represents 'something of an enigma' for social and political scientists (Hyman 2010, p.57). Perhaps at the heart of the tension is the self-constraining principal of 'subsidiarity', which arose as a means to cope with increased diversity and complexity by granting primacy to local levels in the regulation of employment and social policy. However this failed to stem the effects of social dumping in Western Europe, nor did it promote progressive social partnership in the newer member states (Scharpf 1999). From a skeptical position this is unsurprising as the guiding logic of the EU project is economic rather than social integration—subsidiarity merely absolves the supranational state (all the more conveniently in the name of democracy) from protective measures at the same time as downward pressures are brought to bear on national labor market and employment systems. In any case, the role of the state (and its reinvention under neoliberalism) has been fundamental to the 'restructuring' of markets and social regimes (Le Gales 2012; Levy 2006; Faucher-King and Le Gales 2010). Again, this was visibly brought home in the wake of the financial crisis of 2007/2008, when states that were supposedly 'weak' in the face of global capital were suddenly expected to bail out the financial sector and socialize its private debt.

A more fundamental concern is that economic integration almost inevitably weakens social integration in conditions of heterogeneity and weak oversight. In this sense there is a contradiction between the 'broadening' and 'deepening' of the EU (Hyman 2010). Initially it was assumed—probably too quickly— that economic integration would bring social progress. However, what we observe is that European integration involves a contradictory mix of (concentrated) market liberalization and (diluted) social regulation, with a focus on the reduction and readjustment of wages and unit labor costs (Schulten 2012; see also Pulignano and Keune and Vandaele in this volume). Notwithstanding the significance of a number of European Directives, and experimental forms of governance such as inter-professional and sectoral social dialogue as well as the open method of coordination, the overall result is a rather limited space for the social versus the economic dimension of European integration. Hence the common pressures for labor market flexibility and cuts to social benefits and wages in response to the crisis. The result is a threatened reversal of the earlier approach to work and welfare based on security and social rights, including for those outside the labor force on grounds such as age, disability, unemployment or parental status.

An important part of the transformation of employment relations under the EU involves the transfer of risk to workers and potential workers (Crouch 2007). Just as policy goals such as employment gave way to employability, and job security to flexicurity, so have firms used layoffs, cuts in pay or working hours, reductions in pension rights and other benefits to handle the uncertainty created by the crisis. This came after a process of European integration which 'normalized' lower pay in Europe and viewed collective bargaining institutions as obstacles to competitiveness and economic recovery (Dufresne 2012; Schulten 2011). The function of employment law has also shifted. The now familiar mantra of flexibility originated in a context where employment protection was robust in shielding workers from insecurity. Under the Second Great Transformation the objective is now one of fitting workers to market needs and maximizing labor force participation (Davies and Freedland 2007). Even legislation that seems to be about giving workers new rights (such as antidiscrimination on the basis of age or sex) is concerned with increasing the supply of labor. As Crouch (2011, p.5) puts it, '[I]f earlier labour law was concerned with human rights, today's law is concerned with human resources'.

Though it is hard to predict the future direction of employment relations within Europe, it is likely that the ambiguity and contradictions at the heart of the process of integration makes its social model vulnerable to further erosion in the medium to long term (Jepsen and Serrano Pascual 2006). At the organizational level, rapidly changing technologies, as well as the sectoral shifts away from manufacturing and the public sector, continue to have major implications for the management of the people (Wilkinson and

Townsend 2011). The workforce and its working patterns have been transformed in recent decades in such a way that the classic image of a principally male, full-time, and permanent employee no longer generally applies. On the other hand, it can also be argued that people too are changing in their preferences for types of work, their involvement in unions and politics and what they seek from their work and nonwork experiences.

Despite all the change in the structure and content of work, one thing seems to remains constant. This is the requirement for the great majority of the population to carry on working perhaps longer and harder than before. A considerable amount of policy activity in recent years has already started to direct growing attention to how to handle with these 'unexpected' consequences of change. Societal challenges such as demographic change, globalization and internationalization, decollectivism and new technologies will mean that future research and policies will need to focus more on working conditions and how best to realize social benefits in companies, industries and countries. According to Schwab (2012, p.13), 'Today the European Union is in the throes of an existential crisis threatening its very survival'. This is because the political and social Europe envisioned by Spinelli, Monnet and Delors has been eclipsed in a one-sided process that truly represents 'the last great world-historical achievement of the bourgeoisie' (Anderson 2009, p.78). It is to be hoped that the eventual outcome of these profoundly testing times will be the revitalization of the substance as well as institutions of social partnership that represent one of the greatest achievements of postwar social democracy and a cornerstone of the EU itself.

REFERENCES

Anderson. P. 2009. *The New Old World*. London: Verso.

Baccaro, L. and Howell, C. 2011. 'A common neoliberal trajectory: The transformation of industrial relations in advanced capitalism', *Politics and Society*, 39:4. 521–563.

Bieler, A. and Lindberg, I. (eds.) 2010. *Global Restructuring, Labour and the Challenges for Transnational Solidarity*. London: Routledge.

Bohle, D. 2011. 'Trade Unions and the Fiscal Crisis of the State'. Paper prepared for the workshop 'Economic Integration and Political Fragmentation? Parties, Interest Groups, and Democratic Capitalism in Eastern and Western Europe', June 4–5, Florence, European University Institute.

Crouch, C. 2007. *The Governance of Labour Market Uncertainty: Towards a New Research Agenda*. Annual Hugo Sinzheimer Lecture, Hugo Sinzheimer Institute, University of Amsterdam.

———. 2011. *The Strange Non-Death of Neo-Liberalism*. London: Wiley.

Davies, P. and Freedland, M. 2007. *Towards a Flexible Labour Market: Labour Legislation and Regulation since the 1990s*. Oxford: Oxford University Press.

Demetriades, S. and Welz, C. 2012. *Role of Social Partners in Addressing the Global Financial Crisis*. Dublin: Eurofound.

Dufresne, A. 2012. 'Less pay for the workers', *Le Monde Diplomatique*, February. Available at <http://mondediplo.com/2012/02/03lesspay>

Faucher-King, F. and Le Gales, P. 2010. *The New Labour Experiment*. Stanford: Stanford University Press.

Hassel, A. 2009. 'Policies and politics in social pacts in Europe', *European Journal of Industrial Relations* 15: 1. 7–26.

Howell, C. 2006. Varieties of capitalism: And then there was one? *Comparative Politics*, 36:1. 103–124.

Hyman, R. 2010. 'British industrial relations: The European dimension', in T. Colling and M. Terry (eds.) *Industrial Relations: Theory and Practice, 3rd edition*. Chichester: Wiley.

Iversen, T. and Soskice, D. 2009. 'Distribution and redistribution: The shadow from the nineteenth century', *World Politics*, 61. 438–486.

Jepsen, M. and Serrano Pascual, A. 2006. 'The concept of the ESM and supranational legitimacy building', in Jepsen, M. and Serrano, P. (eds.) 2006. *Unwrapping the European Social Model*. Bristol: Polity Press. 25–45.

Kallenberg, A. 2009. 'Precarious work, insecure workers: employment relations in transition', *American Sociological Review*, 74. 1–22.

Kaufman, B. E. 2011. 'The future of employment relations: Insights from theory' in A. Wilkinson and K. Townsend (eds.) *Research Handbook on the Future of Work and Employment Relations*. Cheltenham: Edward Elgar.

Le Gales, P. 2012. 'State in transition, research about the state in flux' in L. Burroni, M. Keune and G. Meardi (eds.) *Economy and Society in Europe*, Cheltenham: Edward Elgar.

Lehndorff, S. and Haipeter, T. 'Negotiating employment security: innovations and derogations', in S. Hayter (ed.) *The Role of Collective Bargaining in the Global Economy: Negotiating for Social Justice*. Cheltenham: Edward Elgar. 20–46.

Levy, J. (ed.) 2006. *The State after Statism: New State Activities in the Age of Liberalisation*. Cambridge, MA: Harvard University Press.

Martin, C. J. and Swank, D. 2012. *The Political Construction of Corporate Interests: Cooperation and the Evolution of the Good Society*. New York: Cambridge University Press.

Polanyi, K. 1944. *The Great Transformation: The Political and Economic Origins of Our Time*. Boston: Beacon Press.

Pulignano, V. 2012. 'Identity, solidarity and non-market values: Prospects for social democracy in Europe?' in F. Garibaldo, C. Casey, M. Baglioni and V. Telljohann (eds.) *Workers, Citizens, Governance: Socio-Cultural Innovation at Work*. Brussels: Peter Lang.

Sapir, A. 2006. 'Globalization and the reform of European social models', *Journal of Common Market Studies*, 44:2. 369–390.

Scharpf, F. 1999. *Governing in Europe: Effective and Democratic?* Oxford: Oxford University Press.

Schulten, T. 2012. 'Minimum Wages in Europe under Austerity', WSI minimum wage report 5/2012.

Schwab, K. 2012. *The Re-emergence of Europe*. Cologne: World Economic Forum. Available at <http://www3.weforum.org/docs/WEF_KSC_Re-emergenceEurope_2012.pdf>

Seifert, H. and Tangian, A. 2008, 'Flexicurity: Between theory and empirical evidence' in F. Hendrickx (ed.) *Flexicurity and The Lisbon Agenda: A Cross-disciplinary Reflection*. Antwerp: Intersentia.

Sisson, K. 2009. *Employment Relations Matters*. Industrial Relations Research Unit, Warwick Business School. Available at <http://www2.warwick.ac.uk/fac/soc/wbs/research/irru/erm/>

Standing, G. 2011. *The Precariat: The New Dangerous Class*. London: Bloomsbury Academic.

Streeck, W. 2009. *Re-forming Capitalism*. Oxford: Oxford University Press.

Streeck, W. 2011. 'The crisis of democratic capitalism', *New Left Review*, 71. 5–29.

Teague, P. 2009. 'Path dependency and comparative industrial relations: The case of conflict resolution systems in Ireland and Sweden', *British Journal of Industrial Relations*, 47:3. 499–520.

Thelen, K. 2012. *Varieties of Capitalisms: Trajectories of Liberalization and the New Politics of Social Solidarity*. Max Weber Lecture n. 2012/3.

Trampush, C. 2009. *Der erschopfte Sozialstaat: Transformation eines Politikfeldes*. Frankfurt: Campus.

Wilkinson, A. and Townsend, K. (eds.) 2011. *The Future of Employment Relations*. London: Palgrave-Macmillan.

Contributors

James Arrowsmith is Professor in the School of Management at Massey University, New Zealand, and Discipline Leader for the HRM Group. He has conducted international research funded by the Economic and Social Research Council (ESRC), European Foundation and the ILO and has published extensively across his primary research areas of flexible working-time systems, variable pay, employee engagement and comparative industrial relations. He is also an Associate Fellow of the Industrial Relations Research Unit, Warwick University in the UK.

Heejung Chung is Lecturer in Sociology and Social Policy in the School of Social Policy, Sociology and Social Research at the University of Kent. Prior to her current position, she worked in various international labor institutes and research centers. Her main research interests concern cross-national studies of European labor markets and welfare states.

Giuseppe Della Rocca is Emeritus Professor of work and industrial sociology at the University of Calabria, Italy. He has published widely on union organization, workplace industrial relations and management. Amongst his many publications is *Strategic Choice in Reforming Public Service Employment, an International Handbook* (C. Dell'Aringa, G. Della Rocca, B. Keller, Palgrave 2001).

Nigel Haworth is Professor of Human Resource Development and Chair of the Department of Management and International Business at the University of Auckland Business School. Trained as an economist, Nigel became a specialist in Latin American Studies and the international labor market. He has led the Capacity Building Network of the APEC HRD Working Group since 2001. A former national president of the Association of University Staff, he is currently a member of the ILO Century Project and Chair of the Partnership Research Centre, in the New Zealand Department of Labor.

Maarten Keune is Professor of Social Security and Labour Relations and Co-Director of the Amsterdam Institute of Advanced Labour Studies,

University of Amsterdam. His research focuses on the inter-relations between industrial relations, the labor market and the welfare state. Recent publications include Burroni, L., Keune, M. and Meardi, G. (eds.) (2012) *Economy and Society in Europe: A Relationship in Crisis* (Edward Elgar); Pochet, P., Keune, M. and Natali D. (eds.) (2010) *After the Euro and Enlargement: Social Pacts in the EU* (ETUI).

Miguel Martínez Lucio is Professor at the University of Manchester, Manchester Business School. His research focuses on regulation and institutions in the context of globalization, managerialism, and socioeconomic uncertainty. Much of this work has a comparative and international perspective, and has been published widely in leading journals and book contributions. His research has been supported by the ESRC, the Leverhulme Trust, the Anglo-German Foundation, the British Council and various trade union and public policy bodies.

Guglielmo Meardi is Professor of Industrial Relations and Director of the Industrial Relations Research Unit at the University of Warwick, UK. Recent publications include *Social Failures of EU Enlargement* (Routledge, 2012) and he is currently working on a comparison of industrial relations change in the six largest EU countries.

María C. González Menéndez is Associate Professor of Sociology at the University of Oviedo, Spain. Her research interests include workers' participation, HRM, gender and employment, and subnational socioeconomic governance. Recent publications include *Women on Corporate Boards and in Top Management: European Trends and Policy* (Palgrave) and *Gestión de Recursos Humanos: Contexto y Políticas* (Thomson-Civitas).

Ruud Muffels is Professor of Labour Market and Social Security at the Department of Sociology and Professorial Research Fellow at the Labour Market Research Institute ReflecT at Tilburg University. He is also a research fellow at DIW in Berlin and IZA in Bonn. His research interests concern labor market dynamics, industrial relations, comparative welfare states, inequality and subjective well-being and panel methodology. He has published widely in economic, sociological and multidisciplinary journals and edited a number of books, the latest in 2008, *Flexibility and Employment Security in Europe*, with Edward Elgar.

Ludger Pries is Professor of Sociology at the Ruhr-Universität Bochum, Germany, and he has previously taught and researched in Brazil, Mexico, Spain and the US. Research interests concentrate on the sociology of organizations, work and labor regulation, migration and transnationalization in international comparison. He has authored fifteen books (five coauthored) and edited nineteen books in German, English and Spanish.

He has also published some seventy journal articles and eighty chapters in books. He is on the editorial boards of five scientific journals and is Regional Editor for Europe of the journal *Global Networks*.

Valeria Pulignano is Professor in Labour Sociology at CESO (KU Leuven), Associate Fellow at IRRU (Warwick University), and a core researcher at the Interuniversity Research Centre on Globalization and Work (CRIMT). She has published widely in comparative industrial relations. In 2008 she coedited a book entitled *Flexibility at Work* (Palgrave Macmillan).

Keith Sisson is Emeritus Professor in Warwick Business School's Industrial Relations Research Unit (IRRU), having previously been its director for many years. He has published widely on the role of management in industrial relations, and has been extensively involved in cross-national comparative research funded by the ESRC and the European Foundation. Between 2003 and 2005 he was the Head of Strategy Development at the UK Advisory, Conciliation and Arbitration Service (ACAS), responsible for a range of initiatives designed to boost the organization's delivery of advice and information. In 2010, he completed a ten-chapter text, *Employment Relations Matters*, that is freely available on the Internet under a Creative Commons Attribution-NonCommercial-ShareAlike license.

Kurt Vandaele is a senior researcher at the European Trade Union Institute (ETUI) in Brussels, Belgium. His research interests include the history and sociology of the trade union movement in Europe, union organizing and transnational union strategies, workers' mobilization and strike activity and the political economy of Belgium and the Netherlands.

Ton Wilthagen has a chair in Institutional and Legal Aspects of the Labour Market at Tilburg University, the Netherlands. He is also the director of the ReflecT Institute at Tilburg University. Wilthagen's main themes of research include flexicurity, labor law, industrial relations, employment strategies and European and regional governance. He is an advisor to many European and national bodies and institutions.

Jonathan Winterton is Professor of Employment and Director of International Development at Toulouse Business School, where he also coordinates the research group *Travail Emploi Santé*. He has been researching labor market issues for thirty years, often in association with the trade unions and the European Commission and its agencies, and is currently working on restructuring in the crisis, as well as international comparisons in employment and training policy. He is editing a book comparing union-led learning in eight European countries, *Trade Union Strategies for Competence Development,* to be published by Routledge.

Index